MY VOICE

MY VOICE

A DECADE OF POEMS FROM
THE POETRY TRANSLATION CENTRE

Edited by Sarah Maguire

poetry
translation
centre

BLOODAXE BOOKS

ISBN: 978 1 78037 107 8

First published 2014 by
Bloodaxe Books Ltd,
Eastburn,
South Park,
Hexham,
Northumberland NE46 1BS
in association with
The Poetry Translation Centre Ltd,
Free Word Centre,
60 Farringdon Road
London EC1R 3GA

www.bloodaxebooks.com
www.poetrytranslation.org

This book has been selected to receive financial assistance from
English PEN's Writers in Translation programme supported by Bloomberg.

Designed in Albertina by Libanus Press Limited.
Cover design: North Kuras, Exploded View.
Printed in Great Britain by Bell & Bain Limited, Glasgow, Scotland,
on acid-free paper sourced from mills with FSC chain of custody certification.

CONTENTS

INTRODUCTION

'My Voice', Afghan poet Partaw Naderi's incisive jewel of a poem, articulates a profound paradox. In it, the 'silenced' poet 'from a distant land' laments as he watches how his voice is '(like Jonah) / swallowed by a whale'. Yet in mourning the annihilating loss of his voice – 'my very life lived in my voice' – the poet once again reclaims his voice. And now, in this anthology celebrating the first decade of translations produced by the Poetry Translation Centre (PTC), his voice will be heard by more people than Partaw ever could have imagined when he wrote 'My Voice' in 1989 – trapped as he then was in a desecrated Kabul that, following the withdrawal of the occupying Soviet army, was ringed by squabbling warlords who treated the city, its people and its magnificent architecture as their personal shooting range.

Partaw Naderi's is just one of 45 voices that can be heard in these pages, many of whom – poets revered and famous in their own countries – have been translated into English for the first time by the PTC. I founded the Centre in 2004 with two aims: to ginger up poetry in English through translating contemporary poetry from Africa, Asia and Latin America; and as an attempt to engage with the countless thousands of people now settled in Britain for whom poetry is *the* highest art form, as is the case for those people from Islamic backgrounds, for example.[1] What better way to make our new neighbours feel welcome than to translate their most highly esteemed poets into English, using the skills of talented linguists working closely with leading British poets (such as Jo Shapcott, Sean O'Brien, Lavinia Greenlaw and W. N. Herbert), with the additional hope that these brilliant translations might engage English-speaking audiences too? And that meetings between these remarkable international and local poets might change the writing and, perhaps, the lives of everyone concerned?

All revolutions in English poetry have occurred via translation, when poets have unequivocally embraced what is distant and unfamiliar. English poetry simply wouldn't be English poetry without poets absorbing influences from abroad. From Chaucer's version of *The Romance of the Rose*, via Wyatt's introduction of the sonnet by translating Petrarch, Dryden and Pope's reclaiming of the Classics for their Augustan ends, to the influence of Chapman's Homer on John

---

1 I'm using the term 'Islamic' here in the way European societies are characterised as 'Christian': as a matter of history and culture, not necessarily of belief.

Keats – poets writing in English have flourished in response to translation. The publication of Ezra Pound's *Cathay* (1915) – a translation of the eighth-century Chinese poet Li Po via versions provided by the scholar, Ernest Fenollosa – had a transformative effect on Modernist poetry that continues to this day. And, more recently, think of the impact of the Penguin New European Poets series on present-day English poetry: how it made the great eastern European poets into our contemporaries, as well as introducing us to some of the major poets of Latin America and western Europe.

Translations are a product of their particular historical moment; they come into being because the interests of the translator and the opportunities they're able to seize coincide, opportunities that arise from a conjunction of historical circumstances and individual ability. Thomas Wyatt, for example, travelled to Italy as a diplomatic envoy for Henry VIII and there encountered Petrarch's poetry. And it was international politics that played a key role in the appearance of the translations that I grew up reading. Throughout the Cold War, the CIA covertly funded magazines such as *Encounter* and *Partisan Review*, enabling them 'to offer large sums in payment for single poems by East European and Russian poets'.[2] The CIA actively encouraged the translation of East European poetry into English as a (very effective) means of countering Stalinist propaganda. I'm not suggesting that the poets themselves were not worth translating, nor that their translators knew how their work was being supported. The point is that the CIA recognised that the translation of poetry could be a political act with significant consequences.

What *doesn't* get translated and published is, of course, as fascinating as what does. The translation theorist, André Lefevere, has noted that 'of all the great literatures of the world, the literature produced in the Islamic system is arguably the least available to readers in Europe and the Americas.'[3] (One famous exception, of course, is Edward Fitzgerald's *Rubaiyat of Omar Khayyam* [1859] which, as Lefevere reminds us, 'introduced the *roba'i*, or quatrain, into European poetics', a form popular with many poets until it fell out of favour in the 1920s.[4]) Yet, despite the ferment of the 'War on Terror', the present-day CIA seems to have little interest in translating poetry from Islamic countries into English.

As a young poet who began to write during the Cold War, I was fortunate to have benefitted from the CIA's (then unknown) largesse. But, growing up in

2   Frances Stonor Saunders, *Who Paid the Piper?: The CIA and the Cultural Cold War* (London: Granta Books, 1999), p.355.
3   André Lefevere, *Translation, Rewriting and the Manipulation of Literary Fame* (London & New York: Routledge, 1992), p.73.
4   *Ibid.*, p.74.

London (a city where, today, more than three hundred languages are spoken and more mixed-race babies are born than anywhere else in the world), with a widening circle of friends from Africa, the Middle East and Central Asia, I was also beginning to be aware of other poetries that were having a far harder time making their way into English.

Somalis are arguably the most poetry-obsessed people on earth. When the explorer Sir Richard Burton visited Somalia in 1854, he was immediately struck by the Somalis' devotion to poetry. 'The country teems with poets,' he wrote, 'the fine ear of this people causes them to take the greatest pleasure in harmonious sounds and poetical expressions, whereas a false quantity or a prosaic phrase excite their violent indignation.'[5] Nothing since then has changed – other than the fact that Somali became a written language in 1972 – and poetry is still the supreme achievement of Somali society, wielding a power and fascination that's difficult for us westerners to grasp.

The UK is home to the largest Somali community in Europe: an estimated 100,000 Somalis were thought to be living here in 2010. They routinely feature at the very bottom of all those indicators of well-being: health, housing, employment and education opportunities. I yearn for the day when, instead of being a byword for instability, ceaseless war and piracy, it's Somalia's exceptional poetic tradition that brings it universal renown.

My Voice includes the poetry of three outstanding Somali poets. In the perceptive essay concerning his experience of co-translating the late Maxamed Xaashi Dhamac 'Gaarriye' (see pp.348–51), British poet W N Herbert records how he found himself describing the 'long, loping poems' he was translating as 'non-lyric'. By this he meant,

> not that they failed to be lyrical in either their thought or their musicality (actually, they succeeded, often compellingly so), but that they were manifestly not reliant, as much of our poetry is, on a device of romantic intimacy: one person deploying that musicality to 'sing' to another, with the reader either pretending to overhear, or to be the person addressed. (p.350)

The 'non-lyric' Somali poem, that always exists within the communal experience of performance, has designs on its audience. It wants to persuade you of its position, or reveal the world anew from a fresh perspective. It achieves this not only through the logic of its reasoning, but also through the virtuosity of its technical brilliance, the complex mastery of which will bewitch a Somali audience.

---

5 Cited in B. W. Andrzewjewski (ed.), *An Anthology of Somali Poetry* (London: John Wiley, 1993), p.1.

The first Somali poem you'll encounter in *My Voice* is 'The Sea-Migrations' by the remarkable young poet, Caasha Lul Mohamud Yusuf, who is fast gaining a following among Somalis both here and at home, a significant achievement for a young woman poet living in the diaspora. 'The Sea-Migrations' is a *gabay*, the most prestigious – and difficult – of Somali verse forms. English-speakers, unable to appreciate the rich complexities of the original, will immediately grasp from Clare Pollard's fine co-translation its crucial formal component: alliteration. The opening line makes clear the poet's method: 'Declaiming this poem, a *gabay*, I alliterate in D to start debate'; and, in the final line of the stanza, we grasp her argument and aim: 'Sea-migration disables my people, I want to drive it back'. Caasha's poems all passionately engage with the plight of her community. As she writes here, she's moved to make her poems because

> I can't endure what's happening, it's like I feel the damage,
> my body jerks, distressed, every time I see them desolate,
> tears stream down my face, I chew blood from my lips.

'The Sea-Migrations' is part of the *Deelley*, a famous 'chain' of poems composed by many leading Somali poets in the late 70s and early 80s that were highly critical of the military regime of Siad Barre. The chain was inaugurated by Maxamed Xaashi Dhamac 'Gaarriye' and Maxamed Ibraahin Warsame 'Hadraawi' – the latter universally regarded as the greatest living Somali poet – both of whom received death threats from the regime as a result, both of whom are also featured in *My Voice*. Caasha's contribution to the *Deelley* is a mark of her confidence as a poet, and of her growing status.

As I said above, translations are created at a particular historical moment as a result of the interests of the translator and the opportunities they grasp. My growing curiosity about poetry of the Islamic world was stimulated by three things: reading Adrienne Rich's 'Ghazals: Homage to Ghalib' in her collection *Leaflets*; meeting a Somali man called Osman who worked at my local Tesco's, who informed me of his country's poetic heritage and illicitly borrowed *An Anthology of Somali Poetry* for me from the library of the School of Oriental and African Studies (SOAS) where he was doing a PhD on forestry; and being the first writer the British Council sent to Palestine (in 1996) and then the only writer they've ever sent to Yemen (in 1998).[6]

It was in Palestine that I first decided to try to use my skills as a poet to

---

6 Adrienne Rich, *Leaflets: Poems 1965–1968* (New York: W. W. Norton, 1969); see also, Aijaz Ahmad (ed.), *Ghazals of Ghalib: Versions from the Urdu* (New Delhi: Oxford University Press, 1994) which contains translations of Ghalib by Rich and other US poets.; B. W. Andrzewjewski (ed.), *An Anthology of Somali Poetry* (London: John Wiley, 1993).

co-translate Palestinian and Arabic poetry. And then, from 2001 to 2003, I was lucky enough to be the Royal Literary Society's Writing Fellow at SOAS. Perfect timing, since I'd just read a special edition of *Modern Poetry in Translation*, edited by Stephen Watts, called *Mother Tongues: Non English-Language Poetry in England.*[7] *Mother Tongues* opens with a selection of poems translated from Somali by Martin Orwin, Senior Lecturer in Somali and Amharic at SOAS – who was now my colleague. SOAS, of course, is bursting with students and faculty who have specialist knowledge of some of the most vibrant traditions of poetry around, and I was determined to mine their expertise. To this end, I instigated fortnightly poetry translation workshops; and it was the enthusiastic response they received that encouraged me to approach Arts Council England (ACE) with a view to establishing the PTC. Without ACE's generous support, the PTC could not possibly have come into existence.

To this day, our workshops remain the core activity of the PTC. The workshops are where we've discovered the majority of the poets we've gone on to translate at length and invite to the UK. They also induct people into the art of translating poetry, something that's had a transformative effect on many of our gifted participants – who range from absolute beginners to senior academics, from professional translators to language students and from teenagers to people in their eighties. The workshops are enormous fun, profoundly stimulating and they give a fascinating insight into the language and culture of the poets we translate. The format is as follows: each session, a workshop member brings along copies of poems in the original language, plus their very basic 'literal' translations that we then try to turn into new poems in English. Our objective is to stay as close as possible to the original poet's intentions, while also making our translation an effective poem in English. In the process we all learn an enormous amount not only about the poetry of many different cultures, but also about the structure of a wide variety of languages and the small, but telling, details concerning weather, food, music, politics, custom and history.

There is, of course, an absolutely vast literature on the subject of translation, stretching back centuries, and I am very far from being an expert on what is often an extremely vexed subject with many vested and competing interests. Translation, it seems to me, is as much about ethics as linguistic niceties. In other words, the starting point is deciding who is more important: you, the translator, or the poet you're translating. Of course, there's a long tradition of

7 *Modern Poetry in Translation, Mother Tongues: Non English-Language Poetry in England*, New Series, Vol. 17, 2001. No one in this country has done more to promote poetry and support poets from abroad than Stephen Watts.

translating poetry in English that unequivocally puts the translator-poet above the translated-poet, the most famous example of which is Robert Lowell's *Imitations*, a book that's had a significant impact on many poets writing today.[8] However, in contradistinction to Lowell, all the translations included in *My Voice* begin from the assumption that no one is as important as the poet being translated; and that our privileged task is to translate them with as much respect and attention to their original poems as we can muster. In other words, what I've asked of all the brilliant poets who've co-translated with the PTC is to put their considerable poetic talents at the service of the poet they're translating in order to render their work into English as faithfully as is possible. Nick Laird talks of the 'weird pleasure' of this, which is 'like opening your mouth and finding someone else's voice coming out'.

If you read the essays on translation at the end of the book, written by our translators, you'll get an insight into the intricate negotiations entailed. Negotiation, of course, being the key term. Translating poetry is the opposite of war. It depends on a deep attempt to fully engage with the 'otherness' of that poet, their culture and their language in order to find effective ways of admitting that otherness into English, thus expanding the boundaries of English poetry. The more open you are to the rich heritage of the poet you're translating, the better and more effective your translation will be as a new poem in English. As Umberto Eco argues in his detailed and practical examination of translation, 'Negotiation is a process by virtue of which, in order to get something, each party renounces something else, and at the end everyone feel satisfied since one cannot have everything.'[9]

Many of the poets included in *My Voice* (and, indeed, their translators) have had brutally direct experiences of war. In January 2012, we translated Fouad Mohammad Fouad's remarkable poem, 'Aleppo Diary', written shortly before he was forced into exile in Beirut by the civil war consuming his city. As well as confronting the horror he has no choice but to witness ('women waiting for children who are already numbers in a news report'), the poet is attentive to how 'The clatter of crockery in the dark means life goes on'; and he mourns how war has cancelled the simple pleasures of life: 'Aleppo. No oud plucked. . . . No drinkers. No song.'

A debate has longed raged in the English-speaking world about the role and relevance of 'political poetry', some claiming – bolstered by (a partisan reading of) Keats – that poetry with 'designs on us' can't be poetry at all (try telling that to a Somali!); others, that poetry has a duty to be 'useful' in a Stalinist,

8 Robert Lowell, *Imitations* (London: Faber & Faber, 1962).
9 Umberto Eco, *Mouse or Rat: Translation as Negotiation* (London: Weidenfeld & Nicolson, 2003) p. 6.

tractors-and-wheat kind of way.[10] The greatest Marxist poet of the twentieth century, Bertolt Brecht, confronted this dilemma head-on when he found himself, in exile from Nazi Germany, unsettled by the power of Wordsworth's 'Lucy' poems – poems that, Brecht admitted, he'd have been tempted to dismiss as 'petty-bourgeois'. But Wordsworth's lyrics moved him. Attempting to analyse why, he argued that 'precisely in this inhuman situation "a lovely apparition sent / to be a moment's ornament" may awaken a memory of situations more worthy of human beings'.[11] In other words, in the midst of the worst, something as simple and beautiful as a lyric poem may awaken in us a sense of our own humanity. Indeed, in a journal entry from two years later, Brecht claimed that 'the battle for Smolensk is also a battle for lyric poetry' – which, on first reading, is a truly startling claim.[12] But what Brecht realised was that something as tender and unassuming as Wordsworth's small lyrics are the antithesis of what Hitler was then attempting to inflict on Europe by brute force. Just as Fouad's 'Aleppo Diary' gives weight to the significance of lost, simple pleasures in his catalogue of destruction. The battle for Smolensk – indeed, all battles against totalitarian, fascist regimes, be they fought with armies and ordnance, or solely with the weapons of metaphor – can be viewed as battles for lyric poetry: for the right to experience and express the delight we find in the ordinary world around us. Strange as it may seem to those of us fortunate to have lived our lives in comfort and peace, the right to joy is a potent threat to totalitarianism.

One of the most lyrically intense poets included in *My Voice* is the outstanding Sudanese poet Al-Saddiq Al-Raddi, whose complex, multi-layered poems are imbued with the mystical traditions of Sufi poetry. Sufism has a particularly strong presence in Sudan (as it does in Somalia, Pakistan and the three Persian-speaking countries of Afghanistan, Iran and Tajikistan). Until forced into exile in 2012, Al-Saddiq Al-Raddi lived in Omdurman, one of the three cities that form greater Khartoum. Omdurman, famous for its richly diverse culture, sprang from the routed army of the Mahdi, the Sufi leader responsible for one of the most humiliating defeats in British military history when he vanquished 'Gordon of Khartoum' in 1885. (Nowadays, Sufism, famous for its celebration of music and poetry, is the 'acceptable' face of Islam in the West, held up as a peaceful alternative to Islamic fundamentalism. But it's worth remembering

---

10 'We hate poetry that has a palpable design upon us', John Keats, letter to John Hamilton Reynolds (3rd February, 1818).

11 Bertolt Brecht, quoted by David Constantine in 'The usefulness of poetry', in *Bertolt Brecht's Poetry of Political Exile*, edited by Ronald Speirs (Cambridge: Cambridge University Press, 2000), p.41.

12 *Ibid.*, p.42.

that, once upon a time, the Sufis, not the Wahhabis, were the West's Islamic bugaboos.)

Al-Saddiq Al-Raddi is famous among the Sudanese not only because of his avowedly political poetry (not translated since the density of its contextual references makes it impenetrable to outsiders) but because his lyric poems express a yearning for transcendence that speaks to his community. An African poet writing in Arabic, his writing subverts the 'purity' of the official tongue of Sudan's Islamist regime by referencing the multiracial plurality of his country's heritage and its history of proud, ancient kingdoms (see 'Poem of the Nile' and 'In the Company of Michelangelo'), a vision that directly challenges the mono-cultural ideology of Sudan's dictatorship – and which led to his imprisonment and torture in 1990.

Al-Saddiq Al-Raddi's poems consistently scrutinise the boundaries of the self. In 'A Body' he answers the question 'What is there?' with the lines,

A body transcending my body.
A body exiled by desire.
A body sheltered by the wind.

This questioning of the nature of the self – its shifting identities, its permeable boundaries – is common to the poets included in *My Voice* who, like Al-Saddiq Al-Raddi, come from poetic traditions infused with Sufism, notably the Persian poets, Reza Mohammadi (from Afghanistan) and the astonishing Farzaneh Khojandi, Tajikistan's national poet, both of whom – like all the Persian poets represented here – are nourished by their immersion in the magnificent traditions of Classical Persian poetry.[13] You will notice that the poems of these Sufi-influenced poets (Noshi Gillani from Pakistan is another) are widely represented here, not only because we have translated them at length (we've translated 33 poems by Al-Saddiq Al-Raddi who, since 2005, has been actively involved in some of the most inventive and exciting of our community-based projects) but also because of the anthologist's prerogative: these are the poets and poems I most admire.

Inevitably, the PTC's programme has been very much affected by my personal interest in the poetry from the Islamic world. But you'll also see the influence of the PTC's ex-Assistant Director (from 2004-2007), Tom Boll, who has a strong interest in Mexican poetry. Tom co-translated the wonderful Mexican poet, Coral Bracho – six of whose sinuous, sensual lyrics (beautifully co-translated by Katherine Pierpoint) are included here; and he was responsible

---

13 Persian culture traverses three present-day countries – Afghanistan, Iran and Tajikistan – in each of which the Persian language has a local variant: Dari, Farsi and Tajik (respectively).

for setting up our extremely successful Mexican Poets' Tour 2010 that brought Coral Bracho, David Huerta and the extraordinary Zapotec poet, Víctor Terán, to the UK.

Regrettably, the poetry of many countries and languages is under-represented. This linguistic lopsidedness is a result of opportunism and contingency since, almost exclusively, the poets we've translated have been brought to our attention by our workshop members. For example, we've only ever had one translator from Swahili, Thai, Georgian, Korean, Shuar, Pashto, Chinese, Siraiki, Hebrew or Zapotec offer to bring translations along to our workshops. And, of course, there are very many other languages I hope we will translate from in future.

As any anthologist will tell you, the selection process is both agonising and joyful. Few things are more painful than having to exclude outstanding poems for want of space. At the time of writing, the PTC website – where all our poems are displayed in three different versions (original, literal and final translation) – houses 397 poems written in 27 different languages by 84 poets from 38 countries. No doubt by the time you read this, there will be many more. I sincerely wish I could have included them all – but at least you'll be able to read our complete list of translations online.

And, as any anthologist will tell you, few things are more pleasurable than creating an order for the poems you've selected. Here, as you'll discover, I've arranged the poems so they take us on a journey from exile to ecstasy. The first group of poems is concerned with poets who 'migrate in vain' ('In Vain I Migrate' by Abdellatif Laâbi, p.23), from Shakila Azizzada's bitter lament at having the 'ground pulled from under my feet' ('View from Afar', p.25) via Dilawar Karadaghi's almost hallucinatory recreation of the loved details of a world he has been forced to abandon ('An Afternoon at Snowfall', p.29) to Al-Saddiq Al-Raddi's painful realisation that, left behind in Khartoum as he then was, 'the streets are empty of my friends' ('Lamps', p.55). It is striking – and shocking – how many of our poets have been forced into exile. Equally striking is their courage in mining their dislocation in order to create transformative poetry.

It is tempting to offer signposts to all the poems that follow this initial group concerning exile. But, on reflection, I've decided to leave you to make your own journey through the 111 poems by 45 poets from 26 countries writing in 23 different languages that make up *My Voice*. I hope these poems will both delight and instruct you, and that they will lead you to explore more deeply the extraordinary cultures and magnificent poetic traditions from which they spring.

MY VOICE

صدا

من از سر زمین غریب می‌آیم
با کوله بار بیگانه‌گی ام بر دوش
و سرود خاموشی ام برلب
من یونس صدایم را
آن گاه که از رودبار حادثه می‌گذشتم
دیدم

درکامی نهنگی فرورفت
و تمام هستی من
در صدایم بود

شهرکابل
دسامبر ۱۹۸۹

My Voice

PARTAW NADERI · AFGHANISTAN

I come from a distant land
with a foreign knapsack on my back
with a silenced song on my lips

As I travelled down the river of my life
I saw my voice
(like Jonah)
swallowed by a whale

And my very life lived in my voice

Kabul, December, 1989
Translated from the Dari (Persian) by Sarah Maguire and Yama Yari

En vain j'émigre

J'émigre en vain
Dans chaque ville je bois le même café
et me résigne au visage fermé du serveur
Les rires de mes voisins de table
taraudent la musique du soir
Une femme passe pour la dernière fois
En vain j'émigre
et m'assure de mon éloignement
Dans chaque ciel je retrouve un croissant de lune
et le silence têtu des étoiles
Je parle en dormant
un mélange de langues
et de cris d'animaux
La chambre où je me réveille
est celle où je suis né
J'émigre en vain
Le secret des oiseaux m'échappe
comme celui de cet aimant
qui affole à chaque étape
ma valise

In Vain I Migrate

ABDELLATIF LAÂBI · MOROCCO

I migrate in vain
In every city I drink the same coffee
and resign myself to the waiter's impassive face
The laughter of nearby tables
disturbs the evening's music
A woman walks by for the last time
In vain I migrate
ensuring my own alienation
I find the same crescent moon in every sky
and the stubborn silence of the stars
In my sleep I speak
a medley of languages
and animal calls
The room where I wake
is the one I was born in
I migrate in vain
The secret of birds eludes me
as does my suitcase's magnet
which springs open
at each stage of the journey

Translated from the French by André Naffis-Sahely

دورنما

باز خالی می شود پشتم
خالی می شود باز زیرپاهایم
دستم به شانه های آفتاب نمی گیرد

نافم را
بر پایه ی عادت گره زدند
مویم را بر طشت بایگانی بریدند
در گوشم اذان گفتند:

" همواره پشت تو
همواره زیرپایت خالی باد"
همواره اما
بالاترک زمینی ست
سچه تر از نیایش ابلیس

با دست آفتاب بر شانه هایم
پا می کنم هزارو یکم باره
از مانده های من

View from Afar

SHAKILA AZIZZADA · AFGHANISTAN

I'm left again with no one standing behind me,
ground pulled from under my feet.
Even the sun's shoulders are beyond my reach.

My navel chord was tied
to the apron strings of custom,
my hair first cut over a basin of edicts.
In my ear, a prayer was whispered:
'May the earth behind and beneath you
be forever empty'.

However, just a little higher,
there'll always be a land
purer than any land Satan could wish on me.

With the sun's hand on my shoulder,
I tear my feet away, a thousand and one times,
from the things I leave behind me.

Translated from the Dari (Persian) by Mimi Khalvati and Zuzanna Olszewska

Viajantes

Traziam poentes e estradas
A sede do horizonte os chamava.

– A quem pertences tu?
Quem são os da tua casa?

Assim estendia nossa avó
A caneca de água ao viajante.

Travellers

CONCEIÇÃO LIMA · SÃO TOMÉ AND PRÍNCIPE

They bore sunsets and roads
Thirst for the horizon called them

– Who do you belong to?
Who are your people?

That's how our grandmother held out
A mug of water to the traveller

Translated from the Portuguese by Stefan Tobler and The Poetry Translation Centre Workshop

سەعات کرێوەی عەسرێک

لێرە نیم
حەیفێک ... سبەینێ ڕۆژ دەبێتەوە و
ئیدی من لێرە نیم
حەیفێک لێرە نابم
کە کەسێک سبەینێ
پەنجەرەکە دەکاتەوە
کە کەسێک سبەینێ ناوێک لەسەر
هەڵمی شووشەکە دەنووسێ
کە کەسێک سبەینێ ئینجانەکان ئاو دەدا و
بە چاوانێک ... پڕاوپڕی ڕووانین
لە دوودڵیی چۆڵەکە وەریوەکان ڕادەمێنێ!

لێرە نیم
حەیفێک لێرە نابم
کە کەسێک سبەینێ
شەلاڵ لە خەونێکی شین
لۆژ لۆژ دەچێتە بەر ئاوێنە
بەلوعەی دەست شۆڕییەکە دەکاتەوە و
بە پیاوی تەنیای ناو ئاوێنەکە
بەو پیاوەی کە ئیدی بۆتە تەپ ونم
کە ئیدی بۆتە دەنکێک لم
کە بۆتە دڵۆپێک شەونم
دەڵێ: وای مەیموون
چ خەونێکی سەیرم پێوە بینیت
سوێند دەخۆم ..... تۆ ئەمشەو زیاتر لە سەد کەڕەت
هاتییە خەونم!

28

An Afternoon at Snowfall

BY DILAWAR KARADAGHI · KURDISTAN

I'm not here.
What a shame, tomorrow day will break
and I won't be here anymore.
Shame, I won't be here tomorrow
when someone opens the window,
when someone writes a name
on the window's mist,
when someone waters the flower pots
and, with an intense gaze,
observes the confusion of fallen sparrows.

I'm not here.
What a shame, I won't be here tomorrow
when someone,
still drenched in a blue dream,
slowly staggers towards the mirror,
runs the tap,
and tells the lonely man in the mirror –
a man who has turned to mist,
to a grain of sand,
to a drop of dew –
You silly thing, what a strange dream I had about you!
I swear, you came into my dreams
more than a hundred times last night.

لێره نیم
حەیفێک لێره نابم
که سەعات پڕوشەی بەیانییەک
کەسێک
لەخۆوه دڵی دەکەوێته مەراقەوه
لەخۆوه دڵی هەزار شت دەکات
لەخۆوه خەیاڵی بۆ هەزار شت دەچێ
له خۆوه حەز دەکات کەسێک،
کەسێک که ئیتر به ڕێگاکاندا ناڕوات،
کەسێک که ئیتر له دەرگاکانەوه نایەته دەرێ
کەسێک که ئیتر له پەنجەرەکانەوه
ناڕوانێ
بەلایدا تێپەڕێ و
پێی بڵێ:
ئەدی ئەوه دیار نیت هاوڕێ!

لێره نیم
حەیفێک لێره نابم
که کەسێک سبەینێ
لەنێو قیتارێکی تیژڕۆدا
بەلای گەواڵەیەکی چکۆڵه هەوری
ڕاماو لەبەر وێستگەیەکی خەمگیندا
تێدەپەڕێ و
دڵی وەخورپه دەکەوێ
کوتوپڕ بانگی دەکا و
کوتوپڕ دەستی بۆ هەڵدەبڕێ و
کوتوپڕ تا دوورترین خاڵی دونیا
ئاوڕی بۆ دەداتەوه و
کوتوپڕ لەبەرخۆوه دەڵێ:
ئەدی بڵێی خۆی بێ؟
ئەدی بڵێی کەسێک بێ
که نییه،
کەسێک بێ که ئیدی

I'm not here
What a shame, I won't be here
when, in the light snowfall one morning,
his heart racing,
somebody suddenly starts worrying without reason,
wishing that someone,
someone who no longer walks the streets,
someone who no longer walks out the door,
or stares out the window,
will walk past
and say:
I haven't seen you for ages, my friend!

I'm not here.
Shame, I won't be here tomorrow
when someone in a fast train
passes by a small brooding cloud
above a mournful station
and, having a sudden premonition,
calls to the cloud,
raises his hand,
turning round to look back
as it vanishes out of sight,
muttering under his breath:
Maybe that's him?
Maybe that's the one who doesn't exist,

لەهیچ وێستگەیەکی دونیادا
ڕاناوەستێ!

لێرە نیم
حەیفێک لێرە نابم
کە سەعات نمەی بەیانییەک
لە کتێبخانەیەکدا،
کتێبخانەیەک بۆیمباخ لە مل و
سیدارە بەسەر و
بۆنخۆش بە ئارەقەی کتێب،
شیعرێک مەلوول .... دانیشتوو لەنێو بانیژەی
تەنیایی خۆیدا
شیعرێک کە هێشتا دەنۆڕێ و
کە هێشتا
ڕوون وەکو ئاوێنە دەپەیفێ،
کەسێک .... میهرەبانترین کەسی دونیا
دەچێتە ژێر بالّی و
لەسەر ڕەفەکە دایدەگرێ
پێکەوە دەچنە دەرێ
پێکەوە لە چاخانەکەی پالّ کتێبخانە
لەژێر هەتاودا دادەنیشن
پێکەوە لەبەر باراندا پێدەکەنن
پێکەوە دەست دەنێنە گیرفان و
لەژێر بەفردا فیکە دەکێشن
پێکەوە دەنۆڕن و هێلّ بەژێر ژیاندا دەهێنن
هێلّ بەژێر
هەر هەموو ئەو شتانەدا
کە گرنگن
کە سادەن
کە تازەن
هێلّ بەژێر هەر هەموو ئەو شتانەدا
کە گەمارۆ دراون
کە دیار نەماون

32

someone who can't ever stop
at a single station anywhere.

I'm not here.
Shame, I won't be here
when in a drizzly hour one morning
in a library –
a library dressed in a *tarboush*
and a suit,
a library stuffed full of musty books –
a sad poem, sitting in
its own attic of solitude –
a poem which still gazes expectantly
and speaks as clear as a mirror –
is picked up by someone,
the kindest person in the world,
who takes it by the hand
and helps it off the shelf.
Together they leave for
a teahouse near the library
where they sit in the sun
and laugh in the rain,
and putting their hands in their pockets,
they whistle in the snow.
As the world passes by,
they think about life, considering
all the things that are important
all the things that are simple
and new.
They consider the things
that have been fenced off,
that have been disappeared

که له پەراویّز نراون

هیّل بەژیّر شیعریّکدا
که گەورە نەبووە
هیّل بەژیّر ساوایەکی لە پەنتۆیەکی پڕ
لە پەپوولەوە پیّچراو
هیّل بەژیّر بەقالیّکی پرتەقالیی
هیّل بەژیّر کۆلارەیەکدا ... گریّدراو
لە پەتی منالیی
هیّل بەژیّر بەیانیانی چایەکی شیرین
هیّل بەژیّر تەلیّک گیا
هیّل بەژیّر چۆلەکەیەکی تازەدا
که بەتەمایە
بۆ یەکەمین جار
بەنیّو باراندا بفریّ
هیّل بەژیّر قوتوویەکی قووپاودا
که لە نیوەڕوانی هاوینی جۆگەیەکدا
ستران دەچریّ!

لیّرە نیم
حەیفیّک لیّرە نابم
که دەرگایەک دەکەویّتە سەر پشت و
کەسی لیّ نایەتە دەریّ
که پەنجەرەیەک دەکریّتەوە و
هیچ پەپوولەپایزەیەک
پیاسەیەک بە ئیّوارەیدا ناکا
که پەیژەیەک چاوەڕوانیی دەیکوژیّ و
کەس بە دوو بۆل تریّوە
بۆ هاوینانی سەربان
پیایدا هەلّناگریّ
که کۆلانیّک لە تەنیاییدا سویّی دەبیّتەوە و
کەس توند توند بەخۆیەوە نایگوشیّ
که دەرەختیّک دەڕوخیّ و
کەس ڕەنگیّکی بۆ خۆی نابات

34

and pushed to one side.
They consider a poem
that has not come to life.
They consider an infant
wrapped up in a blanket patterned with butterflies.
They consider an orange seller.
They consider a kite threaded to childhood.
    They consider their morning sweet tea.
       They consider a blade of grass.
They consider a baby sparrow
risking its first flight through the rain.
    They consider a crushed can
       tinkling downstream at siesta-time.

I'm not here.
Shame I won't be here
when a door is opened
but no one walks through.
When a window is open
but no pollen-down drifts in with the evening.
When a ladder dies from waiting
for someone to climb it
carrying a bunch of grapes
up to the roof on a warm summer night.
When a road pines away from loneliness
and no one gives it a hug.
When a tree collapses
and no one remembers its colours.

که باخچەیەک پیر دەبێ و
کەس گوڵێکی لە یەخەی خۆی نادات!

لێرە نیم
حەیفێک لێرە نابم
که ئێوارەیەک دێبیتە حەوشه و
ئەوە من نابم
که پەنجەم لەسەر زەنگه و
دوو دڵ وەک بەرسیله
لەودیو دەرگاوه وەستاوم
لێرە نیم
حەیفێک لێرە نابم
که سەعات زستانی عەسرێک
شپرزه دێبتە دەرێ و
ئەوە من نابم
که منداڵانه ...لە بەرایی (با) و
لە درێژبوونەوەی باران ڕاماوم
لێرە نیم
حەیفێک لێرە نابم
که سەعات ڕەهێڵەی عەسرێک
شارم بەدوادا تەی دەکەیت
ژێر باڵی پەڕەسێلکەیەکی تەرم
بۆ دەگەڕێی
لەدەرگای ماڵی مێروولەیەکی ڕەفیقم
دەدەیت
شپرزه دەڵێیت: ئەری نەتان دیوه؟
دەست لە پیکابی سمۆرەیەکی مەست ڕادەگریت
خۆت به دوکانی پەپوویەکی گوڵفرۆشدا
دەکەیت
لەگەڵ کۆترێکی ڕەشبیندا
دەکەویتە گمه گم
لە باغێکی خزمم لادەدەیت
نێو مستی نوقاوی گوڵێکی ژێوانم

36

When a garden is overgrown
and its flowers are never worn anymore.

I'm not here.
Shame I won't be here
when you come out to the courtyard one evening
and it isn't me
whose finger presses the doorbell,
waiting by the door
with a heart full of doubt like green grapes.

I'm not here.
Shame I won't be here
when in a cold hour one winter afternoon
you walk out all worried
and it won't be me
who stares like a child at the rising wind
and the falling rain.
I'm not here.
Shame I won't be here
when one afternoon at snowfall
you walk through the city looking for me.
You search for me under the wing of a swallow.
You knock on the door of an ant friend of mine;
worried, you ask, Haven't you seen him today?

You stop a drunk squirrel's truck.
You enter an owl's florist shop.
You coo along with a pessimistic pigeon.
You stop by a garden related to me
to look through the closed fists of flowers.

بۆ دەگەڕێی
ژێر پووشێک لە بەرهەیوانی مالّی لەقلەق
نێوان دەنووکی زەرنەقووتەیەک
ژێر نینۆکی ژێرژکێک
قولّایی قەترەیەک ئاوم بۆ دەگەڕێی
ژێرپێی خالّخالّۆکەیەک
بن دەنکێک گلّ
ناولەپی گەرمی گولّە گەنم
نێو مزرایی دەنکێک گۆیژ
بن لاسکی رەشە رێحانەیەکی زیز
ژێر زوبانی زیکزیکەیەکی لالّ
بن گیرفانی خوساوی حەکایەتێک
بیلبیلەی چاوانی مورووویەک
نێو فەقیانەی تەلێک رێواس
سەر سەربانی بۆنێک منالّ
نێو بوخچەیەک پر لە خەیالّ
ژێر تویّژالّی کلووە بەفرێک
ترپەی دلّی دەنکێک هەنار
هەر هەمووی
هەر هەمووی دەگەڕێی
حەیفێک لەو سەعات وەیشومەی
عەسرەدا
تۆ بەدوامدا دەگەڕێیت و
کەچی من لێرە نیم
حەیفێک لەو سەعات کرپێوەی عەسرەدا
ئیدی من

ن

ی

م

!

زستانی

38

You search through the straw under the house of a stork,
in the beaks of fledgling sparrows,
in the claws of a hedgehog.
You look through the depths of a drop of water for me,
you search under a ladybird's feet,
beneath a crumb of clay,
inside the warm heart of a stalk of wheat,
in the bitterness of a haw,
under a bruised leaf of basil,
beneath the tongue of a speechless cicada,
in the corner of a dank pocket of a story,
in the iris of a bead,
in the sleeve of a rhubarb stalk,
on the roof of a fresh smell,
in the middle of a bundle of dreams,
under the skin of a snowflake,
in the heartbeat of a pomegranate seed –
in everything.
You will search for me in everything.
What a shame that at that sad hour of the afternoon
you'll be looking for me
but I won't be here,
what a shame that
on this afternoon as snow falls
I'm
    not
       here
          anymore.

*Translated from the Kurdish by Choman Hardi and The Poetry
Translation Centre Workshop*

Tarboush: Arabic name for a fez, a traditional red felt Turkish hat with a tassel.

Tahriib

Da'da gabayga dabuubtiyo murtida, doodda hadalkayga;
Waxaan uga danleeyahay inaan, danaha sheegaaye
Dadweynow waxaan doonayaa, inan dadaalaaye
Dulmigan dhacaayaan rabaa, inaan dillaacshaaye
Tahriibtaa dadkeennii rogtaan, deyr ku xidhayaaye.

U dulqaadan kariwaayay oo, waan damqanayaaye
Jidhkaa iga dubaaxiya markaan, dib u jalleecaayo
Inta aan ilmada daadiyaan, dibinta ruugaaye.

Afrikaa dhib deris looga dhigay, daayin abidkoode
Soomaaliduna ka daran oo way, ugu dambeeysaaye
Qalbigaa intuu daxal ka galay, daamur wada yeeshey
Dareenkii waddanigaa lumoo, waa dad baabba'aye
Damiirkii waxaa garanayaan, digigixoonayne

Dabin laysu dhigay weeye oo, duul kalaa xidhaye
Diiwaanka waxaa noogu qoran, doorkii Falastiine
Ma daneeye aan diirran baa, dooxay shacabkiiye
Dillaal iyo mallaal baa midiba, dacalka haystaaye.

Haddii laga dareeroo dalkii, doonni laga raacay
Deebaaq qadhaadh iyo hadduu, dacar inoo yeeshey
Dullin iyo abaar iyo hadduu, diirato horseeddey
Daad laga ordaayiyo hadduu, degel madow yeeshey
Duufaan kacaysiyo haddii, duumo laga qaaday
Duqaydiyo carruurtii hadday, dibed u soo yaacday.

Dalka yaa u hadhi tolow markaa, waa dareen yimiye?
Waa xaajo duudduuban iyo, sheeko duluc dheere
Da'yartaa dhammaatiyo waxa, dumar idlaanaaya
Diricyada tahriibaaya ee, dabargo'aa taagan
Diihaalka gaajada kuwaa, dibed wareegaaya
Badahay dul-heehaabayaan, damalladeenniiye.

The Sea-Migrations

CAASHA LUL MOHAMUD YUSUF · SOMALIA/SOMALILAND

Declaiming this poem, a *gabay*, I alliterate in D to start debate,
to disseminate, to disclose to you: the public.
Hey, you – be diligent! I'm trying though it's difficult
to destroy the injustice, demolish the status quo.
Sea-migration disables my people, I want to drive it back.

I can't endure what's happening, it's like I feel the damage,
my body jerks, distressed, every time I see them desolate,
tears stream down my face, I chew blood from my lips.

All Africa has dilemmas, there are always disputes
but in this distressed continent, Somalis sink down to the bottom.
Their hearts only detest, they have rusted and deadened.
Love for their country's disappeared, they self-destruct.
The conscience has departed, the compassion is mislaid
in a trap laid by others; they act despite their interests.
Acts seem pre-determined; we're destined to be like Palestine.
People don't give a damn, civilian deaths hold no interest.
The dealer and middleman draw the deadly game out.

If people abandon their homes and decamp by boat,
hurt by discrimination, unable to stand delay;
if thugs dispossess and murder, and there's disaster and drought;
if dust-storms blow, dispersing infection and plague;
if children make a dash, the elderly decide to go –
then my people, I demand: who'll stay behind in our country?
Interesting question I've asked, isn't it? A matter to consider.
Look at the hordes of women, all the young who drown,
all those deprived of life's basics, adrift outside their country:
our future floats bloated in sea, is a corpse dragged on sand.

They are devoured, picked dry by sharks and sea creatures,
wild dogs eat them like *darib*, the best camel fat,
and many dead bodies lie decaying on our shores

Diibkiyo yaxaaskaa cunoo, daaqay lafahooda
Dugaaggiyo waraabaa daldala, darib sideediiye
Duleedkaa la soo wada wadhiyo, dacalka xeebaaye
Iyagoo dubkiyo diirku baxay, baa la daawadaye
Waa kuwaa darxumo le'day een, duugan kari waynnay.

Damac baa dadkaygii galoo, waa dawamayaane
Dayow baynnu noqonnay iyo ways, dabammaryaynaaye
Dib-u-socod ayaan wada nihiyo, dawlad jaahil ahe
Dawarsiga ku naaxdaan nihiyo, doonis ruux kale
Diif aan dhammaanaynnin baa, loogu dawggalaye.

Afartaa intaan dabar ka furay, diirad ma ku eegey
Darajada Ilaah baa baxshee, mawga furay daaha,
Doorkaa abwaannadu horey, uga daliilsheene
Deelleeyda maansada horey, uga daqiiqsheene,
Aniguna ka dabaggeeyey oo, waan ku darayaaye
Waanadu kuway deeqdo ee, raacda danahooda
Iyo kuwa dariiqii wacnaa, diinta ku ekaada,
Daayinow Ilaahow ka yeel, dabargo' weeyaane!

Waxba gabaygu yuu ila durkine, waan dabrahayaaye;
Haddii dalagga aan beerannoo, doogga la abqaalo
Nimcadaa inoo dararaysan iyo, badaha duudduuban
Buurahan Ilaah noo dejee, godol la soo daatay

Baadroolka diliq laynayee, dixaya hoostooda
Macdantaa dingiigtiyo haddaan, dahab ka soo saarno
Duunyada haddaan dhaqannoo, doobi laga buuxsho
Duruusta iyo cilmiga lays baroo, diinta la adkeeyo
Dalku wayna wada deeqi laa, aynnu dib u joogno
Daaquudka aan naarno iyo, ducufka shayddaanka
Khayraadku waa dihinyahee, aan dibnaha saarno.

London, 2008

defiled by strangers' eyes, skin peeled off their carcasses,
their lives end in distress, and there will be no decent burial.

My people are dull with greed, they get-rich-or-die trying.
We are filled with bewilderment, disordered and backbiting.
A state that can't read, a reactionary herd,
we only do well at begging, pleading for dollars and food.
We are snared in a cycle, in endless poverty. . . .

Declaiming these lines, I am undoing the camel's hobble,
Allah has raised me here, so I can draw open the curtains.
Decades ago, poets first stated the truth of this debate:
they devised a chain of poems, which we called the *Deelley*.
And I've drafted this poem, and I add it to the chain:
let us use words as a prayer, let the advice be followed.
Let us tread Allah's path, devote ourselves to his order.
Oh, deathless Allah! Change us before we are destroyed!

Let me not drag out my poem, but deliver an ending:
if we cultivate our land, if we dig in our crops,
if we discern our natural wealth, and the rich, deep ocean,
the mountains Allah has made for us, ready to be mined,
the fossil fuel that drips in the dark underground,
the mineral deposits, the reserves of gold,
the domestic animals, milked to fill milk-jugs,
if we develop our people, in knowledge and faith,
the country has abundance, let us return and reside.
Let us purge demons, dispose of devils and their deeds –
we have not used our resources, let's do it now.

London, 2008

Translated from the Somali by Clare Pollard and Maxamed Xasan 'Alto'

Gabay: Alliterative Somali verse form usually employed to advance serious argument.
Deelley: A very famous 'chain' of poems composed by many leading Somali poets in the late
1970s and early 1980s that were highly critical of the military regime of Siad Barre. The chain
was inaugurated by Maxamed Xaashi Dhamac 'Gaarriye' and Maxamed Ibraahin Warsame
'Hadraawi', both of whom received death threats from the regime as a result.

Postais do Mar Alto

I

Crioula ! dirás ao violão
Da noite e à viola do madrugar
Que és noiva e morena
      com Lela em Roterdão
Jamais venderás pela cidadela
      De porta em porta
A sede de água doce que balouça
      Em latas de folha-de-flandres

II

De manhã
Nevava sobre as têmporas d'Europa
A lâmpada da minha mão é nave
      Entre os fiordes de Norga
Desde ontem
Chove pela proa
      Aço que entorpece
E nos ossos de abandono
      gnomo de silêncio sem memória

Desde ontem
O navio é paisagem de alma sem retina
E teu nome sobre o mar
      sol + árvore de boca sumarenta

III

Já vendi Kamoca food
      nas ruas de New York

Postcards from the High Seas

CORSINO FORTES · CAPE VERDE

I

Crioula, you will tell the guitar
Of the night, and the dawn's small guitar
That you are a dark-skinned bride
      with Lela in Rotterdam

You'll never sell around the town
      From door to door
The thirst for sweet water that slaps
      In a tin can

II

In the morning
It snowed on the temples of Europe
The lamp of my hand is a caravel
      Among the fjords of Norway

Since yesterday
It's been raining on the prow
      Steel rain that numbs
Our abandoned bones
      gnomon of silence without memory

Since yesterday
The ship is the landscape of a blind soul
And your name upon the ocean
      the sun in a fruit-tree's mouth

III

I used to sell Kamoca
      On the streets of New York

Joguei orim nas vigas
        dos arranha-céus por construir
Num edifício em Belfast
Ficaram ossos e crânios
        De contemporâneos
O sangue ainda retine
        vivo
nas narinas dos telefones

IV

Ouvidos de ilhéu ouviram
A voz solarenga a goela olímpica
De um pilão nas ruas da Finlândia
Vi então patrícios
        vestidos de toga
Falando crioulo
Nas grandes salas de audiência

        Além-Pirinéus
        há negros y negros
Na Alemanha imigrada
os países da sopa
são os negros da Europa

V

Crioula! nas tarde de Domingo
        Ao sol dos arbustos
Dirás aos rostos de boa têmpera
        E velhos jogadores de cricket
Que os nomes
        De Djone
        Bana
        Morais
        Goy
        Djosa

I've played ourin among the girders
      Of skyscrapers under construction

In a building in Belfast
Remain the skulls and bones
      Of my contemporaries
The blood remains
Alive in the telephones' nostrils

IV

The ears of the islander heard
The sun-drenched voice in the Olympian throat
Of a pestle in Finland

I saw patricians
      clad in togas
Speaking Creole
In vast auditoria

      Beyond the Pyrenees
        there are blacks and blacks
Immigrants to Germany
in the soup-making countries
the blacks of Europe

V

Crioula, on Sunday evenings
      with the sun on the bushes
You will say to the good-natured faces
      Of old cricket-players
That the names
      Of Djone
      Bana
      Morais
      Goy
      Djosa

Frank
Morgoda
Palaba e Salibana
Utilizam-se
como
selo branco nos documentos
como
passaporte e livre-trânsito

À porta das embaixadas

VI

É boca probante
que o chão o drama
Emigram connosco debaixo da língua
Atestam-no
joelhos e cotovelos de secura
do colonato de Cabiri

Ao longo dos caminhos de ferro
Dou E recebo socos
Dos vizinhos da regedoria
Por dissídios de terreno
E normas de cultura

Numa noite de loucura
no colonato em Sacassenje
Dividimos a terra
entre pevides & árvores de fruto
entre sangue & cicatrizes

E fiquei previdente na fronteira
Empunhando a tranca da minha porta

Frank
Morgoda
Paliba and Salibana
Present themselves
    as
white stamps on documents
    As
    passport and laissez-passer

At the doors of the embassies

VI

Our mouths testify
    that the earth and the story
Emigrate with us under our tongues
To witness
    the dry knees and elbows
    of the colony of Cabiri

Along the chemins-de-fer
I give blows and receive them
From neighbouring governments
over land disputes
    And cultural norms

In a night of lunacy
In the colony of Sacassenje
We divided the land
    Between fruit-trees and seeds
    Between blood and scars

Having foreseen this I stayed at the border
Gripping the lock of my door

VII

Ora caminho
Olho que nasce: nascente que olha
A sombra da omoplata sobre o mundo
Tocando tambor
      com sangue d'África
      com ossos d'Europa

      E

Todas as tardes meu polegar regressa
      E diz à boca da ribeira
De Adis Abeba vim E bebi
      Nas cataratas de Ruacaná

VII

Now from the road
I watch the birth: the spring that watches
The shade of the shoulder-blades over the world
Striking the drum
> with the blood of Africa
> with the bones of Europe

And

Every evening my thumb returns
> And says to the mouth of the river
From Addis Ababa I came and drank
> In the cataracts of Ruacana

Translated from the Portuguese by Sean O'Brien and Daniel Hahn

قایقی که مرا آورد

پشت صورتی که شکل تو را دارد
اسم های قدیمی غیب می شود
خون   عکس   مچاله دارد
و   باد   پرنده‌ی مسی
انگار بیابان مرا از روی ژاکتم پوشیده باشد

برهنه نیستم
گاهی کلمات در سرفه هایم
و ماه کف آلود در لیوان   گم می شود
این سفر   همیشه دور زبانم چرخید
و رگ هایم از مرگ   چیزی پنهان نکرد
برای کشیدن قدم هایی به خط ثلث
تابستان مرا اقرار کرده بود
این کرک سبز مچاله   بر انگشت های یخ
موج به طرز زیبایی   شبیه عشق می آمد
و پس می نشست

دلم برای قایقی که مرا آورد
گاهی تنگ می شود
و اینجا شاهدم   برابر پلک های زمستان
همین آسمان کهنه است
و چمدانی که نیمرخ آبی ی مرا پنهان می کند.

The Boat that Brought Me

AZITA GHAHREMAN · IRAN

Behind these eyes that look like mine
old names are fading away, the past lies crumpled in my clenched fist –
a coppery bird in coppery wind,
this vast place has covered me from head to toe.

I am not stripped of word and thought
but sometimes what I want to say gets lost
like a moon smudged with cloud, or when I splutter on a drink.
My tongue trips up when I speak of that journey
though the blood in my veins felt the truth of death.
As I traced my footsteps through the tracery of my old language
Summer whispered to me
and my frozen fingers began to put out shoots
even as I began to love the cold ebb and flow of tides.

Sometimes I miss
the boat that brought me here,
now that I am witness to the icy eyes of a Swedish winter,
under these tired old clouds,
while that suitcase still holds a patch of the sky-blue me.

Translated from the Farsi (Persian) by Maura Dooley and Elhum Shakerifar

مصابيح

في الماء
في صَمْتي وقُرْبِكِ
في نارٍ - وَحْدَهَا تجمَعُنا
أطْفُو ..
ووحْدَكِ قد تُنَادِينَ عَلَيَّ!

....

يدخُلُ الطائرُ طقسَ الأخضرِ
مثلَ الوَتَر
بَرْقٌ يَرفُّ على العينِ كالسِّرِّ
تنحني قُبْلَةٌ في القوسْ
يَسْتَمِرُّ المطر!

في الشوارعِ لم يَعُدْ أصدقائي
في البيوتِ البعيدةِ عن بعضِها
لم تَعُدِ المصابيحْ
في القلبِ عادتْ رَجَّةُ النَّبْضِ المبعثر
لكنَّكِ تَرْمِينَ المناديلَ على الرَّاحِلِ
والباقي على نورِ الصباح!

Lamps

AL-SADDIQ AL-RADDI · SUDAN

In the water
in silence at your side
in a fire that draws us close
I drift –
and only you can call me

. . . .
A bird enters spring
like a lance
Your eyes flash their secrets
A kiss grazes the rainbow
The rain rains

But the streets are empty of my friends
Lamps are extinguished
in the far-flung houses
and the lost heart echoes in its lonely chamber

You give your blessings to those who depart
and leave the rest to fate

Translated from the Arabic by Sarah Maguire and Sabry Hafez

Баҳор меояд

Таъми ғурбат чун аст эй бародари дилбанд,
Дарки танҳой чист.
Дарки танҳоии хуршед дар халаҳи фалак
Дарки танҳоии тасвир дар чаҳорчӯби оина.
Дарки танҳоии дил дар сина.
Зиндагй пеш мекашад моро
Ҷониби кӯчае ки барфи баландаш ба сари раҳгузарон мерезад.
Раҳ ба раҳ ойинаҳо
Ҳамчу дар хонае ханда
Тарҳи моро музҳик хоҳанд кард.
Пойҳо мусиқии мавзуни гом заданро аз ёд хоҳанд бурд.
Дастҳо шавқи ҷӯши гардиши сурхобро
Дави чубаҳои кӯчаки кабуд нахоҳанд шунид.
Дилҳо... оҳ дилҳо... қудрати ҳифзи ишқро дигар нахоҳанд дошт
Ё на? Намедонам. Лек медонам эй бародари ҷон,
Роҳи вопас ҳам ҳаст... Роҳи оинабанди хотираҳо.
Ман аз он роҳ ба фасли содагии мӯъчизаҳо боз мерасам.
Ба он баҳори ҳарири малакути ки нахӯстин бор гуфти:
... Салом хоҳаракам
Дар сурати шонздахсолаи ман руҳи нинй мезист...
Нинии ҳазорсола.
Баъдҳо номаҳои ту саводи чашми маро меафрухт.
Номаҳоят хутути маърифати шеъри порсй буд.
Баъдҳо фохтаҳои Маскав
Аз забони ту "Шоҳнома" мешуниданд
Ва ба симург ҳасад мебурданд.
Тусхои сиҳиқад канори барзанҳо
Сарвҳои равони Ҳофизро шодбод мегуфтанд.
Бонги зангулаи калисоҳо
Ҷараси корвони Саъдй буд.
Корвон рафт. Дар ғубори биёбон гум шуд.
Инак эй сорбони маҳмили танҳой! Эй бародари ман!
Таъми ҳичрон чист?
Дар чаҳон панч рақам ҳаст ки чун пахш куни,
Садои шоди касе гуяд: сабр кун эй бародар! Дил банд!
Баҳор меояд...

Spring Is Coming

FARZANEH KHOJANDI · TAJIKISTAN

What does exile taste like, my darling,
what is it to know loneliness?
To know the sun's loneliness in the empty sky,
to know a reflection's loneliness inside the mirror frame,
to know the heart's loneliness in the breast.
Life pulls us
towards an alley where drifts of snow fall on us.
Path after path leads through
a mocking hall of mirrors.
Feet will forget the melody of stroll,
Hands will no longer hear blood bubbling
through narrow veins.
And hearts, O our hearts, will be so weak love leaks away –
or not – I do not know. But I do know, my love,
there is a way back – through memory's mirror.
I reach for the chapter of simple miracles:
the spring was heavenly silk when you first said,
'Hello my little sister'.
Behind my teenage front lived a baby – a thousand-year-old pupil.
Later, your letters flooded my dark eyes with light:
those letters were the gnosis of Persian poetry.
Years later, the nightingales of Moscow
heard the Epic of the Kings from your tongue
and envied the phoenix.
Soaring tuse trees on the verges
saluted the poet Hafez's flowing cypresses,
the chime of church bells
was the tinkle of camel-bells of the poet Sa'di's caravan.
The caravan has gone – lost in desert dust.
And now, O camel-driver, carrier of loneliness, O my brother,
what does separation taste like?
In this world are scattered letters
that spell out loud and clear – this:
Wait, my darling, spring will come. . . .

Translated from the Tajik (Persian) by Jo Shapcott and Narguess Farzad

مهاجر قاچاقی

حتمن آفتاب
تازه از ستیغ کوه قد کشیده است
حتمن
ابرها هنوز ابر
باد ها هنوز باد
خانواده ها هنوز خانواده اند

صدای پارتی
صدای رقص و پایکوبی وشکستن پیاله
صدای خنده
هر دقیقه انفجار می کند
مردم است
شادمانی است

من با دلی بزرگ
در
کشتی بزرگ پادشاهی
زیر سرد کامیون
مرز را لمیده ام
لحظه لحظه
با شکوه
وارد خاک انگلیس می شویم

Illegal Immigrant

REZA MOHAMMADI · AFGHANISTAN

it is possible
the sun has risen
and over the mountains
the clouds are there still,
that winds are driving
and families arriving
and there is the sound of a party
sound of dancing, chanting,
and glasses smashing,
the laughter exploding
in every minute and people
and happiness and also
me, with my big heart,
in a ship or strapped under
the truck, I am crossing
the border and moment
by moment am entering
with glory England

Translated from the Dari (Persian) by Nick Laird and Hamid Kabir

باڵنده

به پێی تازهترین پۆلێن، کوردهکان
سهر به رهگهزی باڵندهن!
ئهوهتانێ...
لهسهر پهڕهی زهرد و دڕاوی مێژوو
کۆچهرین و
به کاروانی سهفهردا دهناسرێنهوه

بهڵێ کوردهکان باڵندهن!
شوێنیش نهمێنێ ئازاریان بگرێتهخۆ
وههمی گهشتی
نێوانی گهرمیانهکان و
کوێستانهکانی نیشتمان دهدۆزنهوه
بۆیه من لام سهیرنیه
کوردهکان دهفڕن و

وڵات به وڵات دهگهڕێن و ههرنابن
به خهونێکی سهقامگیرو شارستانی!
نه هێلانه به خۆیانهوه دهبینن
نه لهدوا نیشتنهوهیهکیشدا
سهرێ لهمهولانا دهدهن و دهپرسن له حاڵی
نه خۆشیان دهکهن بهقووربان
توزی رێگای بادێکی خۆش مرور وهک ناڵی.

60

Birds

KAJAL AHMAD · KURDISTAN

According to the latest classification, Kurds
now belong to a species of bird
which is why, across the torn, yellowing pages
of history, they are nomads spotted by their caravans.
Yes, Kurds are birds! And even when
there's nowhere left, no refuge for their pain,
they turn to the illusion of travelling
between the warm and the cold climes
of their homeland. So naturally,
I don't think it strange that Kurds can fly.
They go from country to country
and still never realise their dreams of settling,
of forming a colony. They build no nests
and not even on their final landing
do they visit Mewlana to enquire of his health,
or bow down to the dust in the gentle wind, like Nali.

Translated from the Kurdish by Mimi Khalvati and Choman Hardi

*Mewlana: Name by which Jalal ad-Din Mohammed Rumi is commonly known in
Muslim countries ('Rumi' means 'Roman' in Arabic and is used to refer to people
associated with the Byzantine Empire).*
*Nali: Refers to famous lines from Nali, 17th century poet, 'I sacrifice myself to
your dust – you gentle wind! / Messenger familiar with all of Sharazoor!'*

Hijos del sol y del viento

Aún vivimos en las esquinas
de la nada
entre el norte y el sur de las estaciones.

Seguimos durmiendo
abrazando almohadas de piedra
como nuestros padres.

Perseguimos las mismas nubes
y reposamos bajo la sombra de las acacias desnudas.

Nos bebemos el té a sorbos de fuego
caminamos descalzos para no espantar el silencio.

Y a lo lejos
en las laderas del espejismo
todavía miramos, como cada tarde
las puestas de sol en el mar.

Y la misma mujer que se detiene
sobre las atalayas del crepúsculo
en el centro del mapa nos saluda.

Nos saluda y se pierde
en los ojos de un niño que sonríe
desde el regazo de la eternidad.

Aún esperamos la aurora siguiente
para volver a comenzar.

Children of the Sun and the Wind

MOHAMMED EBNU · WESTERN SAHARA

We still live
on the brink of nothingness,
between the north and south of the seasons

We still sleep
on stone pillows,
like our fathers

We still follow the same clouds,
resting in the shadows of thorn trees

We still drink down our tea while swallowing fire
and we walk barefoot not to frighten the silence

And in the distance
at the edge of the mirage
we still watch, every evening
the sun fall into the sea

And the same woman greets us
while she posts lookout for the dusk
in the middle of the map

She greets us, then is lost
in the eyes of a child
smiling from the lap of eternity

And we still wait
for a new dawn
We still wait to begin

Translated from the Spanish by Tom Boll and the Poetry Translation Centre Workshop

Фаромуши замон

Навҷавоне буд. Колои ҳақири худро
Дар кӯчаи мо мегустард
Неруи Рустамӣ аз шонаҳои солими ӯ
Наъра мекашид
Чеҳрааш як асари дурӣ аз Юсуф дошт
Мӯйҳояш чу машъали Зартушт
Фарру фуруғи бостон мерехт.
Навҷавон рӯи курсии кӯҳнайе нишаста буд
Ва рӯзҳои гулобии зиндагиашро падруд мегуфт
Қандҳои бехаридораш дар пироҳани коғазии хеш арақ мекарданд
Сигорҳои арзонаш медонистанд
Ки саранҷоми зиндагияшон сухтан аст
Собунҳояш орзу мекарданд ки рӯзе
Дар дастҳои зебое об шаванд ва миранд.
Навҷавон чашми бехиёлашро ҷониби раҳгузарон мебурд
Ва бар омадану рафтани мошинҳо меандешид
Вале бар омадану рафтани баҳор намеандешид.
Тобистони ҷавонии ӯ
Дар таҳи офтоб мепажмурд.
Ва зимистон кафани барфи ҷавонии вайро мепечид
Ҷавон хушбахт мезист ё бадбахт.
Зеро зи вуҷуди ишқ ғофил буд.
Зеро дар ҳавошии зиндагӣ занг мебаст.
Зеро ҳоларо асли моҳ мепиндошт
Замонаи бераҳм
Навҷавонро ба руи курсии куҳна нишонда буд
Ва фаромуш карда буд...

Forgotten by Time

FARZANEH KHOJANDI · TAJIKISTAN

There was a boy. He would spread his wares
in our alley. The strength of the hero, Rostam,
roared from his shoulders,
he had the features of a Joseph,
his hair was the torch of Zoroaster,
flaming with ancient times.
The young boy sat on an old stool,
saying goodbye to his rose-scented time.
His sweets had no takers,
sweating in their paper wrappers;
his cheap cigarettes knew
that the point of their lives was to burn;
his soaps longed for the day
they would lather in beautiful hands and die.
The boy turned his eyes
towards passers-by
and, pondering the to and fro of cars,
he didn't think of spring coming and going.
The summer of his youth
was dissolving into sunset
and winter would wrap him in snow.
Happy? Unhappy?
For he was oblivious to love,
for the margins of his life were rusting,
for he mistook the moon's halo for the moon.
Ruthless life had sat a young boy
on an old stool and forgotten him.

Translated from the Tajik (Persian) by Jo Shapcott and Narguess Farzad

Rostam: Epic hero of the story, Rostam and Sohrab, part of the Persian epic of Shahnameh.
Zoroaster: Also known as Zarathustra, Persian prophet and founder of Zoroastrianism.

Emigrante

Todas as tardes o poente dobra
      o teu polegar sobre a ilha
E do poente ao polegar
      cresce
      um progresso de pedra morta
Que a Península
        Ainda bebe
Pela taça da colónia
Todo o sangue do teu corpo peregrino

Mas quando a tua voz
      for onda no violão da praia
E a terra do rosto E o rosto da terra
      Estender-te a palma da mão
Da oral maritima di ilha
      De pão & pão feita
Ajunturás a última fome
      à tua fome primeira

Do alto virão
rostos-e-proas-da-não-viagem
      Assim erva assim mercuro
Arrancar-te as cruzes do corpo

O grito das mães leva-te
       agora
À sétima esquina
      onde a ilha naufraga
      onde a ilha festaja
A sua dor de filha
E a tua dor de parturiente

Que toda a partida É potência na morte
      todo o regresso É infância que soletra

Emigrant

CORSINO FORTES · CAPE VERDE

Every evening, sunset crooks
      its thumb across the island
And from the sunset to the thumb
      there grows
      a path of dead stone
And this peninsula
         Still drinks
All the blood of your wandering body
From a tenant farmer's cup

But when your voice
      becomes a chord on the shore's guitar
And the earth of the face and the face of the earth
      Extend the palm of the hand
From the seaward edge of the island
         A palm made of bread
You will merge your final hunger
      with your first

From above there will come
The faces and prows of not-voyage
      So that herbal and mercury
Extract the crosses from your body

The screaming of mothers carries you
               now
To the seventh corner
      where the island is shipwrecked
      where the island celebrates
Your daughter pain
The pain of a woman in childbirth

So that all parting is power in death
    all return a child's learning to spell

Já não esperamos o metabolismo
    Polme de boa fruta fruta de boa polpa
A terra
    aspira
        teu falo verde

E antes que teu pé
        seja
            árvore na colina

E tua mão
    cante
        lua nova em meu ventre

Vai E planta
    na boca d'Amílcar morto
Este punhado de agrião
E solver golo a golo
    uma fonética de frescura
E com as vírgulas da rua
   com as sílabas de porta em porta
Varrerás antes da noite
Os caminhos que vão
    até às escolas nocturnas
Que toda a partida é alfabeto que nasce
    todo o regresso é nação que soletra

Aguardam-te
    os cães e os leitões
    da casa de Chota
    que no quintal emagrecem de morabeza

Aguardam-te
    os copos E a semântica das tabernas

Aguardem-te
    as alimárias
    amordaçadas de aplauso e cana-de-açúcar

No longer do we wait for the cycle
      Pulp from good fruit, fruit from good pulp
      The earth
          breathes in
              your green speech

And there before your feet
              should be
                  a tree on a hill

And your hand
        should sing
            a new moon in my heart

Go and plant
      in dead Amilcar's mouth
This fistful of watercress
And spread from goal to goal
      a fresh phonetics
And with the commas of the street
      and syllables from door to door
You will sweep away before the night
The roads that go
      as far as the night-schools
For all departure means a growing alphabet
   for all return is a nation's language

They await you
      the dogs and the piglets
      at Chota's house
      grown thin from the warmth of the welcome

They await you
      the cups and semantics of taverns

They await you
      the beasts
      choking on applause and sugarcane

Aguardam-te
> os rostos que explodem
> no sangue das formigas
> novos campos de pastorícia

Mas
> quando o teu corpo
> > sangue & lenhite de puro cio

Erguer
> Sobre a seara
A tua dor
E o teu orgasmo
> Quem não soube
> Quem não sabe
> > Emigrante
Que toda a partida É potência na morte
E todo o regresso É infância que soletra

They await you
     faces that explode
     on the blood of ants
     new pastorals to cultivate

But
     when your body
          of blood and lignite, on heat

Raises
     Over the harvest
Your pain
And your orgasm
     Who didn't know
     Who doesn't know
          Emigrant
That all of parting is power in death
And all return is a child learning to spell

Translated from the Portuguese by Sean O'Brien and Daniel Hahn

چەند وشەیەك دەربارەی تەمەنی خۆم

کاتێ ڤالیا لێم دەپرسێ:

«کەی پێت نایه ئەم دنیایه؟»

پێکەنینم، وەکوو چووزەرە ڕێواسێك،

لەژێر بەفری دەم و لێوما سەر دەردێنێ.

پێکەنینم – گریانێکە،

زەردەخەنەی هەموو دنیا دەگەچلێنێ!

بەڵێ، ڤالیا!

نیاندرتاڵ بووم

کاتێ پێی خۆم نایه دنیا.

بە چاوی خۆم

چاخی هەموو پێغەمبەرەکانم دیوه.

کاروانی مێژووی شەرمەزار

بەسەر لۆچی ناوچەوانما تێپەڕیوه.

کەچی هێشتا...

ئۆفیسە قۆڵبڕەکانی

ئەم چاخە ویژدان تۆپیوه

لە دەفتەری زیندووواندا

ناوی منیان نەنووسیوه!

72

A Few Lines About My Age

ABDULLA PASHEW · KURDISTAN

When Valia asked me,
'When did you first set foot in the world?',
my laugh, like a rhubarb shoot
pokes its head through the snow of my mouth.
My laugh is a sob
that crumples all the smiles in the world.
Yes, Valia!
I was Neanderthal
when I first set foot in this world.
With my own eyes
I witnessed the era of the prophets,
the shameful passage of history
marched down the wrinkles on my forehead.
And yet . . .
the swindling institutions
of the rotting conscience of the age
did not record my name
in the book of life.

*Translated from the Kurdish by Mahsn Majidy and The Poetry
Translation Centre Workshop*

Tarih-Coğrafya

Kimse ilk basmaz bir toprağa
Sırtlanırsın geçmiş ruhları
Tanrılar Tanrıçalar da bir
zaman sen gibi canlardı
İçinden geçer hepsinin gücü, zaafı
Aşağıda toprağın üzerinde
kafilelerce çoğaldı
ölü ölümlüler
Gıkları çıkmadı
Allah'ın unuttuğunu kimse anımsamadı

Tarihimsin bir miktar kabul
ama coğrafyam değil
Yer kaplayanların adıdır coğrafya
ve kalmak yürek ister

Ölülerimle kaldım coğrafyamda
Sen kendini inkâr ettin
resmî oldun, hakikatinden boşaldıkça

Hayatımla kaldım coğrafyamda
kendi tarihimi yazmaya

History-Geography

KARIN KARAKAŞLI · TURKEY

No one is the first to set foot on any soil
You're always borne by souls who passed before
Time was, gods and goddesses
were alive just like you
Their strengths and weaknesses flow through you
into the earth
trodden underfoot by the procession
of the mortal dead

Granted some of you are my history
yet not my geography
Geography is the name of those who occupy the land
and it takes heart to stay

I stayed in my geography with my dead
Yet you denied your very self
Turned official, emptied of truth

I stayed in my geography with my life
to write my own history

*Translated from the Turkish by Canan Marasligil and The Poetry
Translation Centre Workshop*

Entropia en Wiesbaden

Por el romano muro te asomaste
a ver la calle alemana
bajo la lluvia tenaz y declinante.
Lo que viste fue el bullicio, la fractal
escritura del desgaste europeo.
Mucho dinero, finas ropas,
edificios cuidadosos, gestos agrios,
mala comida -Goethe, en fin,
en su áulico, nemoroso
y patriarcal papel de santo doctus, poeta
enciclopédico.
Nada que contar de regreso,
nada sino la lluvia ahora pertinaz
y final. Un soplo del Espíritu Santo
entraba por la boca de los minutos-
pero tú, presente, más cuidadosa
que las Edades Medias
de la Selva Negra,
atestiguabas el sermón puritano
y el sedimento postindustrial,
las palabras eclipsantes
de cualquier académico, los consejos
de algún editor
despistado en Francfort. La entropía
se apoderaba de Wiesbaden
y tú renacías incesante
contra el fulgor del tiempo.

Entropy in Wiesbaden

DAVID HUERTA · MEXICO

You peeped out over the Roman wall
into the German street
battered by the slant, stubborn rain.
What you saw was Europe worn away,
its crowded, fractal script.
Lots of money, well-cut clothes,
prim dwellings, curt gestures,
ghastly food – and, finally Goethe
in his memorious, courtier mode,
patriarch, santo doctus, mode
of the all-enlightened poet.
Nothing to tell on your return
except for the now constant,
final rain. A breath of the Holy Spirit
entered the mouth of the passing moment –
but you, present, more diligent
with detail than the Middle Ages
of the Black Forest,
bore witness to the puritan sermon
and the post-industrial dust,
the overbearing views of
some academic, the counsel
of an editor astray
in Frankfurt. Entropy
engulfed Wiesbaden
while over and over you were reborn
against the blaze of time.

Translated from the Spanish by Jamie McKendrick

آب سیاه

شقایق‌ها اول آمدند و
ملخ ها
بعد وقت باد
این تمام کودکی ی چشم‌های تو بود
پیش از آب سیاه و تیغ
رشته‌های هزار مسجد
از گل‌های دیوانه رد می‌شد

اول شقایق‌ها رفته‌اند
بعد مادربزرگ و
اتاق نمور شازده
عکس اوپنهایمر و پاتریس لومومبا
مبل قرمز در حراجی‌ی الیاس

چارقدهای بته‌دار آبی رد شدند
آکاردئون و پرچم‌های عزا
ترک ها   کردها
عموهایم   با عکس‌شان   ته قلیان
مادرم در صف اول نماز جمعه   پشتش به من
برادرم عضو بسیج

اول ملخ‌ها می آیند و بعد شقایق‌ها
نه
اول شقایق‌ها رفته بودند
و ملخ‌ها...

گودی چشم   از برف پر می‌شد
دره‌های زمستان سفید است

بعد تیغ و آب‌های سیاه...

Glaucoma

AZITA GHAHREMAN · IRAN

The corn poppies came first,
then the locusts
and after that the unravelling wind.
That was how childhood looked to you
before the dark water, before the thorns,
before the mountain range of a thousand mosques
cast shadow over those wild flowers.

First the poppies went
then grandmother,
then the royal rooms grew shabby,
the photos of Oppenheimer, Lumumba,
the red furniture – everything went to the second hand shop.

Joyous accordions and flags of mourning,
Turks and Kurds,
little blue patterned headscarves –
all passed us by in the street.
'By Appointment to . . .' the Princes, my mother's brothers,
was stamped on every cup and *shisha*,
my mother, first in line for Friday prayer, kept her back to me,
my brother joined the *Bassij*.

First the locusts come, then the poppies
no
first the poppies went
then the locusts . . .

The hollow of the eye   fills with snow,
the valleys of winter are white,
then come the thorns and the dark waters. . . .

Translated from the Farsi (Persian) by Maura Dooley and Elhum Shakerifar

Bassij: Iranian secret police.

نص

رَأَيتُ المِلاكْ

والعَصافِيرَ مَذْبُوحَةً
ورأُيتُ الحِصانْ
العَساكِرَ
والشَّجَرِ المِّيتِ
السيِّدَاتِ الحَزينَاتِ
السيِّدَاتِ الوَلُوفَاتِ عَلَى الوَلْوَلاتِ – الصُّراخْ

رَأَيتُ الشوارِعَ والعَرَبَاتِ الأَنيِقَاتِ مُسرِعَةً
رأَيتُ المَرَاكِبَ و"الشُّفَّعَ" الأَبْرِيَاءْ

قلتُ كيف هو الطِّينُ يا سيِّدي الماءْ
في هذه الحَالْ
كيف الدُّخَانُ – الظِّلَالُ – الروائِحُ
لكنَّني
لم أَقُلْ – عَامِداً – كيفَ حَالُ البيوتْ

80

Poem

AL-SADDIQ AL-RADDI · SUDAN

I saw the angel
and the singing birds slaughtered.
I saw the horse,
the soldiers,
the grieving women,
the dead trees, and other women
inured to screams and wailing.
I saw the streets, the gusting wind,
the sports cars
racing by, the boats, the innocent kids.

I said, 'Master of the Water, this is
how things are: tell me about the clay,
the fire, the smoke, the shadows, the smell
of reality'. Deliberately, I did not ask
about our homes.

Translated from the Arabic by Mark Ford and Hafiz Kheir

يوميات حلب

(1)

الكتابة ألم.

والدم الذي ينقط على الشاشة يلوث المشهد ويترك على الكنبة مايشبه بقع القهوة الجافة نلمسها بأصابع مرتجفة كي لا تنتقل الينا العدوى

نستند بظهور مكسورة كأننا ذاهبون الى الجحيم بعيون مغبشة بالاحمر الداكن.. لكنه بنيٌّ أيضاً ويترك على الروح مايشبه الصدأ

نمسح على الرؤوس الهرمة ونهرب من لفظها ثم نلعق الملح الذي يسيل من العيون.

الذين يزحفون من طرف الشارع الى طرف الشاشة يتركون على الاسفلت أثراً أخضراً سرعان ما يكبر مثل سياج من الحبق، يرموننا بوردة ويموتون على عجل كي لانخجل منا

...اخلعْ نعليك الآن وامشٍ على قطع الزجاج.. إنك في الوادي المقدس.

(2)

"رفاق القراءة نائمون.

تتجول وحيداً بين رفوف المكتبة

دون إشارات تدل على المخرج.

الأنين على اليمين من الرف الثالث

فصل كامل مطرود من الرواية،

والضحك عنوان مأساوي

لكتاب في الفلسفة.

تسيل السياسة كالمخاط من رف لآخر

لا وقت للملاحم

لكتاب الإمتاع والمؤانسة

حيث ماتشادو يدفع الغلاف المقوى برفق

كي لاتسقط الصحون

..

نحن أشبه ما نكون بمسودات الكتب

Aleppo Diary

FOUAD MOHAMMAD FOUAD · SYRIA

(1)

Writing is pain.

And the blood that drips down the screen pollutes the atmosphere staining the couch with what looks like dried coffee, which we touch with trembling fingers so we don't get infected.

We manage with broken backs as if going to hell seeing dark red, no brown as well, which deposits a residue like rust in the soul.

We stroke their old heads then turn aside to lick away the tears.

Those who crawl from street to screen leave green traces on the asphalt that spring into bushes of basil; they toss us a flower and die in haste to spare our shame.

Now you've entered the sacred valley, take off your shoes and walk on broken glass.

(2)

The comrades in reading have fallen asleep.
You wander alone through the book stacks
with no sign of an exit.
From the third shelf on the right comes a groan
a whole chapter expelled from a novel.
Laughter the tragic title
for a book of philosophy.
Politics flows like phlegm from one shelf to another.
There is no time for epic
for *The Book of Delight and Intimacy*
as Machado eases open the book covers
gently, so as not to startle the ornaments.

مليئين بالمقاطع التي تحتاج الى تنقيح"

(3)

على شرفة البيت أجلس، حلب أمامي سوداء وموحشة، قرقعة صحون في العتمة تعني ان ثمة حياة تحدث على طاولة. لا نأمة سوى رشقات رصاص متقطعة من مكان ما وقذيفة واحدة يسبقها صفير غريب... ثمة من يترك الان هذا الكوكب بحلق جاف.

حلب أمامي سوداء وساكنة، الظلال العملاقة هذه ربما لأشجار ربما لغيلان قادمة من حكايات بعيدة في الطفولة ربما هو بخار اسود تنفثنه الآن نساء ينتظرن اولاداً صاروا أرقاماً في نشرة الاخبار حلب.. لا نقرة عود.. لا قدٌّ يميس.. لا كأس في " العندليب"* .. لا ندامى .. ولاغناء

..

..

واحداً فواحداً
يستيقظون،
وحوش العتمة

(4)

مارينا شحوارو
أنا مارينا قسطنطين
أرملة الخوري جورج شحوارو
ورفيقة مارسيل في الطريق – متأخرين- الى البيت
المزودة بأسرار الكنيسة المقدسة
وحبات الكرز في قعر كأس العنبرية
المشغولة بالضحك في الخمسين
وعقصات الشعر الضائعة في الجوارير

..

..

أنا مارينا
العائدة من الكارلتون
حيث الحياة تتشبث في الموسيقى

We are the proofs of books
full of paragraphs in need of revision.

(3)

I sit on the balcony. Aleppo spread before me black and deserted. The clatter of
crockery in the dark means life goes on. No sound save sporadic gunfire from
somewhere, then a single shell preceded by a peculiar whistle. Someone is leaving
this planet with a dry throat. Aleppo before me black and still. These huge shadows
might be trees or childhood goblins or black vapours exhaled by women waiting
for children who are already numbers in a news report.

Aleppo. No oud plucked. No 'Swaying Silhouette'. No drinks in The Nightingale.
No drinkers. No song.

One by one
they awaken
the beasts of darkness.

(4)

Marina Shihwaro

I am Marina Constantine
widow of the priest George Shihwaro
companion of Marcel as we walk, late at night, to our home;
I am she, endowed with secrets of the holy church,
with cherries at the bottom of a glass of liqueur,
busy with laughter at the age of fifty,
hair braids forgotten in an old chest of drawers.
..
..

I am Marina
returning from the Carlton
where life clings to music

وتتصلب كشجرة الصمغ

على راحتي
أرش الملح
وأنا أعلم ان المائدة لن تفسد
وأغمس إصبعي في النبيذ ليفرح القلب

..

..

أنا مارينا
التي شمت في المنعطف الخطأ
رائحة الخوف تنز من القبضات العرقانة
وتخترق الهواء كمعدن رصاصي
قبل أن تغيب القلعة في قبعة الساحر

..

..

أنا مارينا
التي لم تعلم أنها ماتت
الا حينما أصغت مع الآلاف الذين يرتدون الابيض ويلوحون بالورد
الى صوت الكاهن في كنيسة النبي الياس:
يا أحبائي
لنردد جميعا بين يدي الرب
وبقلب خاشع
لراحة نفس ابنتنا.. حاملة الإكليل الى الذي في السموات.......
....
....
الفااااااااتحة.

and thickens like frankincense
Freely
I scatter salt
even though I know that meat will not spoil
I dip a finger in wine to rejoice my heart.

..

..

I am Marina
who, at the wrong turn, smelled
the odour of fear exuding from sweating fists
piercing the air like lead
before the Citadel vanished in a magician's hat

..

..

I am Marina
who did not know she had died
until, alongside the thousands bearing roses wearing white,
she heard
the words of the priest in the church of Prophet Ilyas:
O dearly beloved,
in God's hands and with humble hearts
let us pray:
May the soul of our daughter
who ascends with the crown to our Lord in Heaven
rest in peace.

…

…

Al-Fatihah.

Translated from the Arabic by Samuel Wilder and the Poetry Translation Centre Workshop

Swaying Silhouette: a famous Syrian song. The bar, The Nightingale, was where Aleppo's artists and thinkers would congregate.
Marina Shihwaro was killed in Aleppo on 18th June, 2012.
Al-Fatihah: Opening Sura of the Qur'an.

فوتبال

سیاست رودخانه بزرگی است
که قریه های ما را از هم جدا می کند

هی سربازان!
تفنگ هایتان را جمع کنید
بی سیم هایتان را ببندید
دستبند و هشدار و کمین چه به کار است
ما از شما نیستیم
تنها می خواهیم از رودخانه رد شویم
توپمان آن طرف افتاده است

...سیاست رودخانه غمگینی است

The Football

REZA MOHAMMADI · AFGHANISTAN

Politics is a river that divides the villages.
Hey soldiers!
Put down your guns and still your radios.
There is no need for handcuffs,
for warnings, for an ambush.
We are not one of you.
We are not one of them.
We just want to get across and get back our ball.

Translated from the Dari (Persian) by Nick Laird and Hamid Kabir

Les loups

J'entends les loups
Ils sont bien au chaud dans leurs maisons de campagne
Ils regardent goulûment la télévision
Pendant des heures, ils comptent à voix haute
les cadavres
et chantent à tue-tête des airs de réclame
Je vois les loups
Ils mangent à treize le gibier du jour
élisent à main levée le Judas de service
Pendant des heures, ils boivent un sang de village
encore jeune, peu fruité
à la robe défaite
le sang d'un terre où sommeillent des charniers
J'entends les loups
Ils éteignent à minuit
et violent légalement leurs femmes

The Wolves

ABDELLATIF LAÂBI · MOROCCO

I hear the wolves
nice and snug in their country homes
staring gluttonously at their televisions
counting bodies out loud
howling at the top of their lungs
for hours on end
I see the wolves
without their sheep's clothing
stuff their faces with fresh game
elect their token Judas by show of hands
drink the blood of a village
that is still young, a little fruity
the blood of a land strewn with mass graves
for hours on end
I hear the wolves
switch the lights off at midnight
and lawfully rape their wives

Translated from the French by André Naffis-Sahely

Hal la qalay

Hal la qalay raqdeedaa
Lagu soo qamaamoo
Qalalaasihii baa
Nin ba qurub haleeloo
Laba waliba qaybteed
Qorraxday ku dubatoo
Qoloftiyo laftii baa
Lagu liqay qallaylkee
Qosol wuxuu ka joogaa
Qubannaa danbeeyee
Weli qaba hamuuntee
Buuraha qotada dheer
Ka arkaaya qiiqee
Qarka soo jafaayee

Qalwadii mas baa galay
Qodax baase hoos taal
Fule quudhsigii diid
Geesi qoorta soo dhigey
Faras qaayihiisii
Qurux buu ku doorsaday
Qabqab dhaafay baa yimi
Qosol qoonsimaad noqoy
Qabyo waa halkeedii

Qarandidu libaaxbbay
Ku qadhaabataayoo
Soo qabo tidhaahdaa
Qaankiyo biciidkoo
Qaybtana shan-laab bay
Qoondeysataayoo

The Killing of the She-Camel

MAXAMED IBRAAHIN WARSAME 'HADRAAWI' ·
SOMALIA/SOMALILAND

How they came rushing to that place
where the carcass of the she-camel lay,
and what a commotion there was
as each caught at her flesh
pair by pair clawed off their share
frying it in the glare of the sun
and cramming down dry
its crisp skin, crunching the bones.
You'd bare your teeth too to see
their scattered followers come
still cramped with greed, ravenous
at seeing the smoke ascend
from the colossal mountain's top,
scrambling up cliffs and ravines.

The snake sneaks in the castle:
although it's carpeted with thorns
still the coward casts off his curses
so the courageous must stretch out his neck;
the cob stallion sells his values
in order to cut a fine figure.
When such cockiness struts forth
and even laughter becomes a crime
our country has unfinished business.

When the aardvark tells the lion
how it's supposed to hunt
and orders it, 'Go catch
the young camel and the oryx';
then carves five times its share
setting this aside

Isagana qorshaha guud
Qanjidhkiyo xumaystay
Ha qawedin tidhaahdaa
Aarkuna ma quustoo
Ma qarsado xanuunkee
Hadba qaran-jabkiisiyo
Qiirada xasuustuu
Kolba dibin qaniinaa

Qalwadii mas baa galay
Qodax baase hoos taal
Fule quudhsigii diid
Geesi qoorta soo dhigey
Faras qaayihiisii
Qurux buu ku doorsaday
Qabqab dhaafay baa yimi
Qosol qoonsimaad noqoy
Qabyo waa halkeedii

Weligay cad quudheed
Anna qaadan maayoo
Qalanjadan faraa dheer
Wax la qaybsan maayee
Bal inay qabuuruhu
Saddex-qayd ka maarmaan
Ama qoor-tol jeexaan
Labadaas mid quudhaan
Xilka qaawan saaraan
Hadba qaylo-doon baan
Ka horow qiyaamaha
Ku qulaamin maydkee
Aan qoofallaadee
Qarqarsiga ha iga furin.

while granting for the lion's role
glands and offal,
commanding it, 'Don't quibble,'
the lion can't cave in
and doesn't hide its hurt
but now and then remembering
the loss of its prestige
it bites its lip in bitterness.

The snake sneaks in the castle:
although it's carpeted with thorns
still the coward casts off his curses
so the courageous must stretch out his neck;
the cob stallion sells his values
in order to cut a fine figure.
When such cockiness struts forth
and even laughter becomes a crime
our country has unfinished business.

Never will I ever accept
a single insulting slice
from those grasping commissars –
I won't share a thing with them.
Until the grave's prepared
to forego its three-yard shroud
or a collar round the neck,
since one at least is needed
to cover the naked dead,
I'll keep rallying and calling
until the Day of Judgement,
pray my cries can comfort the dead:
tie me to this task, and don't
release me from its harness.

Qalwadii mas baa galay
Qodax baase hoos taal
Fule quudhsigii diid
Geesi qoorta soo dhigey
Faras qaayihiisii
Qurux buu ku doorsaday
Qabqab dhaafay baa yimi
Qosol qoonsimaad noqoy
Qabyo waa halkeedii

The snake sneaks in the castle:
although it's carpeted with thorns
still the coward casts off his curses
so the courageous must stretch out his neck;
the cob stallion sells his values
in order to cut a fine figure.
When such cockiness struts forth
and even laughter becomes a crime
our country has unfinished business.

*Translated from the Somali by W. N. Herbert, Said Jama Hussein
and Maxamed Xasan 'Alto'*

تشجيع القرويات (8)

الحروبُ النحيلةُ غداً
صدفةً في الظلام
أقفاصُ الفاكهة تخيف

أعرف بعد شارعين من الأسى
ملائكة
وطرقاً وخيمةً إلى الرب
أعرف الماء قبل أن يكتئب
في الثديات المرحة
يومياً بأجر زهيد

اليأس شيئاً فشيئا
على هيئة ماعز
أعرف فضلةً من يمامٍ غريب
قبل أن يشبع الأفق:
تعتقدين في البحر
نضع الحكايةَ في الملح
أعتقدُ في الشمس والصداع النصفي
في المشاط الغليظ أوقات السلم
السبرانو ينبعث من يدٍ حانية
والهوائي منفعلاً على سقف قرية:

Exhortation to the Village (8)

ATEIF KHIERI · SUDAN

Tomorrow the straitened wars
In darkness, suddenly,
the crates of fruit terrify

After two streets of grief
I know
Angels
and treacherous paths toward the Lord

I know water before it is sullied,
cheapened by carefree mammals every day

Piece by piece
I know despair in the form of a goat
I know the leavings of a homeless dove
before the horizon has had its fill

You believe in the sea
We preserve the story in salt
I believe in the sun and a split head
in wearing camouflage at a time of peace

In the caress of your hand
a soprano
an aerial quivering on the roof of the village

Translated by Samuel Wilder and the Poetry Translation Centre Workshop

Бояд фарор кард

Оқибат метаркад вожаи фарёд рӯи дафтари ман
Оҳ аз ин иҷтимои носолим,
Ки сояхо зи бузургии хеш менозанд.
Касе набудани хуршедро намефаҳмад.
Касе намедонад ки ин рӯшнойии маснуъ
Сароби субҳи дуруғин аст
Касе набудани маъниро
Дар шаклҳои буқаламун пай намебарад.
Ин шабаҳҳои беҳаюло
Бо либоси қашанги чашмрабо
Бо шуъои баланди гарданбанд
Бо нафасҳои муъанбар зи атри афранги
Бо суханҳои мунаққаш зи манбари замони риёро
Чун хақиқат муъаррифи карданд.
Ман аз бузургии бархе ки ҷавҳараш ҳақорат аст, сахт дилгирам.
Ман зи худ низ сахт дилгирам.
Чаро ки хеч намефаҳмам.
Аз ин заъифии шакл ва шаҳомати маъно.
Чаро равонаам аз пушти бебасиратхо
Ба шодбодии деве ки бо нигини Сулаймонӣ аст.
Чаро ба ҳеҷ сухан мекунам ки ҳеҷ най
Чаро ҳарфи намозеро чун ҳошия мебандам
Ба домани макруҳ
Бояд фарор кард
Бояд аз ин тилисм сӯи содагӣ гурехт.
Бояд нигоҳи тахтнишинро уруҷ дод.
Бояд намунаи дигари офтоб шуд.
Эй ёр чи гуямат ки ту ҳам бо нигоҳи оламбин
Дигар набудани хуршедро намебинӣ.
Чи гуямат ки ту ҳам ломпи нимбисмилро
Ҷои хуршед мегузинӣ.

Must Escape

FARZANEH KHOJANDI · TAJIKISTAN

At last the word for scream bursts into my notebook.
Damn this sick society
where shadows boast about their own size.
No one understands the absence of the sun.
No one knows that this brightness
is just pretending to be dawn.
No one understands the absence of meaning
in the guises of the chameleon.
These hollow ghosts
with their gorgeous clothes
and dazzling pendants on long chains,
and breath perfumed with the scent of Europe –
from the pulpit of time, with fancy words
they talk deceit as if it were truth.
I am offended by them, offended
by the pretentiousness of the very small.
I am offended by myself, too:
I just don't understand enough
about the weakness of form and the courage of meaning.
Why do I make conversation with nothing
and stitch my words into the hems of the mediocre
like margin prayers or footnotes.
Must escape
must run away to simplicity,
must elevate the best,
must become another example of the sun.
O darling, what can I say, for even you,
choose a dim light-bulb over daylight,
even you with your perceptive glance,
no longer see the absence of the sun.

Translated from the Tajik (Persian) by Jo Shapcott and Narguess Farzad

Kifungoni

Kwa kuangulia juu mbinguni
na kulia sana kwa matumaini
samawati imeingia
                    mwangu machoni.
Kwa kuota mahindi mashambani
na kulia sana kwa mahuzuni
manjano imeingia
                    mwangu machoni.

Waache majemadari waende vitani
Wapenzi waende bustanini
Na waalimu mwao darasani,
            Ama mimi, tasubihi nipeni
            Na kiti cha kale, za zamani
            Niwe vivi nilivyo duniani:
                    bawabu mlangoni
                    katika kingo ya maumivu ya ndani
            maadamu vitabu, sheria na zote dini
zitanihakikishia mauti
                    nikiwa na njaa au kifungoni.

In Prison

ALAMIN MAZRUI · KENYA

From looking up at the sky
and crying from so much longing
sky-blue has seeped
                    into my eyes.
From growing maize in the fields
and crying so much from sadness
yellow has seeped
                    into my eyes.

Let soldiers go to war
lovers go to the garden
and teachers to the classroom,
    As for me, give me prayer beads
    and an old chair from the past
    So in this world I would be:
        a gatekeeper
        at the door of inner pain
    while books, laws and all religions
guarantee me death
                    starving or in prison

*Translated from the Swahili by Katriina Ranne and The Poetry
Translation Centre Workshop*

یہ قیدی سانس لیتا ہے

اِن آوازوں کے جنگل میں
مرے پر باندھ کر اُڑنے کا کہتے ہو
رہا کرتے نہیں لیکن
رہائی کے لیے بینائی کو اِک جُرم کہتے ہو
مری پلکوں کو سی کر
موسموں کو جاننے پہچاننے کی شرط رکھتے ہو
مرے پاؤں کو زنجیروں کی بے چہرہ صداؤں سے ڈراتے ہو
مری آزادئ پرواز کی خواہش کو جنگل کے لیے آزار کہتے ہو
مرے جذبوں کی کشتی کو جلاتے ہو
مرے افکار کے دریاؤں کو صحراؤں کا قیدی بناتے ہو
مگر سُن لو
کوئی موسم ہو
حبس و جبر کا، صحرا کا، جنگل کا
یہ قیدی سانس لیتا ہے

104

This Prisoner Breathes

NOSHI GILLANI · PAKISTAN

I am trapped in a jungle of voices
In which I cannot spread my wings
Even so, you insist that I take flight
You will not set me free
And are so offended by my point of view
That you stitch my eyelashes closed
You insist that I must explain the weather
Terrorise my feet with echoes of chains
You say that my desire to be free
Is too much for your precious jungle
Yet you set fire to the boat carrying my feelings
Surround this sea of feeling with desert sand
But listen!
Whatever happens . . .
Suffocation, torture, desert or jungle
This prisoner breathes

Translated from the Urdu by Lavinia Greenlaw and Nukhbah Taj Langah

بەرد باشترە

شپرزەتر لە گەڵای سەر باڵی "با"
ناائومێدتر لە مەودای نێوان گەردیلەکانی "خۆڵ"
شەهوەتبازتر لە نیگای "ئاگر"و
بێزرەنگتر لە فوستانی "ئاو"، رۆژەکان رەتدەبن.
بەرد باشترە...
ژیانی مردووانەی ئەو سەنگینترە
لەقسەی ئەو فەیلەسوفانەی قەدەرێ
فریویاندینو بەتەنیا جێیانهێشتین!
حیکمەتیشی وەک قردیلەی خوێندکارێکی سەرەتایی
دڵبەرو سادەیە. ئەو کەویستی پیرۆزبێت وەچەی وەکو
بەردە قارەمانی شێخو بەردە مۆرو
بەردە رەشەکەی پێغەمبەری خستەوە...
کە ویستی نەمر بێت بوو بە میعمارو پەیکەرتاش
هەر بۆ ئەوەی بەدرێژایی رۆژەکە لەگەڵ کچان بێ
خۆی کرد بە بەردی هەڵماقۆو خەتخەتێن
توانی وا لە ژنان بکا رازی دڵیانی پێ بڵێن
بەرلەوەی بینێن بە گڵکۆی رزیووی پیاوچاکانەوە.
بۆ ئەوەی دەستی بگاتە مەزنیی پیاو
چووە سەر شانی سیزیفو کردی بە هێما بۆ عەبەس
لەراستیدا، بەردی سەبرو بەردی رەجمو
بەردی ئەلحەدو بەردەباز برادەرن.
بەردی نیازو دەستارو یاپراخو حەمام
دەستە خوشکی یەکترن.
جوگرافیای بەردینی ئێمە
حەقیقەتێکی سەرکێشی لەشاخزاوە
من دەمخواست نەوەی بوونێکی ئاویی بم
کە ژیانی لێ برژێ.
هەروەها کۆژراوی بوونێکی هەوایم
کە تا بڵێی مەزاجیی بێ.
شێتی بوونێکی ئاگریم
وەک هەموو ئەو پەرستگایانەی بۆ ئەبەد زەردەشتین.

Stone Is Better

KAJAL AHMAD · KURDISTAN

Bewildered as leaves on the wind's wing,
drear as the space between motes of dust,
lustful as the gaze of fire, colourless
as water's dress, the days pass.

Stone is better, its dead life weightier
than the words of philosophers who
for a while deceived us, then left us bereft.
Its wisdom, like the hair ribbons
of primary-school children, is simple and lovely.
When it wishes to be holy, it gives birth
to descendants like the 'hero stone' of Sheikh,
the prayer stone and black stone of the Prophet.
When it longs for eternity, it becomes
an architect and sculptor. Whenever
it wants to play with girls all day, it becomes
a fivestone and hopscotch pebble; it makes
women tell it their secrets before they press it
against the crumbling headstone of holy men.
To reach man's greatness, it sits on Sizeph's shoulder
until he stands for all human futility.
In fact, the stone of patience, the stone of stoning,
the burial and stepping stones, are brothers.
The wishing stone, the grinding stone,
the *dolmeh* and *hammam* stones, are sisters.
Our rocky geography is a defiant truth
born from a mountain. I wish I had been born
from a watery being, brimming with life.
Or from an airy substance, ever-changeable
and moody. Or descended from a living fire,
like all temples that are forever Zoroastrian.
Our geography is rocky which is why
our poems brim with talk of seas, captains
and ships we've never seen.
Our geography is defiant too which is why

جوگرافیای ئێمه بهردینه، بۆیه شیعرهکانمان پڕن
له باسو خواسی ئهو دهریاو ناخوداو کهشتییانهی که
نهمانبینین! ههروهها یاخیشه.. بۆیه گیرفانی مێژوومان
لێوان لێوه له مێوژی شۆرشو قووربانی
ههروهها کهللهرهقیشه..

دیرۆکی ئێمه بهردینه
بۆیه خهونهکانمان به کوشتار ئاوسن
من زمانو خهڵکێکی نوێم دهوێ
زمانێ که شاعیر بێتو خهڵکێکیش که شیعر بن.
شهقامێکی دیکهم دهوێ که سپێده پێیدا رۆشتم
خهیاڵم لای جریووهو گمهبێ نهک لهلای تیرۆرکردنم.
لهبهرئهوهی شتێکی جیاوازم دهوێ
بووم به سێوێکی چاوهڕوان
تاقهتم چوو..
ئهمهوێ به عهشق بڵێم خودا حافیز
بهرد باشترێکه له مرۆڤ
کردنی ئهو ههموو دڕۆو شهڕو زوڵمه
وایلێکردم ئهوه بڵێم.
ئێمه تهنیا بهناوی عهشقهوه دهکوژرێین
بهناوی خهباتهوه ههڵدهخهڵهتێین!
جورئهتمان هێنده بچووکه
جار ههیه لهنێو گیرفانی
بهرینی ترسنۆکیدا ون دهبێتو
دهبین به ئۆف. تاقهتم چوو..
حهزدهکهم ئیدی به ژیان بڵێم شهوباش
من دهمهوێ جیاببمهوه
مهرگ باشتره له مرۆڤ!!!

pockets of our history are caked
with the crumbs of revolution and its victims.
It is also stubborn.

Our history is rocky which is why
our dreams are rife with massacre.
I want a new era and a new people,
a people who are poets and an era that is poetry.
I want a different road, a road
I will walk in the morning thinking of
birdsong and cooing, not of my own murder.
Because I want something different,
I am like a waiting apple.
I am worn out. I want to say goodbye to love.
Stone is better than humanity.
It's only because of all the lies, wars,
and oppression, that I say this.
We are killed only in the name of love,
deceived in the name of struggle.
Our courage is so small,
it gets lost in great pockets of fear
and we give up. I am worn out.
I want to say goodbye to life.
I want to be divorced from life.
Stone is better than humanity.

Translated from the Kurdish by Mimi Khalvati and Choman Hardi

'Hero stone' of Sheikh: a large boulder in Bazian (near Suleimanya) where the wounded Sheikh Mahmud Barzanji (who led the Kurdish Revolts against the British in 1919 and 1922–24) took shelter.

Prayer stone: used by some Shi'a in private prayer.

Black stone of the prophet: the eastern cornerstone of the Kaaba, the ancient stone building toward which Muslims pray, in the centre of the Grand Mosque in Mecca.

Sizeph: Sisyphus.

Dolmeh and hammam stones: used for making stuffed vegetables and for washing clothes.

A cesariana dos três continents

Antes
da moeda do corpo Ao capital da alma
Antes da luz
no mar da memória
E da pedra & vento na erosão do rosto
Éramos no verão da terra
A semente sem primavera
Éramos a exclamação
Do lon na lonjura

Dando
Pernas aos montes E braços às montanhas
Dando face & sentido
Às dunas do mar alto
Que respiram
as coxas
os seios
o sexo de Sahel

Lembro-me de ti! na África do teu ventre
Interrogando-se
sobre o istmo + a
proa do nosso destino
Quando pólos e penínsulas de maremoto
Rasgaram & rasgavam
No vórtice da vida! na fractura da terra
A cesariana dos três continentes

Ficamos umbigos de pedra
Em rodopio
Entre a pele e o osso das estações
Ficámos então ilha + ilha

The Caesarean of Three Continents

CORSINO FORTES · CAPE VERDE

Before
the body was coin and the soul Kapital
Before the light
on the remembered sea
And the erosion of the face by stone and wind
We lived inside the summer of the earth
The seed that had no spring
We were the exclamation
Of the 'di' in distance

We gave
Legs to the hills and arms to the mountains
Gave a face and a meaning
To the dunes of the high seas
That breathe out
the thighs
the breasts
the sex of the Sahel

I remember you! In Africa your womb
Enquiring of yourself
about the isthmus + the
prow of our destiny
When poles, peninsulas and tidal waves
Tore and tore in the vortex of life! In the fracture of earth
The Caesarean of the three continents

We became navels of stone
revolving
Between the skin and bone of the seasons
We became island and island

sobre o vento
pelo arquipélago da evasão

*

Assim! foi a pronúncia
Antes & depois do 1.º dia + a
Erosão da crónica
na boca da "Rotcha Scribida"

beyond the wind
in the evasive archipelago

*

Thus it was pronounced
Before & after the 1st day + the
Erosion of the chronicle
In the mouth of the Written Stone

Translated from the Portuguese by Sean O'Brien and Daniel Hahn

Agoon

Ararta gabayga waayadaan, eeg isma lahayne
Ma aloosin maansooyinkii, aan astayn jiraye
Alifka iyo Miimkaba ma curin, iba furkoodiiye
Asaaski murtida waanigii, daayay illinkeede
Allaylee markaan uurxumada, eegi kari waayay
Inaan erey idhaahdaa kolkaa, way ekoontahye.

Waddan aabbihii waayay oo, wada agoomoobay
Ay ooridiisii mar hore, aakhirow hoyatay
Afka oodda laga saaray oo, aqal madow taagan
Oo aan adeer iyo abtiyo, eeddo kale haysan
Oo ehelka kii ugu xigaa, iilka wada geeyey
Oo ay ayaaniba ayaan, ugu amaah doontay.

Abris aadunoo laba afle ah, odayadiisii dheh!
Wixii aan aqoonyahan lahaa, aaway magacood dheh!
Isma dhaanto bay wada noqdeen, inan raggeedii dheh!
Ergadoodu waa taa iyaga, uubta gelinaysa
Amley baa wadnaha laga sudhaa, amarka kii diida
Iyagays arkaayee cid kale, kuma ilduufteene
Indho beeshey Soomaali oo, waa ogsoonnahaye
Awood hadday lahayd beri iyagays, jaray unuunkiiye

Abeesow inkaaraa dhiciyo, aafadiyo hoogga
Awaaraha iyo boodhkaa ka kaca, arladi Soomaale
Uuradaa ka boodaysa oo, aadmi geli waayey
Adduunyadaa ku tababbarata oo, waa iskuul furane
Ummaddii ku noolaydna waa, kala abraareene.
Argaggaxii ku dhacay waa kuwaa, inniba meel aadday;
Inna waa intaa ooyaysee, wada itaal beeshey
Inna waa intaa ololaysee, loo arxamahaynnin
Inna waa intaa aay cidla' ah, lagu ugaadhaysto
Inna waa intaa aayo li'i, arad Carbeed daadsan

Orphan

CAASHA LUL MOHAMUD YUSUF · SOMALIA/SOMALILAND

Lately, I haven't attempted poems, or arresting public attention.
I've stopped articulating verses, advancing my words,
haven't recited the initials – the alliterative letters of Alif.
I've stopped being involved, playing by form's essential rules,
but how can I stand useless, whilst my people grieve and ache?
With affairs as they are, I must utter a few words.

A country has lost its father. It is entirely orphaned.
Long ago his wife crossed over. She passed from this earth.
The land's sealed off by fences, behind them dark acts happen.
There are no uncles to help, there are no aunts,
instead kin kill each other; they dig each other's graves
as life undermines life; one day occurs after another.

Say it: snakes are toxic-tongued, assuming human masks.
Say it: we can't observe those we once called intellectuals.
Say it: no one is different, they are all equally bad.
Where are the envoys? Cast into a pit.
Those who refused orders? Blades stabbed their arteries.
They antagonise each other, ignore the others,
these unseeing Somalis, who can't tell good from evil.
If once they were mighty, today they engage in self-slaughter.

Hey Abees! There's been curses, affliction, sorrow.
Above Somali ground, clouds of dust unspooled.
Humans couldn't endure it, the heat-blast of awful burning
or the dumping ground, where a world practises shitting.
An urgent stampede, no abode here for the living.

A terror so intense, they fragmented, fled apart:
some of them are impotent, they are howling out for help,
some of them are attacked, bombs aim at them without pity,
some of them are hunted, hiding in the jungle,
some of them are hopeless, flung across the Arab World,

Inna waa intaa aradkan Gaal, eeridhaban keeney
Inna waa intaa eedadday oo, ubuc badeed jiifta.

Ayaandarrada ina haystaan, la anfariiraaye
Eerigo'anka aan taagannaan, la amankaagaaye
Is afgarad la'aantaa ayaan, ka istixyoodaaye
Asaraarka diintii galee, loo abtirinaayo
Arday iyo macallinkii ayaa, wada alhuumaysan
Astaantii Kitaabkay wataan, iyo Axaaddiise
Nin waliba intuu doonayuu, ku andacoodaaye
Abdo beeshayoo waydinkaa, aan u tudhahayne
Waxa aan galnee uumiyuu, innagu eedeeyey
Af-ku-xoogle mooyee nin kale, waa ogsoonyahaye.

Aheey sow qalbiga kama ilmeeyn, umal la taaheenna!
Aheey sow qalbiga kama ilmeeyn, aayo li'idiinna!
Aheey sow qalbiga kama ilmeeyn, aniga ii daada!
Aheey sow qalbiga kama ilmeeyn, aano nagu raagta!
Aheey sow qalbiga kama ilmeeyn, ayaan li'ideeda!
Aheey sow qalbiga kama ilmeeyn, 'aayar tali!' diidka!

Hooyada sidii igadh maqaar, wayday ubadkeeda
Hooyada halkay eeg tidhaa, lagaba awdaayo
Hooyada 'ax!' iyo 'way!' ku nool, oogtiyo allaylka
Hooyada halkay addin dhigtaba, adhax wareegaysa
Hooyada agteedii madfaca, lagu asiibaayo.

Waxba arami bay jiifsatee, yaanan urugoonnin
Isticimaar hadduu ii dhashiyo, amar-ku-taagleeyne
Addoonsigaan ka baxay waanigaa, galay albaabkiise
Afrikada madow bayga daran, aarka saanta cade
Asqow baa raggii iga noqdoo, wuu anbanayaaye
Sidii awrta raraygoo kalaa, 'ooh!' la leeyahaye
Ama adhi xayeeysoo kalay, wada ekaadeene.

Afgembiga wax igaga daran, amal la'aantayda
Aayar baa wixii layla rabaan, oofinahayaaye
Ilig baa la dhaafsaday Abees, udubdhexaadkiiye
Asaaggay haddii aan ka hadhay, eegmo xumadayda

some of them are running to asylum in the west,
some of them take boats, sink to death in the unfathomable sea.

I'm altogether bewildered. Don't understand this misfortune.
I'm angered in isolation – it feels like we're all alone.
I'm embarrassed at the lack, how there is no understanding –
wrongly interpreted religion, and the constant contradictions.
How insecure the student and educator's situation –
they're both aware of symbols in the Hadith and Qur'an
and select the lines of text that suit their assertions.
With your absence of mercy, the Qur'an loses eternity.
Other nations accuse us, and we've performed those acts.
Everyone knows this, but those who act.

Oh don't I weep and mourn in my heart, out of rage and agony?
Oh don't I weep and mourn in my heart, for the empty future?
Oh don't I weep and mourn in my heart, for their 'leave-me-alone-to-have-it-all'?
Oh don't I weep and mourn in my heart, at idle hate and revenge?
Oh don't I weep and mourn in my heart, that we're not assigned to Paradise?
Oh don't I weep and mourn in my heart, when power's not quiet or easy?

Think of a mother, like the she-camel whose offspring has died –
they fill its skin up with grasses, trick her into giving milk.
The mother looks everywhere, but her searches are ended,
from dawn until it's dark, she moans her ah and oh.
Every time she steps, an explosion rips her spinal cord,
every time she steps, heavy artillery shells fall.

Let me not eat out my heart, though distress accompanies me
and colonialism and dictatorship are reborn in my country.
Though owning slaves is over, inequality's door creaks open –
the black Africans are worse than white colonisers earlier.
Our men have lost awareness and also their way
like calves instructed to take the burden, to slow up at whoa!

Animate skeletons, undernourished goats, their bones show.
But our hopelessness is the worst act, in this upside-down society,
how, unresisting, we execute malevolent orders.
Hey Abees! The nation's trust was ensnared by selfish wealth.

Waa inaan illoobaa naftaba, way eekoontahaye
Waa inaan abaadaa sidaan, aakhirow kacaye
Waa inaan adduunyada dhammaan, kaba ag guuraaye.

Waxba alifku yuu ila gudbine, waxaan ku soo ooday;
Eebbow iyagays eersadee, cidi ma aanayne
Eebbow is aamminid la'aan, uurxumada taalla
Eebbow iyagays wada arkee, adigu soo oolli,
Eebboow abaaraha dhiciyo, omoska jiilaalka
Inuu ubuxu noo soo baxaan, kaa igmanayaaye,
Nabad baan u oonnee Allow, adigu noo oofi,
Neecow udgoon badan inaad, uga dambeeysiisid
Isnacayb ayaa kala galee, mid isu keenaaya
Oo Eebbihii garanayaan, hadal ku soo ooday.

London, 2009

If we're far behind our peers and looking so appalling,
maybe the appropriate thing is not to keep on living,
not to endure as if it's already after,
to move away entirely from this earth.

Let me halt my Alif alliteration. I could go on and on.
Oh God, no one else is responsible. The blame ends with Them.
Oh God, the suspicions, the endless ill will.
Oh God, the collusion, the grudges against each other.
Oh God, the parched season, the drought occurring now.
This is a prayer for flowers and leaves.
Oh God, bring ease. We thirst after peace!
And later, usher in new starts, fresh air –
release from intense hatred. I end now:
may a leader, obeying Allah, bring us together.

London, 2009
Translated from the Somali by Clare Pollard and Maxamed Xasan 'Alto'

قصيدة النيل

سورة:

تصعدُ الجدرانُ في اللبلاب

والخرطوم واقفةٌ

على ساقٍ تغنّي

هل ينامُ النيل؟!

كُنَّا عاشقَيْنِ نَهدهدُ الأطفالَ

– ما أُسمّي؟!

– أُسمِّيكِ حضورَ الأرضِ فاقتربي

– وما طعمُ البكاءِ؟!

– ... ...

إفترقنا!.

سورة:

النيلُ يمضي هادئاً

ينسابُ في صمتِ المدينةِ

واحتراقاتِ القرى

والأصدقاءُ الآن

لا يتبادلونَ تحيةَ الصُّبْحِ

ولا يتعارفونَ

وأنبياءُ الفَقرِ في كُلِّ الأماكنِ

يرشفون الشّايَ والحزنَ

ولا يتحدَّثونَ

يخبِّئونَ الموتَ في أطرافِهِم

ويوزِّعونَ الصَّبْرَ للأطفالِ

ينتشرونَ في الأشجارِ عَبْرَ الأرضِ

120

Poem of the Nile

AL-SADDIQ AL-RADDI · SUDAN

Prelude:

Walls climb the ivy
And Khartoum, poised on its unamputated foot
     Singing
Will the Nile ever escape into sleep?
We were the most loving of lovers, children trickling from us
          –   What name do you give me?
          –   I call you Presence of Earth
          –   Come closer then
          –   What will be the taste of grief?
          –   ....
And we parted!

Sura:

The Nile flows quietly
     Seeping through the city's silence
          And the burning sorrows of villages.

Now friends no longer exchange greetings each morning
     No longer recognise each other.
          Everywhere one sees them, these one-time prophets,

Poverty-stricken, sipping their tea, their tears,
     Speechless.
          They hide death in their fraying clothes,

And all they can say to our children is: patience.
     They fade into the trees, commit suicide
          At night, derive from alcohol

Their arguments, embark on futile wars
     With their women, give up
          Their prayers, then disappear.

ينتحرونَ في اللَّيلِ احتجاجاً
ثمَّ يَنْتَحِلُونَ عَقْلَ زَجاجةِ الخَمْرِ،
ويفتعلونَ حَرْباً في النساءِ،
ولا يقيمونَ الصَّلاةَ
ويرحلونْ.

تصعدُ الجدرانُ في اللبلابِ
والخرطومُ جالسةٌ على مقهىً تدخِّنُ
إستوى في اللَّيلِ قُطَّاعُ الطَّريقِ
وعابرو نصفَ المسافةِ
هل يكونُ الشارعُ الآن امتداداً
لاختناقِ اللَّيلِ بالعرباتِ والعُهرِ
وكنَّا عاشقَيْنِ، نفتِّش الأطفالَ
والأطفالُ في رئةِ المخابز

يسرقونَ النَّارَ
– ما اسْمي؟!
– أُسمِّيكِ احتراقَ الأرضِ، فانتفضي
– وما طعمُ الرَّمادِ؟!
– ... ...
إفترقنا!.

سورة:

الماءُ ضدَّ النَّارِ
والأمواجُ خارطةٌ تفرُّ من البلادْ
النَّارُ ضدَّ الماءِ
والدخان ذاكرةٌ تؤسِّسُ للرمادْ
الصَبِيَّةُ بين سِكِّيني وقلبي

Walls climb the ivy
And Khartoum, sitting in a café
                    Smoking
In the dark you can't tell apart
Muggers from those whose journeys they'd cut short.
We were lovers, looking for our children
Who were breaking into bakeries, stealing fire
From the ovens' throats.
                              –   What name do you give me?
                              –   I call you earth's Fiery Anger
                              –   So rise up
                              –   What will be the taste of ashes?
                              –   ……………………
                                    And we parted!

Sura:

Fire is the opposite of Water
And Smoke is a memory that prepares us only for ash.
Water is the opposite of Fire
And the waves are like maps, rippling across the land.
And the girl? She is somewhere between this heart and this knife. . .

City – you're a handful of grains of wheat, tucked
            Into the purses of usurers and slave-traders.
                    And the black men

Are approaching, approaching. River Nile
            To what deserts are you taking my reflections? You depart
                    And I stand among the horses, by your gate,

And my soul would embark on a holy journey too,
            For the silence suspended between us
                    Is a language floating among the ruins of a beautiful, vanished past.

والمدينةُ قبضةُ القمحِ

بحافظةِ المرابينَ وبجَّارِ العبيدْ

والرِّجالُ السُّمْرُ يقتربون يقتربون

يا نيلُ ..

إلى أيِّ الصَّحارى

تحملُ الآن تصاويري وتمضي

وقفتي بين الجيادِ أمامَ بابِكَ

عُمْرَةٌ للرُّوحِ

والصَّمْتُ المعلَّقُ بيننا

لغةٌ من الزمنِ الجميلِ إلى الزمانِ المستحيلْ

يا أيها النيلُ – أبي

هل كانت الأشجارُ نافذةً

لأحزانِ النساءِ

أم المرايا هشَّمت في الماءِ

تاريخَ الحضورِ الأنثويِّ

وثَبَّتَتْ في العشبِ لونَ الفقرِ

إنَّ الفقرَ ينبُتُ في أراجيحِ الصِّغارِ

يورِّثُ الأطفالَ

صمتَ اللعنةِ الكبرى وكُفْرَ الأوَّلينْ.

سورة:

النيلُ يفتح ساعديه

يحدِّثُ الطَّيْرَ المهاجرَ

ثم يصمُتُ

يعتلي عرشَ المكانِ

ولا ينامُ ..ولا ينامُ

النيل يَسْكَرُ بالنفاياتِ

124

O River Nile, father
Were the trees merely windows reflecting women's sorrows,
Or have your waters shattered their images,
Drowned the history of women,
And painted forever their meadows the colour of poverty?
Poverty invades the children's playgrounds, leaving
Them silent, accursed, their heritage
Only anger and disbelief.

Sura:

The Nile opens his arms
Speaks to the migrant birds
                    Falls silent
Reigns
          And never sleeps
          Never sleeps

The Nile drinks dry the desert's tavern,
Gets drunk on dumps of toxic waste,
Must survive in the city, falling apart
Each night, rising up through its history
          And never sleeps
          Never sleeps

The drums began with the sun
And its light filtered songs that entered into the pores of the soul.
In the river's shallows boats sheltered from toil and wind.
Now the carnivals of the blacks take fire
And the Nile has burst through the layers of time.

ويَقْنَعُ بالمدينةِ وانكسارِ اللّيل

يصعدُ في الزّمانِ

ولا ينامُ ..ولا ينامْ

طلعتْ من الشمس الطُّبولُ

ورقرقَ الضوءُ الغناءَ على مَسامِ الرُّوحِ

والماءُ استراحاتُ المراكبِ من عناءِ الرِّيح

فجَّرَ النيلُ الزمانَ

وقد أطلَّتْ – فجأةً– مَرَوِي

ووجه العاشقِ النوبيُّ

إذْ يمشي على حزنِ السواقي

وهو يبحثُ في الجيادِ عن الرجولةِ

أين تبدأُ دورةُ الدَّمِ يا بعانخي

أين يحتدمُ النزيفُ

وأنت مستندٌ على "كُوْشَ"

التي اهترأَتْ من الصمتِ المريْ

قل للجياد تحرّكي ،

تَقِفُ المياهُ على أناملِها

وتنشطرُ الخرائطُ هل تضيعُ الأرضُ،

والنيلُ اكتمالٌ للقرون القادمةْ؟!

النيلُ يعرفُ سوءةَ المدنِ التي ضاعتْ

ويعرفُ موقفَ الزّمنِ القَديمِ

ولا يحدِّثُ

إنه النيلُ

وللأجيالِ أن تمضي

وللأطفالِ أن يقفوا على الشَّطِّ طويلاً في انتظارِ العاقبة!

126

And, see, the kingdom of Meroë appears
And the face of the Nubian lover
Who walks among the sorrows of the waterwheels
Searching for warriors among the horses.
Where does the line of ancestral blood begin
And when does the blood loss reach its climax,
O King Piankhy, enthroned ruler of Kush,
A kingdom unravelling in bitter silence?

Shout at the horses, and let
The waters ready themselves.
Let the maps explode. How can the land be lost
When the future belongs to the Nile?

The Nile knows of the disgrace of cities
That have vanished.
Knows of the old times
Yet never speaks.
It is the Nile...
Generations will pass, and there will always be children
Lingering on its banks,
Waiting
For it all to end.

Translated from the Arabic by Mark Ford and Hafiz Kheir

Meroë: Capital city of the ancient Sudanese Kingdom of Kush.
King Piankhy: Kushite king who conquered Egypt.

لکه للمي ګل

لکه للمي ګل د باران په تمه
لکه ګودر د منکو لمس ته تږی
لکه سپیدې

د رڼایې په ارمان

او لکه یو کور..
لکه یو کور چي
بې له ښځي وي
وران
داسي زموږ د وختو ستړی
انسان

یوه شېبه غواړي چي:
ساه وباسي

یوه شېبه غواړي چي:
خوب وکي
د آرامۍ په لېچو
د آرامۍ په لېچو

128

Like a Desert Flower

PARWEEN FAIZ ZADAH MALAAL · AFGHANISTAN

Like a desert flower waiting for rain,
like a riverbank thirsting for the touch of pitchers,
like the dawn
longing for light;
and like a house,
like a house in ruins for want of a woman –
the exhausted ones of our times
need a moment to breathe,
need a moment to sleep,
in the arms of peace, in the arms of peace.

Translated from the Pashto by Dawood Azami and The Poetry Translation Centre Workshop

Plegaria

Señor, salva este momento.
Nada tiene de prodigio o milagro
como no sea una sospecha
de inmortalidad, un aliento
de salvación. Se parece
a tantos otros momentos...
Pero está aquí entre nosotros
y crece como una luz amarilla
de sol y de encendidos limones
-y sabe a mar, a manos amadas,
huele como una calle de París
donde fuimos felices. Sálvalo
en la memoria o rescátalo
para la luz que declina
sobre esta página,
aunque apenas la toque.

Prayer

DAVID HUERTA · MEXICO

Lord, save this moment.
There's nothing outlandish or
miraculous about it, unless it holds
a hint of immortality, a breath
of salvation. It looks like
any number of other moments . . .
But it's here now among us:
it casts its yellow light and swells
like the sun or like flaming lemons
– and tastes of the sea, of loved hands
and smells like a street in Paris
where we were happy. Save it
in your memory or deliver it
into the light that sets
on this page,
barely touching it.

Translated from the Spanish by Jamie McKendrick

살아남은 자의 배고픔

마치 자기가 어디로 가고 있는지 안다는 듯 완벽한
하나의 선으로 미끄러지는 새

그 새가 지나며 만든 부시게 푸른 하늘

그 하늘 아래 포스트머던하게 미치고픈 오후,

자리를 잡지 못한 사름들은 식당 입구에 줄 없이 서
있었다

Survivors

CH'OE YOUNG-MI · SOUTH KOREA

As if tracing a perfect, pre-destined route,
the bird soars

through the air,
turning that clichéd blue sky blindingly blue —

an afternoon sky
under which I am going postmodernly mad

A gaggle of customers stuck outside the restaurant
throngs round the entrance
not able to queue

Translated from the Korean by Sarah Maguire and Kyoo Lee

Golondrinas

Enganchadas al cable como pinzas de ropa,
gaviotas de madera diminutas,
ágiles y minúsculas contra la brutalidad del azul,
fijas al mediodía cayendo una tras otra,
moviendo ropas, brazos, sonrisas,
el pecho blanco, la capucha negra,
las alas afiladas y en lista, mínima agitación.
Hasta que vuelan todas excepto una,
que se plantó un momento y arañó el regreso,
como una ligerísima despedida,
axila de golpe la mañana.
Quedan los cables, el cielo en abandono intenso,
como una boda de domingo de pueblo,
después nada.

Swallows

PEDRO SERRANO · MEXICO

Gripping wires like clothes pegs,
small seagulls made of wood,
agile and tiny against the brutal blue,
bound to midday, they fall, one then another,
moving clothes, arms, smiles,
white breasts, black hoods,
pointed wings aligned, minimal agitation,
until they all fly off but one –
which takes wing then flits back,
like a swift goodbye,
breaking free of the morning.
The wires stay put, the sky in intense abandon,
like a Sunday village wedding,
then it's done.

Translated from the Spanish by Sarah Maguire and Gwen MacKeith

นรกและสวรรค์ของคนอื่น

นรกและสวรรค์ของคนอื่น...
เราหยิบยื่น, เป็นชนวนด้วยส่วนหนึ่ง
ผูกโยงสายใยไว้ลึกซึ้ง
ทุกการกระทำกระเทือนถึงซึ่งกันและกัน

อาจทั้งหมดสิ่งที่เห็นที่เป็นอยู่
ดูคล้ายชีวิตต่างปิดกั้น
ขวางโลกเฉพาะไว้ไม่สัมพันธ์
เหมือนไร้สิ่งยืนยันถึงสายใย

คิด กระทำ ดำเนินไปไม่รู้สึก
ลึกลึกสอดคล้องเคลื่อนไหล
เลือดเนื้อ, จังหวะเต้นของหัวใจ
อกหนึ่งอกใด — จังหวะเดียว

จังหวะเดียว — แต่แบ่งแยกแตกต่าง
สร้างทั้งหมดทั้งมวลจากส่วนเสี้ยว
เปลี่ยนแปลง แพร่งทางเลือกท่องเที่ยว
เกี่ยวพันสูงส่งหรือเสื่อมทรุด

นรกหรือสวรรค์ของคนอื่น...
เราหยิบยื่นข้างเป็นอยู่ไม่รู้หยุด
ไม่ว่าโสมมเพียงสมมุติ
หรือสุดสง่างาม — ความจริง

วันนี้โลกเลือกข้างแตกต่างขั้ว
ทั่วไป, สืบเสาะเฉพาะสิ่ง
มวลอดีตฝากอนาคตกาลอิง
ชิงชังหรือรักผลักไป —

เป็นนรกหรือสวรรค์ของคนอื่น...
เราหยิบยื่น, เป็นชนวนส่วนหนึ่งได้
ไม่ว่าเด็ดดอกไม้, ปลูกดอกไม้,

ไม่เลือกเปลงไฟของสงคราม...

Other People's Hell, Other People's Heaven

ANGKARN CHANTHATHIP · THAILAND

Other people's hell, other people's heaven
we pick up, like a spark
that fuses a deeply-held bond
all actions move each other

Perhaps everything we can see
looks like lives held back
only disconnected worlds are blocked
as though they lack strengthening bonds

Think   act   go on without feeling
cast an anchor deep in the flow
blood and flesh   the rhythm of the heart
whichever heart – one rhythm

One rhythm – taking many forms
creates the whole from each chamber
change   the crossroad offers a choice of journeys
reap a thousand heights or sink

Other people's hell or other people's heaven
we can't help but take in
whether they are repulsive
or glorious – truth

Today the world usually takes sides
seeks only the present
ignoring the future
continues to love or to hate

It is the hell or heaven of other people
we pick up that can be a spark
whether they are beautiful flowers, flowers in bloom
never choose the flames of war

Translated from the Thai by Tracey Martin and The Poetry Translation Centre Workshop

قضا

بارانی بی وقتم
که خیابان ها درکم نمی کنند

زمان گذشته دورم
که ارواح سیاحان گمنام و ملاحان نامدار
که ارواح همه گذشتگان در من مدفون است

کلمه ای مطرودم
که کودکان از من می گریزند
و شاعران ترکم کرده اند

صورت کنده بتی در بامیانم
که کشتی کشتی کشتی
از وطنم دست به دست
دزدیده می شوم

شغالی مرده ام
در خیابان های لندن
که از یاد شهرداری رفته ام

Providence

REZA MOHAMMADI · AFGHANISTAN

I am a rain that nobody wants.
Even the streets don't understand me.
I am the past perfect tense

and deep down inside me are buried
the ghosts of anonymous travellers,
of infamous seadogs and all of the dead.

I am a certain word small children fear
and which the poets have forgotten.
I'm Buddha's face in Bamiyan,

stolen, sold on from my homeland,
and I am a corpse, knocked down
in Stockwell, ignored by the binmen.

Translated from the Dari (Persian) by Nick Laird and Hamid Kabir

Je suis l'enfant de ce siècle

Je suis l'enfant de ce siècle pitoyable
l'enfant qui n'a pas grandi
Les questions qui brûlaient la langue
ont brûlé mes ailes
J'avais appris à marcher
puis j'ai désappris
Je me suis lassé des oasis
et des chamelles avides de ruines
Étendu au milieu du chemin
la tête tournée vers l'Orient
j'attends la caravane des fous

I'm a Child of this Century

ABDELLATIF LAÂBI · MOROCCO

I'm a child of this dreary century
a child who never grew up
Doubts that set my tongue on fire
burned my wings
I learned to walk
then I unlearned it
I grew weary of oases
and camels eager for ruins
My head turned to the East
I lie in the middle of the road
and wait for the caravan of the mad

Translated from the French by André Naffis-Sahely

Найнавоз

Роҳи бозор куҷост?

Ман басе мехоҳам аз чашме меҳрубонӣ бихарам.

Ман басе мехоҳам пироҳане дошта бошад

Руҳам аз ҳарири шодӣ.

Тоҷире ҳаст ки аз шаҳри таманноҳоям меорад

Ранги мунири шодӣ

Лек ҳайҳот дар ин бозор, бозори Хӯҷанд

Чеҳраҳо туршу суханҳо тунданд,

Қанди Табриз дилам мехоҳад.

Роҳи бозор куҷост.

Найнавозе ҳаст дар он ҷо ки ба ман мегуяд:

Гуши нашнида ба ҷуз ҳарфи ҳақорат пеш ор

Бишнав нур, бихонад ба сиёҳии Ёсин

Чашми нодида ба ҷуз ранги қабоҳат бигушо

Ба ҷамоли ҳақ бин.

Роҳи бозор куҷост.

Найнавозе ҳаст дар он ҷо ки диламро ба садо мехонад

Ба кулоҳаш ки пур аз як дурри маҳтобӣ нест

Гавҳари ашк бимонам, биравам.

142

Flute Player

FARZANEH KHOJANDI · TAJIKISTAN

Where is the real bazaar?
I want to buy an eyeful of kindness.
I want to dress my soul in hyperbole.
There's a merchant who brings me
a whole spectrum of leaping colour
from the city of desires.
But here at the bazaar at Khojand,
faces are sour, talk is hot
and I long for the cool sweets of Tabriz.
Where is the real bazaar?
The flute player tells me:
come with your ears used to insults,
and listen to the light recite a prayer to the dark.
Open your eyes used to pale shame
and see the beauty of Truth.
Where is the real bazaar?
The flute player is there
calling my heart towards his hat
full of old change, but not a single pearl,
and since I am the jewel in the teardrop
I must go.

Translated from the Tajik (Persian) by Jo Shapcott and Narguess Farzad

Aadmi

Aadmiyahaw hallaysani!
Ambadyahaw wareersani!
Maqal ereyadaydoo!

Buuraha ag joogsoo
Amakaag daraaddii,
Ilmo gabax ka siiyoo!

Cirka sare u eegoo
Xiddiggaha astaysoo
Arag felegga meeroo!

Onkodkiyo hillaaciyo
Ufadaa dhacaysiyo
Uurada waraysoo.

Ololkeeda Gooraan
Aammus oo dhegeysoo
Shimbiraha la ooyoo.

Badda "aw"-da haysiyo
Waxa uurka ugu jira
Axadhoo garwaaqsoo.

Dhulka aad u baadhoo,
Webiyada ordaayiyo
Daruuraha indheeyoo.

Oogada jalleecoo
Ciirada aroortiyo
Dabaylaha af gara oo.

Uduggooda kaymaha
Urso oo jeclaysoo
Ku ilwaadso dooggoo.

Arrogance

MAXAMED XAASHI DHAMAC 'GAARRIYE' ·
SOMALIA/SOMALILAND

Wandered brood of Adam,
lost, bewildered people,
hear what I have to say.

Stop for a moment before the mountains
and for the simple sake of awe
be humbled, let your tears fall.

Look to, look through the air above,
be moved by the sight of stars,
watch their bodies wheel.

Ask the thunder, see what lightning says,
the rain-bearing wind which blows
the good grey cloud, ask them.

The camel's old keen for her calf,
be hushed and hear it, hear how
the birds' song weeps with it: weep with them too.

How the sea sounds out its old chorus,
what moves in its abyssal womb:
acknowledge these and what they mean.

Examine the earth at your feet,
the rush of the rivers,
raise your eyes to the clouds.

Glimpse what lies above
the auroral mist, the winds,
understand what these things have to say.

The scent of wild acacia –
inhale it, relish it, and
delight in the green of pastures.

U abtiri naflaydoo
Ayaamaha tilmaansoo
Aabiga bilaashka ah,
Waa inaad illowdaa!

Afaggaalayaashiyo
Cadceeddeenna oloshiyo
Awrka samada yaa yidhi,
Aadmigay u shidanyiin?

Ifkoon cidi ku uunnayn,
Miyaan Dirirku oognayn?
Ururradu miyaanay
Kaa ayni weynayn?
Ilayskooda goormaa
Loo daaray awgaa?

Hadmaa felegga oosha ah
Amar buuxa lagu yidhi
Ku ekaw dadkoo qudha?

Haddaad eegga madhataan,
Miyaanuu iftiimayn,
Sidiisaa ahaanayn?

Aadmiyahaw hallaysani!
Amarkaagu waa been!
Waxaad uur wadaagtaan
Ugaadhaa wareegtoo
Ugbaadkiyo caleentaad
Uur wada gasheenoo.

Uumiyaha dhammaantii
Ilma-adeer gudboon iyo
Isir baad tihiinoo;
Noolahaad arkaysaa
Waa ul iyo diirkeed;
Waa sida indhaha oo
Kolkay midi ilmaysaa

Count up the lineage of all life,
mark the endless days and days:
this worthless arrogance of yours,
you have to let it go.

All nebulae and galaxies,
the Camel of the Southern Cross,
our own burning sun, who said these
were lit for humankind?

Before a man was made in this world
didn't Virgo blaze above?
Aren't all those gatherings of stars
far older than us?
Since when was their high light
kindled only for you?

Exactly when do you think the heavens
were told to carry out the order
'Confine yourselves to the human race'?
If you simply ceased to be
wouldn't their light continue?
Wouldn't it be then as it is now?

Wandered brood of Adam,
your bluster is a lie.
You shared this womb with all
wild things that roam,
all roots that flourish,
you entered this world together.

All creation is your cousin,
each creature your equal
and you share an ancestor:
all living things are to you
as stick is to bark, bark to stick.
You and they are like two eyes –
when one sheds tears
the other weeps.

Ta kaleeto ooydaa;
Looma uumin keligaa
Inay kuu adeegaan.
 Ammuuraha badh baa sir ah;
Sida xaal u eg yahay
Ujeeddadu ka xeeldheer.

They were not made for you alone,
nor were they created to serve.

Of everything which is, half is secret –
however things appear
the meaning is always deeper.

Translated from the Somali by W. N. Herbert and Martin Orwin

साधारण कमीज़

दोपहर और शाम के बीच
आता है एक अंतराल
जब थक चुकी होती हैं
आवाज़ें क्रियाएँ

जैसे अब
समाप्त हो गईं सभी इच्छाएँ,
बैठ जाता हूँ किसी भी
खाली कुर्सी पर

पीली कमीज़ पहने
एक लड़का अभी गुज़रा
मुझे याद आई
अपनी कमीज़
उन साधारण से दिनों में

यह संभव था
हाँ यह जीवन संभव था
मैं पहने हूँ अब भी
वैसी ही कमीज़

A Standard Shirt

MOHAN RANA · INDIA

Between midday and nightfall
there comes a time
when the day's noise and actions
are already done with,

just as now,
all desires quenched,
I am ready to sit down
on any chair.

A boy in a yellow shirt
has just passed by
and made me think
of a shirt of mine
in those old ordinary days.

So it was possible.
Yes, this life was possible.
And here I am, still wearing
a shirt just like that.

Translated from the Hindi by Bernard O'Donoghue and Lucy Rosenstein

Aural

Escarcha sucia del *audio*
en la penumbra nómada
del automóvil;
ciénaga de sonidos
en donde la aguja del oído
apenas puede moverse.
De pronto, una *torch singer*
desmenuza a Wittgenstein
con tenedores de Cante...
¿Cómo lo hace? ¿Cómo
desenlaza, destraba los lenguajes,
hace fluir el mundo -y por añadidura
suma la gracia
y la tragedia?
El automóvil
entra en la noche
ungido por la música.

Aural

DAVID HUERTA · MEXICO

Gritty frost from
the radio speaker
in the car's
nomadic shadows:
a swamp of sounds
in which hearing's
needle can
barely move.
Out of nowhere,
a torch singer
slices through Wittgenstein
with the cutlery
of *cante jondo* . . .
How does she do it? –
unstitch, unseam
language itself,
make the world flow and
if that wasn't enough
hit the twin peaks
of grace and tragedy?
The car
anointed with music
slips into the night.

Translated from the Spanish by Jamie McKendrick

Cartão-postal sem fôlego

A natureza não cuida de nada
nem olha pra tás.
Pára-raios e paraísos
e todos os verbos no infinito.
Morro
dentro da paisagem
onde as estações passam
nos relógios ao relento.
Pelas janelas do trem
ao tempo
bruscos recortes rápidos
arrancados pela raiz do ar livre:
o que a lua tira da pedra
pedaços de céu e mar
montanhas, ah! além e alheias
folhas rasgadas, deve & haver o quê?
E em qual caderno?

Breathless Postcard

ARMANDO FREITAS FILHO · BRAZIL

Nature doesn't nurture anything
it never looks back
parasols and paradise
and every verb in the infinite
I die
within a landscape
where stations pass
by clocks fixed in the open
From the windows of a train
through time
brusque cuts quick
plucked by the root from plain air:
what the moon pulls from the stone
pieces of sky and sea
mountains, ah! Beyond and indifferent
torn leaves, thou shall & shall not what?
And in which notebook?

*Translated from the Portuguese by Francisco Vilhena and
The Poetry Translation Centre Workshop*

לְפָנֶיךָ הַגֶּשֶׁם

לְפָנֶיךָ הַגֶּשֶׁם הָעַתִּיק
הַחֹם בְּגַבְּךָ, אַתָּה עוֹמֵד וְחוֹשֵׁב
מַה מְּעַטּוֹת הַמִּלִּים
שֶׁאָדָם צָרִיךְ בְּחַיָּיו
וְחוֹשֵׁב עַל מִי שֶׁרוֹאֶה כָּל אֵלֶּה וְעַל מִי
שֶׁפָּנָיו רוּחַ וּבַשַּׁלֶּכֶת, וְגֶשֶׁם
זֶה הַמַּכֶּה בַּחַלּוֹן.

Before You the Rain

TUVYA RUEBNER · ISRAEL

Before you the ancient rain
warmth on your back, you stand and think
how few the words
a man needs in life
You think of him who sees all this, and him
whose face is the wind, and the falling of the leaves, and rain
tapping the glass

Translated from the Hebrew by Oded Manor and the Poetry Translation Centre Workshop

En la entraña del tiempo

El tiempo cede
y entreabre
su delicada profundidad. (Puertas
ue unas a otras se protegen; que unas en otras entran; huellas,
rastros de mar.) Un otoño
de leños y hojarascas. En su fondo:
La espesura translúcida del placer; sus hiedras íntimas:
Oro:
foliaciones de luz: Fuego que enraiza en el metal florecido,
y un musgo fino,
incandescente.

In the Heart of Time

CORAL BRACHO · MEXICO

Time lets its subtle depths
half-open. (Doors
shielding one another; pushing open, one to another; the spoors
and traces of the sea.) This autumn
of kindling wood, drifts of leaves. At its heart,
forests of pleasure where the light shines through; its ivies, involved:
gold:
light in leaf everywhere: fire raked and rooted, a metallic flowering,
and the finest moss,
incandescent.

Translated from the Spanish by Katherine Pierpoint and Tom Boll

Zamanında

Seramik kabuğumu çatlatınca
Çini mozaik gibi çıktım ansızın
Eski ve zamansızdım
kıymetli ve kalender
Gökyüzü en iyi toprağa
uzanınca seyredilir ya,
Bir bulutun kanatlarında
kıkırdarken sırtım çim nemiydi
İçimde umut saçımda otlarla kaldım.

Kaç yıl önce bir kız yine
ve hep uzanmıştı çimlere
Elinde gereksizce şiir kitapları
mucizesine bakardı gökyüzünde.

Otların kökünü emdiğin
o sakıncasız ânı unutma
Kendinde güzel koca bir şakaydı
Bir dilek tutmuştun
eski ve zamansız
kıymetli ve kalender

İçim geçmiş uyumuşum
yıllar sonraki bir ihtimale
uyandım ağacın altındaki rüyamdan
Böyle tamamız böyle zamanında, demek için
Her kimsen sana

On Time

KARIN KARAKAŞLI · TURKEY

Suddenly I cracked my ceramic shell
and hatched like a Chinese mosaic
I was ancient and timeless
precious and carefree
Clouds are best contemplated
lying on the ground
Flying in the sky
I laughed, the grass warm beneath my back
with hope inside me, with leaves in my hair

How many years since you were a girl
flat out on the grass
superfluous poetry books in your hand
observing their miracle in the sky

Never forget that necessary moment
when you soaked up the wet leaves of grass
What a joke –
you made a wish
ancient and timeless
precious and carefree

I drifted off
and dreamed of the years to come
Waking from my dream under this tree
to say, this is how we become complete
We are on time
Whoever you are, this is for you

*Translated from the Turkish by Canan Marasligil and The Poetry
Translation Centre Workshop*

O Cataclismo e as Canções

Feliz o que de mim restar, depois de mim
Se uma só das canções cantadas
Viver além daquele que em mim agora canta.
Da hecatombe não salvaria contudo
Uma só das canções que cantei e canto.
Às entranhas do olvido
Antes roubaria o riso das crianças
E a idade do provérbio.

Assim aos vindouros
Intacto ofertaria o enigma da luz.

Cataclysm and Songs

CONCEIÇÃO LIMA · SÃO TOMÉ AND PRÍNCIPE

Happy what's left of me after I'm gone
If only one of the songs sung
Lives beyond the person singing in me now.
Yet I would not save from the slaughter
A single one of the songs I sang and sing.
I would steal the laughter of children
And the age of the proverb.
And so to those who come
I would offer intact the enigma of light.

*Translated from the Portuguese by Stefan Tobler and The Poetry
Translation Centre Workshop*

Desde Esta Luz

Desde esta luz en que incide, con delicada
flama,
la eternidad. Desde este jardín atento,
desde esta sombra.
Abre su umbral al tiempo,
y en él se imantan
los objetos.
Se ahondan en él,
y él los sostiene y los ofrece así:
claros, rotundos,
generosos. Frescos y llenos de su alegre volumen,
de su esplendor festivo,
de su hondura estelar.
Sólidos y distintos
alían su espacio
y su momento, su huerto exacto
para ser sentidos. Como piedras precisas
en un jardín. Como lapsos trazados
sobre un templo.

Una puerta, una silla,
el mar.
La blancura profunda,
desfasada
del muro. Las líneas breves
que lo centran.
Deja el tamarindo un fulgor
entre la noche espesa.
Suelta el cántaro el ruido
solar del agua.
Y la firme tibieza de sus manos; deja la noche densa,
la noche vasta y desbordada sobre el hondo caudal,
su entrañable
tibieza.

From this Light

CORAL BRACHO · MEXICO

That delicate flame –
eternity –
is falling, slanting, on this light. From this garden, so composed;
from this shadow.
Eternity lifts its latch onto time
and, there in it, objects
are magnetised.
They sink themselves in deeper,
and it holds them, then renders them back like this:
very clear, full,
abundant. Breezy, brimful of their own sunny selves,
their festival glory,
deep space.
Solid and separate,
they bring places,
time and space together, those neat little gardens,
so that we can feel them fully. Like perfectly-placed stones
in a garden. Like time's blueprint,
overlaid on a temple.

A doorway, a seat,
the sea.
The very old, deep
whiteness
of a wall. The slim lines,
all pointing into it.
The tamarind tree stands, glowing
through the dark.
The water-jug lets stream
the water's own sound, of the sun.
And his hands; warm, firm; the night, tangible,
night vast and brimming over, a profound river-flow,
his intimate, deep
warmth.

Translated from the Spanish by Katherine Pierpoint and Tom Boll

ایں جگ دے بھرے کٹورے وچ

ایں جگ دے بھرے کٹورے وچ
ساڈا عشق گلاب تاں ڈِکھو میاں

بھانویں رَل تے ٹکر نہ کھاوو
بھانویں نال اساڈے نہ باہوو
ساڈے کٹھے خواب تاں ڈِکھو میاں

بھانویں کٹھے بہہ تے نہ پیوو
بھانویں سُونھے ساڈے نہ تھیوو
ساڈا رنگ شراب تاں ڈِکھو میاں

کینویں سجھ گلیاں وچ لاہندا پئے
کینویں دَرتیں دریا واہندا پئے
ساڈا دل بے تاب تاں ڈِکھو میاں

In the Bowl of this World

RIFFAT ABBAS · PAKISTAN

In the bowl of this world
Look at the rose of our passion, my friend

Even if we don't eat together
Even if we don't sit together
We can at least dream together, my friend

Even if we don't drink together
Even if we are strangers
Let us consider the colour of our wine, my friend

The sun is setting on the lanes
The river is almost at my door
Let us examine our restless hearts, my friend

Translated from the Siraiki by Nukhbah Taj Langah and The Poetry Translation Centre Workshop

رفاقت

ما كفش هاي چرمي هم بوديم
وقتي كنار در همراه مي شويم
از خاطرات همدگر آگاه مي شويم

در خاطرات تو گوساله اي ست رومي
پروار گفته هاي خدايان
برواز نقل
پروار دور باطل تاريخ
از زندگي به مرگ
ار سفسطه به عقل
آن گاه
با كلب كلب كلب
با كلبيان رواق رواق آمده به بقل
پس از تو
پادشاهي
كفشي درست كرده
تحفه نموده است به درويشي
من بچه گوزني بودم به كاشغر
در حمله مغول به خراسان سپر شدم
در بلخ كاغذ سبق
در باميان علم
در غزنه زير دست يكي كفشگر شدم
دزدي مرا خريد
تو از زمان كفش شدن
انگار
اندازه مانده اي
درويش و نسل هاي پسين
هر گز ترا نه ديده نه پوشيده اند
تو تازه مانده اي
من
اما
با دزدهاي مختلفي راه رفته ام
دزدان مرا زمان به زمان شب به شب
با خود گرفته اند و به اين جا كشيده اند
اينك من و تو آه
همراه همراه همراه
از خاطرات هم دگر آگاه
......
ما كفش هاي چرمي هم هستيم

168

Friendship

REZA MOHAMMADI · AFGHANISTAN

Two pairs of well-used leather shoes
belonging somehow together,
we sit in the sunlight by the door
and go over each other's past.

You are the afterthought of a Roman calf,
born in the shadows of a goddess's temple,
bred to wisdom and vanity, from life to death
you are grown into the centre of all attention

then a king made two shoes from you and gave you to a monk.

Meanwhile, I was a baby Elk in China.
The Mongols made a shield of me, the Persians
a parchment in Balkh, and in Bamiyan
I acted as a standard all could see.
In Kabul I fell into the hands of a cobbler
before a thief with one eye bought me.
You, from the time you were a pair of shoes,
up to this present moment
have remained essentially the same.
The monk and subsequent generations
neither wore you nor noticed you much.
You're still remarkably fresh

but I have walked among robbers
day after day and night after night
and they dragged me with them to here

where now we sit by this door in the sun
and forever have known each other,
since we are two pairs of shoes made from leather.

Translated from the Dari (Persian) by Nick Laird and Hamid Kabir

صحبة مايكل انجلو

1

الملوكُ الذين مضوا ..
تركوا أثراً اسمه نسيانَهم
مثل (أليس) أو (كوش) ..إلخ .

تركوا: تيجاناً مُمعنةً في غرابةٍ
بقايا هياكلَ عظميةٍ
رؤسَ أسماكَ — أسماءَ يَصعبُ نُطْقُها
مراودَ كُحلٍ — وصايا — مدائحَ منقوشةً على حجرْ

بيدَ أنِّي تركتُكِ
أنتِ المُضاءةُ بي
أينما حملتُكِ عروشُكِ
دماً طازجاً في شرايينَ تَفنَى
و يصعبُ نسيانَكِ !

2

عند روما القديمة — أبواب روما القديمة
تصحبُني مُمعناً في صرامة الدقّة المتناهيةْ
لتصوركَ الخيطَ في ثقبه الأرهفَ
لتصوركَ الخطَّ والمنحني
تصحبُني في صداقةِ الحجرْ
يدٌ ليدٍ

170

In the Company of Michelangelo

AL-SADDIQ AL-RADDI · SUDAN

1

The kings who have gone
left us the remains of their forgettable names –
like Aleece or Kush

They left us their peculiar crowns
shards of skeletons
fish-heads
unpronounceable words
kohl-sticks
commandments
and eulogies graven in stone

Yet I left you radiant,
resplendent, wherever your throne sets down
Live blood in mortal veins –
truly you are unforgettable

2

You accompany me
to the gates of ancient Rome
reaching the ends of perfection
as you envisage grace threading each tender aperture
as you envisage the faultless line, and the perfect circle

أصابعُ لأصابعَ
ثم ..
في مدخلِ الحانةِ
نقرعُ كأساً بكأسٍ
تضعُ النقطةَ التاليةْ
في صفحةِ وجهٍ يتفرَّسُ تاريخَه

3

أينا المفتاحُ – عند بابكَ أو عند بابي ؟!

4

يَسْعَدُ الصمتُ
يَسْعَدُ الحالِ
يسعد نُطْقُ الصورْ

كلما تُركَ المقعد خاليا
كلما توارى صاحب المعطف
كلما سُمعت شهقةُ العتمة الخفيفة

العناق — ميثولوجيا الحضور!

5

ما الحكمة ..؟!

172

Let us be brothers in stone
hand in hand
fingers entwined –
and then,
on the threshold of a bar
we clink our glasses
as you add the last touch
to a face already dreaming its history

3

Which of us is the key?
Your door or mine?

4

Silence is bliss
Life is bliss
Creation is bliss

Even though his chair is empty
even though he is gone
darkness is ablaze
with the presence of his embrace

5

What is the key?

London, 30th March, 2006
Translated from the Arabic by Sarah Maguire and Sabry Hafez

Aleece or Kush: Ancient Sudanese kingdoms.

طلوع

من همزاد روشناییم
از تاریخ آفتاب خبر دارم
ستاره گان
از آبلهٔ دستان من طلوع کرده اند

شهر کابل
فوریه ۱۹۹٤

Star Rise

PARTAW NADERI · AFGHANISTAN

I am the twin of light
I know the history of the sun

Stars
rise from the blisters on my hands

Kabul, February, 1994
Translated from the Dari (Persian) by Sarah Maguire and Yama Yari

कुछ कहना

कुछ कहना क्या उचित है अपने बारे में,
इतना ही पर्याप्त है.

नीली आँखों वाली काले रंग की चिड़िया हूँ
मेरे पंखों में सिमटी हैं सीमाएँ
मेरी उड़ान ने छुआ आकाश के रंग को
मैंने उचक कर देखा उसके परे अंधकार को भी
सूखती हुई नदियों और दौड़ते रेगिस्तान का पीछा मैंने किया है
जलते हुए वनों में झुलसी हूँ मैं कभी,
बारिश में घुलते दुख को मैंने चूमा है,
मैंने देखा बाढ़ से घिरे पेड़ पर जनम देती स्त्री को,
कितनी ही बार बदला है मैंने इस देह को
हर बार मैं नीली आँखों वाली काली चिड़िया हूँ.

कठिन ढलानों पर चढ़ते छुपते
युद्धों से भागते लोग मुझे देख रुकते
सोचते वे नहीं हो सकते कभी
इतनी ऊँचाई पर इतनी दूर फिर भी मैं इतने पास उनके मन में,
लंबी लकीरों में उनके चेहरों की टूटते बनते हैं देश
वे खरीदते हैं नए ताले नई चाबियाँ अपने स्वर्ग के लिए,
क्या सोचा होगा बोअबदिल ने इज़ाबेला को अलामबरा की चाबियाँ सौंपते
बस धीमे से कहा उसने "ये लो स्वर्ग की चाबियाँ"

The Blue-Eyed Blackbird

MOHAN RANA · INDIA

Is it right to speak of myself?
This will do:
I am a blue-eyed blackbird
My wings know all directions
My flight has touched the colour of the sky
When soaring aloft I've glimpsed the darkness beyond
I've tracked drying rivers and swelling deserts
I've been singed in burning forests
I've kissed anguish as it melts in the rain
I've seen a woman give birth in a tree besieged by flood
I've changed my body so many times
and yet I am always a blue-eyed blackbird

People in flight from war, in hiding,
climbing steep slopes, stop when they see me
Stunned they are so high, so far,
even though I live in their hearts
In the deep lines of their faces
countries are shattered and rebuilt
They buy new locks, new keys to new heavens
What did Boabdil think when he handed the keys
of the Alhambra to Isabella,
whispering, 'Here are the keys to paradise'?

This endless flight with no day and no night
when the sun sets and rises at once
Longitude is locked in my eyes
Reading the diary of a poet's dreams
lost in fog, I fall
merging with the earth's dust
a blue-eyed blackbird is born again

यह अंतहीन उड़ान जिसमें न दिन है न रात
कभी डूबता और उगता है सूरज एक साथ
मेरी आँखों में बंद हैं देशांतर,
कवि के सपनों की डायरी पढ़ते
धुंध में खोकर गिर पड़ती हूँ कहीं
मिल जाती धरती के कणों में
जनमती फिर नीली आँखों वाली काली चिड़िया

कभी तीर अब बंदूकें तनी हैं जिस पर
डर नहीं है मुझे, पतझड़ के लाल रंग में घुल जाएगा मेरा रक्त,
किसी और प्रदेश से किसी और दिशा से फिर शुरू करूँगी उड़ान अपनी,
तुम्हारे ही शब्दों से गढ़ती जीवन को
मैं इस दुनिया की चीज़ नहीं हूँ.
कुछ और कहना क्या उचित है अपने बारे में,
इतना ही पर्याप्त है

Arrows, now guns, are aimed at me
I have no fear
My blood will mingle with the crimson of autumn
I'll take flight from another country
Another direction
Casting life from your words
I am not of this world
Is it right to speak more of myself?
This will do

Translated from the Hindi by Bernard O'Donoghue and Lucy Rosenstein

Boabdil: Abu Abdullah Mohammed XII, final ruler of Granada,
the last Muslim-run city in Spain.

Булбуле дар қафаси синаи ман

Булбуле ҳаст дар ин баргистон
Булбуле ки нағамоташ субхро тӯҳфа мекунад бар ман
Ва маро мебарад ба дурдасти нурони.
Ба ҳамон қулла ки Фарҳоде дорад.
Ба маҳалле ки зоғро Маҷнун мегуяд:
Салом эй зи ҳама зебо.
Ба ғори хушбахт зи танҳоии мунаввар зард аст
Ба биҳиште ки Одаму Ҳавво бе донаи гандум хира мешаванд:
Чашем ё начашем?
Ман агар Ҳавво будам намечашидам.
Шукри Ҳавво набуданам вагарна аҳли башар
Бегуноҳии маро ҳеч гаҳ намебахшид.
Оваҳ! Эй гандумаки муъҷиза ва эй себаки шигифт
Аё ибтидойи содайи ман
Булбуле ҳаст ки андешаи шаффофи маро
Ба суи хотираҳои азалӣ мехонад.
Булбуле ҳаст ки бигрехта аст аз қафаси синаи ман
Инак аз бекаронаи субҳ гулбонг мезанад.
Меравам, меравам эй дуст
Бояд вучуди худро ба қадамҳои зиндагӣ густард.
Бояд шитоб кард.
Бояд он Фарҳодро муждаи Ширин гуфт.
Боре ба ғори Зартушт ворид шуд барои ҷабидани нур.
Бояд аз гандуми биҳишт чашид ё намебояд?
Оҳ...
Меравам, меравам охир,
Инак омода кун эй дуст дилатро ба пазироии ман.

A Nightingale in the Cage of My Breast

FARZANEH KHOJANDI · TAJIKISTAN

In this leafy orchard is a nightingale,
a nightingale whose songs are the dawn
and take me into the light,
to the mountains of legendary Farhad,
and to the place where mad Majnun talks to the raven:
'Hello gorgeous!' And to that lucky cave,
luminous with solitude, basking in gold,
and to a paradise where Adam and Eve stare at a wheat grain:
'Shall we taste it or not?' If I were Eve, I wouldn't taste it.
Thank goodness I'm not Eve or else mankind
would never forgive me for not sinning.
O tiny, miraculous wheat grain, O tiny apple of amazement,
O simple beginnings of myself.
There is a nightingale who sings my see-through thoughts,
sings back to the beginning of memory.
There is a nightingale flying out of the cage of my breast;
it's chirping now at the edge of morning.
I am leaving; I am leaving, my friend.
You have to step into life, spread your existence,
you must hurry,
you must bring to Farhad in the story,
the good news about Shirin, his beloved,
you must enter Zoroaster's cave
and taste the light.
To taste the wheat grain of paradise – or not? O . . .
I am leaving, I am leaving at last:
my friend, open your heart for me.

Translated from the Tajik (Persian) by Jo Shapcott and Narguess Farzad

*Farhad: Doomed lover of Shirin who commits suicide when his rival, Khosrow, sends a
messenger with the false news that Shirin has died.*
*Majnun: Famously 'possessed' lover of Layla who dies of a broken heart – as does Layla.
Both stories are recounted in the influential 12th-century Persian romances by Nizami.*

جسد

جُثَّةُ طائرٍ بِفَمِكِ
تَبْعَثُ الأُغْنية.
نَيّاً
من عيونِكَ ينطلقُ الضّوءُ
في عُرْيِهِ الكامِل
عليكَ أَنْ تُرسِل ﴿الأُفْقَ، مَرَّةً كي تُفيقَ، عليكَ
أَنْ تبعثَ نافذةً تِلْوَ أُخرى
تَسْنِدُ الجِّدارْ
أَتْرُكُ الأَبجديةَ تتعلَّقُ بي
وأَنا أَتسلَّقُ خيطَ اللُّغَةِ الرَّفيع
بيني والعالَم.
أَتَجَمْهَرُ في فَمِي
معلَّقاً بين اللُّغةِ والعالَم
بين العالَم والأَبجديةْ .
أَتْرُكُ رأسي
يُنْصِتُ للخرافةِ
أُصغِي لمديحِ الجِّهاتِ لبعضِها
وأُزمجِرُ للرِّيحِ من فُوَّهَةِ الجَبَل
ما لساني يقولُ ليَ أَصْعِدِ المسافةَ
ما المسافةُ بين صوتي وحنيني
ما هناكَ   ؟ !
جَسَدٌ يترفَّعُ عن جسدي
جسدٌ تَنْفِيهِ الرَّغبة
جسدٌ تَعْلُوهُ الرِّيح.

A Body

AL-SADDIQ AL-RADDI · SUDAN

The body of a bird in your mouth
breathing songs.
Raw light spills from your eyes,
utterly naked.

You must breach the horizon, once,
in order to wake up.
You must open window after window.
You must support the walls.

I let alphabets cling to me
as I climb the thread of language
between myself and the world.
I muster crowds in my mouth:
suspended between language and the world,
between the world and the alphabets.

I let my head
listen to the myth,
to all sides praising each other.
And I shout at the winds from the top of a mountain.

Why does my tongue tell me to climb this far?
What is the distance between my voice and my longing?
What is there?

A body transcending my body.
A body exiled by desire.
A body sheltered by the wind.

Translated from the Arabic by Sarah Maguire and Atef Alshaer

رسم

صدا، ز کالبد تن به در کشید مرا
صدا به شکل کسی شد به بر کشید مرا

صدا شد اسپ ستم روح من کشان ز پی‌اش
به خاک بست، به کوه وُ کمر کشید مرا

چه وهم داشت که از ابتدای خلقت من
غریب و کج‌قلق و دربه‌در کشید مرا؟

دو نیمه کرد مرا، پس تو را کشید از من
پس از کنار تو این سوی‌تر کشید مرا

میان ما دری از مرگ کرد نقاشی
به میخ کوفته در پشتِ در کشید مرا

خوشش نیامد این نقش را به هم زد وُ بعد
دگر کشید تو را وُ دگر کشید مرا

من وُ تو را دو پرنده کشید در دو قفس
خوشش نیامد بی‌بال وُ پَر کشید مرا

خوشش نیامد ـ تصویر را به هم زد ـ بعد
پدر کشید تو را وُ پسر کشید مرا

رها شدیم تو ماهی شدی و من سنگی
نظاره‌ی تو به خون جگر کشید مرا

Drawing

REZA MOHAMMADI · AFGHANISTAN

There was a voice and it coursed
from a pair of parched lips,
drawing me out of my body.

The voice was despotic, uncurbed
as a horse dragging my soul
across rocks and up scree.

I don't know why the voice,
the maker, drew me as unroofed,
as a vagrant, a fool,

or why it split me in two
and then drew me from you,
sliding the earth in between us.

It sketched a door of death then
and depicted me nailed to the door –
but that wasn't enough so it rubbed us out

and started from the beginning,
drawing us in the likeness of doves,
caged in separate cages.

It wasn't enough
so it drew me with neither wings nor feathers
but it wasn't enough

so it dashed us to pieces
and drew me as your son, you as my father,
and a moment later I was a stone

and you were a star shining down on me,
making me into the most precious thing . . .
It wasn't enough.

خوشش نیامد؛ این بار از تو دشتی ساخت
به خاطر تو نسیم سحر کشید مرا

خوشش نیامد، خط، خط، خط، خط زد این‌ها را
یک استکان چای از خیر و شر کشید مرا

تو را شکر کرد و در دهان من حل کرد
سپس به سمت لبش برد وُ سر کشید مرا

It drew you as a desert and me as a breeze
on the long wander through you.
It wasn't enough. It erased us

and sketched me as a cup of tea,
full of good and full of evil,
and made you the sugar that sank in me

and got dissolved and finally we
were lifted up to a pair of parched lips
and drank

Translated from the Dari (Persian) by Nick Laird and Hamid Kabir

บ้านเรือนและผู้คน

ทีละจุด ทีละจุดส่องจินตภาพ...
ฝั่งทะเล ทุ่งราบ บนภูเขา
ทุ่งนา ข้างถนน ค่ำหม่นเทา
ที่โน่น ที่นี่เฝ้าจุดดวงไฟ...

วอมแวม เรืองรองของชีวิต
ทุกที่ ทุกทิศ ถึงเมืองใหญ่
ชนบท ย่านบาง ทั้งใกล้ ไกล
ไม่เคยไร้บ้านเรือนและผู้คน

จากผู้คนก่อร่างสร้างหลักแหล่ง
ทุกหนแห่งเก่าแก่มาแต่ต้น
ดึกดำบรรพกาลผ่านพ้น
ล่วงอดีตมาจนปัจจุบัน

ผู้คนก่อร่างสร้างเรือนเหย้า
จากดวงไฟชีวิตเฝ้าสร้างความฝัน
ดำรงอยู่เป็นความจริงทุกสิ่งอัน
ต่อเนื่องแต่นั้น-ตลอดมา

ทีละจุด จุดความฝันในจินตภาพ
ให้ภาพความจริงที่ยิ่งกว่า
ใจกลางความมืดอันหม่นทา
ที่ไหนไหนใต้ฟากฟ้ามีดวงไฟ...

วอมแวม เรืองรองของชีวิต,
คืนมืดมิด คนเดินทาง โลกกว้างใหญ่
ทุกแห่งทุกหนดั้นด้นไป
ไม่เคยไร้บ้านเรือนและผู้คน

ตะกั่วป่า-กรุงเทพ/คืนวันที่ 11 พฤศจิกายน 2548

Houses and People

ANGKARN CHANTHATHIP · THAILAND

Each spot each spot kindles an image . . .
the seashore the plain the top of a mountain
the rice field the roadside the bleak grey twilight
there, then here, the light is tended . . .

Glistening splendour of life
each place each direction arrives in the city
the countryside riversides near far
never without houses and people

The forms of the houses are created by people
everywhere is old from the beginning
the dark ancient times are finished
go beyond the past until you reach the present

People build houses homes
their dreams are built from the light of their lives
the truth of all things is sustained
by that – forever

Each place is the dream of an image
reveals a truth stronger than
the heart of the darkest darkness
everywhere under the sky there is light

Glistening brilliance of life
the deep dark night the traveller the wide world
each place everywhere it breaks through
never without houses and people

Translated from the Thai by Tracey Martin and The Poetry Translation Centre Workshop

Poblaciones Lejanas

Sus relieves candentes, sus pasajes, son un salmo
luctuoso y monocorde;
los niños corren y gritan,
como pequeños lapsos, en un eterno, enmudecido
sepia demente. Hay ciudades, también,
que dulcifican la luz del sol:
En sus espejos de oro crepuscular las aguas abren y encienden
cercos de aromas y caricias rituales; en sus baños:
las risas, las paredes reverdecientes
-Sus templos beben del mar.

Vagos lindes desiertos (Las caravanas, los vendavales, las
noches combas y despobladas, las tardes lentas,son arenas franqueables
que las separan) mirajes, ecos que las enturbian,
que las empalman;
un gusto líquido a sal en las furtivas comisuras;
Y esta evocada resonancia.

Far-Off Settlements

CORAL BRACHO · MEXICO

Their burning, hot-branded outlines, their inner pathways, are all a psalm
sung sad and monotonous;
children run and yell
like little blips, in never-ending quiet,
demented sepia. And there are also cities
which can make this sun's light sweet:
In their dusky golden looking-glasses, water breaks, and lights up
those gathered sweet smells and old caresses; in the warm bathing-places:
the laughter, the walls turning green now once again.
– Their temples sip from the seas.

Ghostly city limits, wavering (the caravans, the strong south winds, the
over-arching nights with no-one there, the long afternoons –
what separates all these are the untrodden sands), mirages, echoes that
cloud them, that connect them;
a sly wet lick of salt in the corners of the mouth;
And this resonance, called forth.

Translated from the Spanish by Katherine Pierpoint and Tom Boll

Mafuriko

Nitaandika wimbo juu ya mbawa za nzi
Utoe muziki arukapo wausikie walio wengi
Ushairi wa jalalani utaimbwa
Juu ya vidonda vya wakulima
Na usaha ulio jasho lao.
Nitaandika juu ya mbawa za wadudu
Wote warukao
Juu ya mistari ya pundamilia
Na masikio makubwa ya tembo.
Juu ya kuta vyooni, maofisini, madarasani,
Juu ya paa za nyumba, kuta za Ikulu,
Na juu ya khanga na tisheti.
Nitaandika wimbo huu:
Mafuriko ya mwaka huu
Yatishia nyumba kongwe bondeni.
Waliomo wameanza kuihama
Na miti ya umeme imeanguka.
Palipokuwa na mwanga, sasa giza.
Mafuriko ya mwaka huu!
Mti mkongwe umelalia upande
Wa nyumba zetu hafifu.
Upepo mkali uvumapo hatulali.
Kila kukicha twatazama mizizi yake
Na mkao wake, na kuta hafifu za nyumba.
Lazima ukatwe kuanzia matawi hadi shina
Mafuriko ya mwaka huu yaashiria. . .
Tutabaki kuwasimulia wajukuu:
Mwaka ule wa mafuriko
Miti mingi mikongwe ilianguka.
Mafuriko ya mwaka huu!
Wengi wataumbuka.

Floods

EUPHRASE KEZILAHABI · TANZANIA

I will write a song on the wings of a fly –
let this song make music when the fly flies, let everyone hear it.
The poetry of rubbish will be sung
on the wounds of farmers
and on the pus they sweat.
I will write on the wings of insects
and everything that flies,
on the zebra's stripes
and the elephant's ears,
on the walls of toilets, offices and classrooms,
on the roofs of houses, the walls of the government,
and on scarves and t-shirts.
This is the song I will write:
This year's floods threaten old houses in the valley;
people have begun to leave;
electric cables have been destroyed –
where there once was light, now it's dark.
The floods this year!
An old tree has fallen down next to
our rickety houses.
We don't sleep when the fierce wind blows.
Every day we examine its roots
the rickety walls of the house,
and the branches that must be severed from its trunk.
The floods this year are a warning . . .
We shall tell our grandchildren:
The floods that year
many trees were felled.
The floods this year
many of us will perish.

Translated from the Swahili by Katriina Ranne and the Poetry Translation Centre Workshop

Dialecte des cyclones

Chaque jour, j'emploie le dialecte des cyclones fous.
Je dis la folie des vents contraires.

Chaque soir, j'utilise le patois des pluies furieuses.
Je dis la furie des eaux en débordement.

Chaque nuit, je parle aux îles Caraïbes le langage des tempêtes hystériques. Je dis l'hystérie de la mer en rut.

Dialecte des cyclones. Patois des pluies. Langage des tempêtes. Déroulement de la vie en spirale.

Fondamentalement la vie est tension. Vers quelque chose. Vers quelqu'un. Vers soi-même. Vers le point de maturité où se dénouent l'ancien et le nouveau, la mort et la naissance. Et tout être se réalise en partie dans la recherche de son double, recherche qui se confond à la limite avec l'intensité d'un besoin, d'un désir et d'une quête infinie.

Des chiens passent – j'ai toujours eu l'obsession des chiens errants – ils jappent après la silhouette de la femme que je poursuis. Après l'image de l'homme que je cherche. Après mon double. Après la rumeur des voix en fuite. Depuis tant d'années. On dirait trente siècles.

La femme est partie, sans tambour ni trompette. Avec mon coeur désaccordé. L'homme ne m'a point tendu la main. Mon double est toujours en avance sur moi. Et les gorges déboulonnées des chiens nocturnes hurlent effroyablement avec un bruit d'accordéon brisé.

C'est alors que je deviens orage de mots crevant l'hypocrisie des nuages et la fausseté du silence. Fleuves. Tempêtes. Éclairs. Montagnes. Arbres. Lumières. Pluies. Océans sauvages. Emportez-moi dans la moelle frénétique de vos articulations. Emportez-moi ! Il suffit d'un soupçon de clarté pour que je naisse viable. Pour que j'accepte la vie. La tension. L'inexorable loi de la maturation. L'osmose et la symbiose. Emportez-moi ! Il suffit d'un bruit de pas, d'un regard, d'une voix émue, pour que je vive heureux de l'espoir que le réveil est possible parmi les hommes. Emportez-moi ! Car il suffit d'un rien, pour que je dise la sève qui circule dans la moelle des articulations cosmiques.

Dialecte des cyclones. Patois des pluies. Langages des tempêtes. Je dis le déroulement de la vie en spirale.

Dialect of Hurricanes

FRANKÉTIENNE · HAITI

Every day I use the dialect of lunatic hurricanes.
I speak the madness of clashing winds.

Every evening I use the patois of furious rains.
I speak the fury of waters in flood.

Every night I talk to the Caribbean islands in the tongue of hysterical storms.
I speak the hysteria of the rutting sea.

Dialect of hurricanes. Patois of rains. Language of tempests. Unravelling of the spiralling life.

Fundamentally, life is tension. Towards something. Towards someone. Towards oneself. Towards the point of maturity where the old and the new, death and birth untangle. And every being is realised in part in the search for its double, a search which may, in a sense, merge with the intensity of a need, a desire, and an infinite quest.

Dogs pass by – I've always been obsessed with strays – they yap at the shadow of the woman I'm pursuing. At the image of the man I'm looking for. At my double. At the hubbub of fleeing voices. For so many years. Feels like thirty centuries.

The woman's gone, without a fanfare. Along with my discordant heart. The man never even offered me his hand. My double is always at my heels. And the unhinged throats of night dogs howl with the cacophony of a busted accordion.

It's then I become a storm of words bursting the hypocrisy of clouds and the falseness of silence. Rivers. Storms. Lightning. Mountains. Trees. Lights. Rains. Savage oceans. Take me to the frenzied core of your articulation. Take me! Just a hint of clarity would give me a living chance. Would let me accept life. Tension. The inexorable law of growth. Osmosis and symbiosis. Take me! The sound of a step, a glance, a touching voice would be enough for me to live happy in the hope that awakening is still possible among humans. Take me! It wouldn't take much for me to speak the sap that flows through the core of the cosmos in motion.

Dialect of hurricanes. Patois of rains. Languages of storms. I speak the unravelling of the spiralling life.

Translated from the French by André Naffis-Sahely and the Poetry Translation Centre Workshop

Biete bi

Biete bi.
Lu neza gui'chi' ne bacuela
nanda saaca' ne xiana.
Ruguubeedxe' ca yoo, ridopa cuuxhu' bi'cu'.
Daabi ti xiixa
bicuininá' huadxí ri',
ti guichi guluxu,
ti guiiba' tini.

Nuu tu laa
gudu'ba' xhaata' gueza guibá',
bisaana ni naté, nagu'xhu'.
Xaguete' ri' guiruti'
nibeezá xpandá',
guirá' zeguyoo ra lidxi
cugaba' xquenda zí'.

Caxidxi zinña,
laaca tuuxa biaanatá'
gudxite xcunaa laa.
Yanadxí guirá'
bietenala'dxi' ladeñee,
málasi gunna binni
nabani guendaruseegu' ra lidxi.

Tu laa nanna
xiñee cazaaca' huadxí ri',
xiñee nisi nuaa'
gudxiga' yaana' xii
bixé' cundubi rarí'.

The North Wind Whips

VÍCTOR TERÁN · MEXICO

The north wind whips through,
in the streets papers and leaves
are chased with resentment.
Houses moan,
dogs curl into balls.
There is something in
the afternoon's finger,
a catfish spine,
a rusty nail.

Someone unthinkingly
smoked cigarettes in heaven,
left it overcast, listless.
Here, at ground level, no one could
take their shadow for a walk,
sheltered in their houses, people
are surprised to discover their misery.

Someone didn't show,
their host was insulted.
Today the world
agreed to open her thighs,
suddenly the village comprehends
that it is sometimes necessary to close their doors.

Who can divine
why I meditate on this afternoon?
Why is it birthed in me
to knife the heart
of who uncovered the mouth
of the now whipping wind,
to jam corncobs in the nose
of the ghost that pants outside?

Cuxidxi ca yaga,
riaba riásaca'
cuxidxica' naa
runi biaanata'ya'.

Latané naa nagasi
guirá' manihuiini' ruunda'
guidxélatu lu yaga,
ti gabe' laatu
pa naye'que' guichalaga binidxaba'.

The trees roar with laughter,
they split their sides,
they celebrate
that you haven't arrived at your appointment.

Now bring me
the birds
that you find in the trees,
so I can tell them
if the devil's eyelashes are curled.

Translated from the Zapotec by David Shook

Пушти анбӯҳи сабз

Вақте ки қосид омад ва хандон паём дод:
... Тобистон дар роҳ аст,
Одамҳо чун обҳои гилолуд
Дар андаруни ҷуйборҳои зиндагӣ
Беэътибор бар сухани қосид
Бо роҳи хеш рафтанд.
Аммо гулҳо
Гармии бӯсаи тобистонро
Дар баногуши худ эҳсос намуданд.
Ҷуҷаҳо аз даруни байзаҳои навшикаста наъра заданд.
Олуҳо аз ҳаяҷон сурх шуданд.
Модарам аз сандуқ
Ҷомаҳои фарбеҳи зимистониро
Берун кашид ва густард дар роҳи офтоб.
Ман низ диламро
Аз сандуқи сина баровардам.
Ман низ диламро ки
Бӯи андуҳи зимистон мекард, офтоб додам.
Баъд аз ин, эй мардум,
Дили ман дар никоҳи хуршед ҳаст.
Вақте ки шумо пардаҳои гафлатро
Дар чашмхои шиша мекашед
Ва бар хоби нимрӯз меравед,
Ман бо офтоб ишқ меварзам.
Медонам, ин мухаббат
Ҳусни ман аст ва ҷурми офтоб.
Зеро касе ба тозагии ман газанд ворид кард.
Касе ба хандаи музҳик
Сукути бикри шабистони маро бишкаст.
Номи мастури маро дар даҳони русбиён андохт.
Бояд нигоҳ кард. Пушти ин анбуҳи сабз касе дигар ҳаст.
Касе ки чашмаш аз ибтидои офариниш то имрӯз
Имон ва ишқи одамро ҳифз кардааст.
Касе ки нафаҳоти нафасаш таҳаййури Исо аст.
Касе ки мӯъҷизаи дасташ воме аст аз Калим.
Касе ки пушти садои пардааш овози ғайб пинҳон аст.
Касе ки дар бағали нахли маърифат нишаста аст.
Ва себи нимаи дасташ

200

Behind the Mass of Green

FARZANEH KHOJANDI · TAJIKISTAN

When the message came with a smile
that summer was coming,
men, sloshing their way
through puddles of muddy water,
carried on oblivious.
But the roses felt the warm kiss
of summer on their necks.

Chicks roared inside cracking shells,
plums blushed with excitement.
My mother lugged our winter clothes
out of the chest of drawers
and spread them in the sun.
I pulled my heart out of my breast,
and laid it in the sun as well,
my heart, smelling of frost, and musty winter.

Listen, from now on, my heart is married to the sun.
While you draw the curtains over it all,
and fall into mid-morning naps,
I make love with the sun.
I'm certain this love is my virtue but maybe it's the sun's sin –
because someone hurt me, recently,
someone with a ridiculous laugh,
which broke into the quiet night,
got my name so drunk even street girls shouted it.
Look. There is someone behind this mass of green.
Someone whose eyes, right from the beginning of creation
until this moment, saved faith and love.
Someone whose breath is the astonishment of Jesus,
someone whose touch is a loan from Moses,
someone whose voice veils the song of eclipses,
someone who is seated in the palm of knowledge
and in whose hands the half-apple

Интизори лаби шакархойе аст.

Касе ки бо гарди пояш офоқ тайяммум дорад.

Оре, пушти ин анбуҳи сабз касе ҳаст,

ва ман ба хотири он кас дубора бар ҳастӣ баргаштам.

waits for sweet lips, someone
who has blessed horizons with dust from his feet.
Yes, behind this mass of green there is someone,
and for him I have come back to life.

Translated from the Tajik (Persian) by Jo Shapcott and Narguess Farzad

العالَمُ – نَسيجُ الأصابع

صُورَةٌ

خَارجٌ من كِهوفٍ بذَاكِرتي للفضاءْ
بعصافيرَ ميّتةٍ عَبْرَ تُقْبِ الظلامِ الوحيدْ
بمَعَادِنَ شَكَّلْتُها بدَمِي شجرَاً
لا يُظِلُّ مرايا تماثيلِها
للهواءِ بنَفْسي وأَجْنِحتي

مَنْ يُخَبِّئُ لي شارعاً
حين أخطو وحيداً إلى وطني
حين أَحمِلُ شمساً
وأمشي إليّ جسدي في عراءِ الحريقْ؟!.

يُتم

لأنّي وحيدٌ هنا بالعراءِ
ولا سِرَّ لي
منذ أكتوبرَ المحْتَرِقْ
كانَ لابدَّ لي أَنْ أُفتّشَ عن قمرٍ
أنْ أواجهَ امرأةً
في الحقولِ البعيدةِ: عُرْياً لِعُرْيِ
أَنْ أُفتّشَ عن وطنٍ يَحْتَمي
مِنْ شِتَاءِ الغيابِ بوهجِ أصابعِها
بالحليبِ المقَدَّسِ من شَطرِهَا
لأُخبِّئَ أبريلَ مِنْ دَمِهِ
في دَمِي

Weaving a World

AL-SADDIQ AL-RADDI · SUDAN

An Image
From the dark spaces of memory
        I emerged, rising through a pinprick of light
        in the gloom, on all sides the falling
        bodies of dead song-birds: these trees
that cast no shadow on their own reflections – I
fashioned them, forging, hammering, working the metal.

        And so I found myself, in the wind, fully fledged . . .
        Who
        will keep clear a road for me, care
        about the solitary journey
        I make, torch in hand, in search of home,
        or stride towards this body when it's
            blackening in the blazing desert heat?

Lost
Out of reach, stripped bare, orphaned,
betrayed by the secret fires
that October ignited,
I set about searching, searching
        for a consoling guide like the moon: for a woman
        also stripped bare, in a distant field,
        whose fingers might cradle, whose body
        might shelter, whose breast
        might nurture this aching for home.

كانَ لابدَّ لي

أنْ أقولَ وداعاً وسَهْلاً

لعرشِ السماءِ المضيءِ

أنْ أُفجِّرَ جُرْحاً بنسيانِهِ

ضِدَّ هذا الفضاءِ!

وقتٌ آخَر

كان لابُدَّ لي

أنْ أُعرِّفَ نَفْسي بأشجَارِها

أنْ أُزوِّجَ نَفْسي فُكَاهتها نَفْسَها

مِنْ تَخيطِ الهواءِ العميقْ

بالدُّمُوعِ التي لا تَخيطُ الكَفَنْ

كان لابُدَّ لي

أنْ أقولَ وأمضي إلى كَهْفِ رُوحي

غَريباً بفاكِهتي وأصَابِعِها

لأنِّي أنا الضُّوءُ يَلْبَسُ أجْنِحَةَ الأرْضِ

والجُرْحُ يَرْفُو دَمَ القَلْبِ

لأنِّي أنا اللَّيلُ وأَسْمي فَسيحٌ على الأمْكِنَةِ

النَّهَارُ الذي يَتَّسِخْ

بالنَّهَارِ على خطوتي

أخْلَعُ اللَّيلَ عنه

وأمْشِي على الوقتِ مُتَّسعاً في طَريقي.

206

Further,
I had somehow to hide
the frail, blood-stained shoots of April
inside me; I had to allow the crimson night-sky
its majesty; I had
to learn how to stain
the space of the present
with what seeps from a forgotten wound.

Another Time

Feeling my way through an inner forest, I practised
the art of self-possession: at times my own jokes
had me laughing out loud.

From the dense air
that surrounded me I gathered
the tears that stitch no shroud.

I bequeath to strangers all
I had to say, and the touch of my loves; the cell
or cave of my retreat is the shape of my soul.

What am I there? The light that floats
or the wound that streams or the dark
itself? Can words name it? What am I there?

To walk through day and night, both in time, and on it . . .

نَسِيجُ الأَصابِع

المُعَلَّقُ سَقْفاً على صَمْتِهِ وحَنينِ سُلالاتِهِ
دائِماً يَشْتَهي دَمَهُ

تُرْبَةً للغِناءْ
دائِماً يَشْتَهي
مَنْ يَقُودُ أَصابِعَه
مَنْ يَكُونُ الطَّيورَ التي لا تُغَنّي جَنَازتَهُ
كَأَنَّ الذي لا يَموتُ وحيداً
هو الكائِنُ الخيطُ
يَخْلَعُ مسمارَهُ عن نَسيجِ الجِدَارِ
كَأَنَّ الذي لا يَكُونُ وحيداً
هو الكائِنُ العنكبوتْ

إضاءة

كيفَ كُنْتِ تقودينَ لي قَمراً
حين أُطفِئُ دَمْعَكِ بين الأَصابِعِ
بين الأَصابِعِ حين أُضيءُ حنينَكِ
حين تَقُودينَ لي خنجراً
كيف كنتِ هنا وهناكْ
كيف كُنّا مَعاً؟!.

حنين

حين كنتُ خليعاً بنَفْسي
بلا هَمِّ قُوتْ
وأنا أشتهي سِرَّكِ المِلْتَبَس
وَرَقُ التُوتِ – نَفْسُهُ – لم يكن نَفْسَهُ
كيف أَلْبَسُهُ
في الحنينِ الغَريبِ إلى كائنٍ لا يموتْ؟!

208

Weaving

Swaying beneath the ceiling, silent, brooding
on ancestors, all the time longing
           to hear
           his blood sing –
or for someone to take and guide
his fingers, and sing songs that refute dying…
he likes to think that those who spin
and weave won't die alone. Slowly
he removes a leg from the wall.
Others may live alone, but not spiders as patient,
as industrious as he is.

Close Up

How beautifully you offered
me the moon, as I caressed
away your tears, and you, alight
with love, thrust
at my vitals with a kitchen knife.
Was I here   or there?
How one we were!

Longing

I got undressed.
I was beyond hunger, obsessed
with the mystery of you.
How, why should I
conceal my longing with senseless
fig-leaves? While I
was naked, you were immortal.

حلم

وَلْتَكُنْ جَسَداً أَخْضَرَ يا أَيُّها الشِّعْرُ
كُنْ لُغَةً أَتغَرَّبُ فِيها بِنَفْسِي وأَجْنِحَتِي

نَفَساً في لِسَاني
لأرْعَى قَبَائِلَ صَوْتِي – على صَمْتِها
سَاهِراً ووحيداً أَرَى

لم تَكُ جَسَداً أَخْضَرَ
لم تَكُ سيِّداً طيِّباً تُشْتَرَى
لم تَكُ رَبَّةً
أَيُّها الهَذَيانُ الذي أَشْتَهي، يَنُها الذَّاكِرَةْ!

هَيْكَلٌ

لِمَ كنتِ معي جَسَداً ظَامِئاً في فِراشي
وعَارِيةً بالسَّمَاء
ومَسْقُوفَةً بالنُّجُومْ؟!
لِمَ كنتِ المِياهَ الغَرِيقَةَ في جَسدِي
حين كنتُ الغُيومْ
الغُيُومُ التي كالحَمَائِمِ تَطَّايَرُ الرُّوحُ مِنها
الغُيُومُ التي أَرْتَوِي نَوْمُها سَاهِياً
في الشِتاءِ البعيدِ عَرَقْ
لِمَ كنتِ سِهامَ الأَرَقْ
ضِدَّ قلبي
وكنتِ الرِّيَاحَ الصَّدِيقَةَ في جَسدي
حين كنتُ الغيومْ!
لِمَ كنتِ الوحيدةَ عَارِيةً تَحْتَ هَيْكَلِ كَيْنُونَتي
حيث أَقْبِضُ – حين أُزِيحُ السَّمَاءَ – طيورَ الأَبَدْ!.

Sacred
You were the thirsty body
next to mine in bed, the sky
your blanket and the constellations your roof: why?

You were the deep waters in my body
when, sweating through winter, I daydreamed I was a cloud
of rain, dove-white, aflutter with souls: why?

You were the barbs of insomnia
tearing my breast, and the friendly winds
coursing through me, driving these streaming rain-clouds: why?

You, naked, were the only one present and sacred
instant when, moving the sky to one side,
I reached out and caught hold of the birds of eternity: why?

Dream
Poem – may you be green
and alive, a world
through which I wander aloft
on wings, with my whole
being. Inspire my tongue
until the tribes that inhabit my voice,
long silent, are fed again.
Poem – alone and sleepless,
I find you are neither green
nor alive, nor a kind master
nor a muse-figure, but an addictive
fusion of delirium and memory!

Translated from the Arabic by Mark Ford and Hafiz Kheir

April and October: References to two successful peaceful uprisings, in October 1964 and April 1985, staged by the Sudanese people against the military dictators, General Aboud (1958–64) and General Nimeiri (1969–85), both of which introduced brief periods of democracy (Sudan has been ruled by the dictator, Omar al-Bashir since 1989).

Uurkubbaale

'Cawdu billoo balooy baydh.'
'Bismillaahi "Yaasiin"'.
Botorkiyo ciyaartoo
Sidaa lagu bilaaboo,
Anna biito-biitiyo
Bille-jire ku dheelaan
Beri hore garaadsaday.

Dadka waxan ka bawsaday:
'Dhool bari ka hirey baa
Dhaanka loo bariiyaa'.
Gabaygana Burhaanoow
Waxa aniga lay baray
Inu laba u kala baxo
Beeshana u kala yahay:

Waxay Biliso igu tidhi:
'Hadday maanso beer tahay
Run baa lagu biyeeyaa.
Bilicsiga dareenkaa
Lagu baalaleeyaa;
Xaq baa lagu bac-rimiyaa.
Baaqbaaqa noloshiyo
Biyo-dhiijinteediyo
Xilligay ku biqishaa.

'Midho waxay u bixisaa
Habka loo barbaarshiyo
Barta lagu abqaalaa.
Sida loogu baahdaa
Loo buushe-bixiyaa;
Ama loo bislaystaa.

Seer

MAXAMED XAASHI DHAMAC 'GAARRIYE' ·
SOMALIA/SOMALILAND

In my cradle I heard the women sing
'In the name of God, "Yaasin"':
this is how we begin,
with the dance step and the dance.
I was playing 'biito biiti',
singing 'Bille-jire'–
this is how Gaarriye grew.

I suckled on hearsay, drank in lore:
'A cloud in the east means rest your feet,
the rain will trek to us.'
Dear friend, dear Burhaan, I was taught
there are two types of poem:
that which tells you how things are
and that with another agenda –
the people know which is which.

When she brought me up, Biliso said,
'If a poem is a farm
then how things truly are, that's water;
the best words for the best thoughts,
that's how it begins.
Justice is your only compost,
life itself is what you hoe:
just squeeze truth from what happens
and in its own time it will sprout.

'Whether a poem brings forth seeds
depends on how it's tended and by whom –
the spot in which it's planted;
depending on who needs it and for what
its husk is hulled or boiled.

'Waxa lagu bardaanshaa
Baqoolkiyo geeddiga
Fac kastaa intuu bogo.
Bullashada dagaalkana
Bunduqay tilmaantaa.

'Waa buun wax lagu hago;
Boodaanta yeedhmada
Bigil ereygu leeyahay.
Caws baar leh weeyaan;
Lana baxay sabool-diid
Soddon laguma baayaco.
Boqor laguma caabudo.
Biidhi-qaatennimiyo
Baqas waa ka xaaraan.

'Waana biime liidda ah,
Boqnihiisa lama xidho.
Nin baqdaa ma halabsado;
Bayd-gaabku kuma galo;
Beentana wax kuma laha.
Waa Bilan ma-geyno ah;
Bog-dooxeedu waa sino.'

* * *

'Waxay bilic wax dheer tahay;
Iyadoon bariidada
Ballankeedi ka hor dhicin,
Kolkay bocorta maansado,
Adoo baalku kaa qoyey
Xadantana u baahnaa,
Sidii baalalleey iyo
Balanbaallis qalimo leh,
Ooy ubax baraarugay
Isku waa-bariisteen.

'A poem is the measure for
that trek beneath the draining sun
each generation adds to;
when you have to stand and fight
it shows you where to point the gun.

'It guides you like a conch shell horn,
the call of the large camel bell;
it is the words' own bugle.
It is the finest matting, woven for a bride,
the one the song calls 'Refuser of poor suitors'.
It's not sold for coppers,
it's not for praising the powerful;
to put a price on it, any price,
cheapens it and is forbidden.

'It's riding bareback on an unbroken horse –
you don't hobble its heels.
Those who fear for their hides
and won't ride without a saddle,
those lacking in the craft, can't get near this:
lies have nothing to do with it.
Poetry is a woman you do not betray,
to abuse her beauty is a sin.

* * *

'It's most lovely when most perfectly timed,
as though, met at morning,
you exchanged greetings
at just the right moment.
When your own wings feel so bedraggled
that you need another's touch,
then the full beauty of a poem
is like a butterfly meeting
a just-wakened flower
at the exact moment of dawn.

215

'Bogga kuu salaaxdee
Burcad kuugu duugtee,
Bu'da leebka kugu mudan
Baydari-abbaartee,
Bulxankeedu laba-dhaca
Sida uur-ku-baalaha,
Boogahaaga hoosiyo
Bayrtaada qoomee.

'Kolba baaq xiloodin ah
Barta aad u nogoshahay
Intuu baac u sii dego,
Tixda miino-baadhkii
Fiix kugu biskootiyo
Dhul bacdii ku taal iyo,
Ku banayso meel aan
Beryahaaba gacal dayin.

'Ee baahi-laawuhu
Adigoo basiiro leh
Intuu boodhka kaa tumo,
Xiisaha basaasiyo
Beer-qaado laabtee,
Tuduc wali gun iyo baar
Meel baas ku taabtee,
Intuu baaxad le'eg yahay
Isagoo banbaane ah
Badhtankaaga ka sanqadho.

'Ee kugu ballaadhee
Markii bayd la sheegaba,
Sidii baal qarsoodi ah
La bac dhabay xogtaadii,
Hadba baallo-daymada
Faraq-bood ka qaaddee.'

'When it seems to caress your flank,
to massage a salve into you;
when the pupil of its arrow pierces you
striking the mark exactly,
splitting your anguished cries in two.
Like a seer who peers inside you,
it homes in on your over-sensitivities,
your innermost wounds.

'When you suddenly hear of your betrothal
it sends the message deeper
into your most vulnerable point.
Poetry is the mine-seeker
opening your old, scarred-over hurt,
discovering your untouched earth,
that place closed off
from those closest to you.

'When Baahi-laawe, that dancing verse,
brushes the melancholy from you
as though it were a dust
that settled on your lust for life,
choked the desire in your chest;
it's like a grenade, a bomb,
its blast-range perfectly judged
so each stanza touches you
from problematic top to troubled toe,
exploding from your core.

'When it permeates you
each time a line is recited
as though from a secret page
on which your own secrets are exposed
so that each time you scan it
you jolt with anxiety.'

Maansada ba'leeyda ah
Ee baadi-soocda leh,
Bog kastoo la soo rogo
Sir aad bixisay mooddee,
Nafta oo baraad li'i:
Kolba 'baga!' tidhaahdiyo,
'Bishmaha Eebbe kuma jaro.
Ninka yidhi run badanaa!
Ma afkaygu kala baxay?'

This poem alliterates in 'b'
but all the best poems are branded
so that each page which is turned
makes you believe you've confessed
and each time your soul
involuntarily cries out, 'Bravo!
Dear God, don't seal this man's lips –
may the truth he speaks continue
as though it burst from my own mouth.'

Translated from the Somali by W. N. Herbert and Martin Orwin

أنا والشِّعر

كُل الْخَطِيئَة أَنِّي لَم أَكُن حَجَراً

وَأَن هَم بَني دِنْيَاي لِي أَرَق

وَأَن لِي فِي فَضَاءِ الْحَرْف مُدَّرعاً

أَسْلُو بِه كُلَّمَا نَاءَت بِي الطُّرُق

وَلِي حَقِيبَة شِعر ظَلْت أَحْمِلُهَا

فِيهَا مِن الْأَرْض طَعْم الْأَرْضِ وَالْعَبَق

فِيهَا مِن الْطَّلْح أَغْصَان مُشَاكِسَة

فِيهَا مِن النَّخْل أَفْنَان لَهَا عَذَق

رَسَمَت كُل حَكَايَا الْحُب فِي لُغَتِي

أَلْوَانُهَا الْطَّيَّف وَالْعُنَاب وَالشَّفَق

وَقُلْت هَاتُوا مِن الْأَوْتَار أَجْمَلَهَا

لِيُعرِف الْكَوْن كَيْف اللَّحْن يَنْبَثِق

لِيَعْزِف اللَّحْن أَنْغَاماً مُهَوَّمَة

لِيُنْصِف الْقَلْم الْمَوْثُورَ مَن عَشِقُوا

دِنْيَاي هَذَى حُرُوف جَد مُثْقَلَة

وَرِيَشَة حِبرُهَا مُسْتَنْفِذ قَلْق

وَرِيَشَة حِبرُهَا مُسْتَنْفِذ قَلْق

شَوْق الْمُحِبِّين أَتْلُوَه وَأَحْتَرِق

Poetry and I

MBARKA MINT AL-BARRA' · MAURITANIA

The sin is that I wasn't a stone
    And the troubles of the world make me sleepless
And I shield myself with poetry
    And it keeps me company when I'm far from home
And poetry is my satchel that I carry with me always
    It holds the taste and fragrance of the earth
It holds thickets of prickly branches
    It holds palm fronds loaded with dates
It paints all the stories of love in my language
    Its colours form the spectrum from grape to dawn
And I said bring the most beautiful of stringed instruments
    So the universe may know how music flows
And play its soothing melody
    That brings justice to those who are in love
Letters burden this world of mine
    Trouble leeches ink from the quill
Trouble leeches ink from the quill
    When I read of the longing of lovers I burn

Translated from the Arabic by Joel Mitchell and The Poetry Translation Centre Workshop

ناونیشان

تا هەڵبەستێک تەواو دەبێ،

من ڕۆحی خۆم پەڕە دەکەم وەکوو هەلاج.

کە تەواو بوو،

خاڵێک دەکەم بە عەرش بۆی،

ناونیشانێک دەکەم بە تاج.

* * *

هەر قورینگێک

جارێک باڵی لە دەریاچەی

ئەڤینی من هەڵکێشابێ،

بۆته وشه بۆ هەڵبەستێک،

کە عومرێکە دەینووسم و تەواو نابێ!

* * *

هاوڕێم، ماندووم!

وا هەست دەکەم،

هەڵبەستم هێنده درێژدادڕ بووه،

دیوانی بوون لێی پڕ بووه...

ئاگام لێیه، لە یادمدا

جێگۆڕکێ دەکەن پەیڤەکان.

ڕێگەم بده خاڵێک دانێم،

تۆی بۆ بکەم بە ناونیشان!

Title

ABDULLA PASHEW · KURDISTAN

Until a poem is finished
I tease my soul like a cotton carder.
When it's done,
its throne is a full stop
and its title a crown.

* * *

Any crane
that once dipped its wing
in the lake of my passion
becomes words for a poem
that I write without end.

* * *

I am tired, my friend!
I feel my poem lengthening
into the epic of existence.
I am aware that, in my memory,
words slip out of place.
Let me assign the full stop
and crown it with a title.

*Translated from the Kurdish by Mahsn Majidy and The Poetry
Translation Centre Workshop*

სიმშვიდე

რა უცნაურად შევიჩვიე სიტყვა " სიმშვიდე",
ხელთათმანებად წამოვიცვი,
კაშნედ მოვიჩგე,
მასში დავიგე ქვეშაგები,
სასთუმალი და სურვილები ავიფუმფულე,
სამოცვოლტიან ნათურასაც ვითვინიერებ,
ტკივილის თხრილით შემოვფარგლე ჩემი კარავი
და კართან შიშის მგელიც დავაბი. . . .
რა უცნაურად შევეჩვიე სიტყვას "სიმშვიდე"
და მაინც,
შფოთვის ალვის ხეზე თვალღიას მძინავს

Tranquillity

DIANA AMPHIMIADI · GEORGIA

Strange how I accustomed the word 'tranquillity' to me.
I drew it on like a glove.
I arranged it like a scarf.
I made my bed on it
And plumped up my wishes.
I also tamed the sixty-watt lamp.
I encircled my tent with a moat of pain
And I tethered the wolf of fear near its entrance.
Strange how I became accustomed to the word 'tranquillity'.
And yet
I sleep in an anxious birch tree
With my eyes wide open.
Strange how I accustomed the word 'tranquillity' to me.

Translated from the Georgian by Natalia Bukia-Peters and The Poetry Translation Centre Workshop

تَنْقِيطْ

يَسْجِنُ نَفْسَه في وَرَقَةٍ بَيْضَاءْ

يَفْتَحُ فيها وَطناً لامرَأَةٍ

تَفْتَحُ فِيهِ العَالَمْ

يُضِيءُ مِنْ عَالَمٍ لا يَدَّعِيهْ

مِنْ عَالَمٍ يشْتَهِيهْ

يَسْكُنُ فيهْ

Writing

AL-SADDIQ AL-RADDI · SUDAN

He has trapped himself in a blank page.
He creates a home in it
for a woman
who unwraps there his own
inner world. He glows
in this world he aches for
and lives in,
yet which is not his.

Translated from the Arabic by Mark Ford and Hafiz Kheir

Post Scriptum

Ingin aku tulis
sajak porno sehingga
kata mentah tidak diubah
jadi indah, pokoknya
tidak perlu kiasan lagi
misalnya payudara, jadi bukit,
tubuh wanita = alam bangat
senggama = pelukan yang paling akrab

yang sudah jelas
tulis sajak itu
antara menyingkap dan sembunyi
antara munafik dan jatidiri.

Post Scriptum

TOETI HERATY · INDONESIA

I want to write
an erotic poem
in which raw words, unadorned,
become beautiful
where metaphors are unnecessary
and breasts, for instance,
do not become hills
nor a woman's body a sultry landscape
nor intercourse 'the most intimate embrace'.

It's quite clear
this poem is written in the space
between exposure and concealment
between hypocrisy and true feeling.

Translated from the Indonesian by Carole Satyamurti and Ulrich Kratz

زندگی سے نباہ کرتے رہے
شعر کہتے رہے، سُلگتے رہے

تیرا آنا تو خواب تھا لیکن
ہم چراغوں کے ساتھ جلتے رہے

کیا بتائیں کہ اب کے ساون میں
ہم تجھے کتنا یاد کرتے رہے

شہر والو! ہوا کی بستی میں
پھُول، خُوشبو، چراغ کیسے رہے

تم نے جگنو سے دوستی کر لی
ہم ستارے تلاش کرتے رہے

وصل جن کو نصیب ہو نہ سکا
ہجر کی داستان لکھتے رہے

Kept on Compromising on Life

NOSHI GILLANI · PAKISTAN

Kept on compromising on life
kept reciting poetry, kept blazing

I burned down with the lamps
Your arrival was only a dream

I cannot explain how much I remember
Of you in this monsoon

City people! Did the breeze convey
Our village of flower, scent and lantern?

You befriended the firefly
We kept searching for stars

Those who could not know union
kept writing the story of separation

Translated from the Urdu by Lavinia Greenlaw and Nukhbah Taj Langah

کلمه

کلمه ی متروکی بودم من
در کتابی کهنه
کلمه ی فراموش شده بودم
از عشق از سیاست از دنیا
شاعران از من می گریختند
حروفم از من متنفر بودند
به کلمات دیگر می رفتند و باز نمی گشتند
کلمه ای تنها بودم
بی حرفی
تنها صدای قرن هابا من بود
صدای بردگان
صدای مردگان
صدای جهات دوار زمان

تو آمدی با لب های خونینت
باانگشتان غمگینت
تو آمدی و مرا پیدا کردی
و تمام جهان از من پرشد

The Word

REZA MOHAMMADI · AFGHANISTAN

I was a word abandoned in an old battered book,
a word forgot by politics, by love and the speaking world.

The poets fled from me. All of my letters detested me,
deserting me for other words without once looking back.

Just like that I was alone, a ghost-word that lacked its letters,
lonely and only the terrible sound of the frenzied centuries

for company, only the sound of the slaves, of the dead,
of the arrows of time flying and flying and flying.

You (o my true love) came with your fierce mouth
and hands of ten desolate fingers and found me,

and so loudly then the whole world did shout me

Translated from the Dari (Persian) by Nick Laird and Hamid Kabir

أتجلَّى

أنا سليلةُ البحَّارةِ المتمرِّدينَ على الشواطئ.

ابنة الموج والذاكرة.

آخر من تبقى ممن تنازل لهم شمشون عن شَعره فانتفض فتاةً بكر

أنا آخر سلالة الأنوثةِ الطازجةِ والمعتَّقة.

أفتحُ ذراعي فيبدأ الكون دورته الأحادية الاتجاه.

أبتسم فيقطر العسل من شفاهي البكر اللعوب.

أخطو فتفقِد الكرة الأرضيّة توازنَها

وحينما تجلْجلُ ضحكتي تسمع أجراس الزلازل.

والبراكين تخلخل أنظمة الطبقات السبع

أنا ابنة اللهو والعفاف

ابنة الفسق والطهارة

ابنة السواد والبياض

على حَدِّ إصبَعي تختلف النُّجوم حول تحديد مواقعها الأولى.

وإنْ أغمضتُ عينيَّ

حلَّ الكسوف بالعالم حتى تتفتحا فتغرقاه أشعَّة بلون الخروب.

وحينما أرمي بخصلات شعري للوراء

يرتجفُ الكونُ إجلالاً وخشوعاً

أنا اليوم والغد

صاحبةُ الجلالة المتوَّجةِ على عَرْش الفضاء

أشيرُ بطرف عيني فتنقلب الحقولُ قمحاً وشموساً خضراء

وأنا القمحُ والشُّموس الخضراء

وأنا الحصادُ الأول

والحصاد الأخير.

234

I Reveal Myself

FATENA AL-GHARRA · PALESTINE

Descendant of raiders who landed on the beaches,
heir to the woman who unmanned Samson,
I am the daughter of waves and of memory,
a fresh shoot from ancient stock.

When I open my arms, the universe sets forth.
When I smile, honey wells from my virgin lips.
I take a step and the earth loses its balance.
In my laugh, earthquakes resound,
and volcanoes spurt from seven tectonic plates.

The child of frivolity and modesty,
I am the daughter of depravity and purity,
the progeny of black and white.

The tip of my finger taps the stars off track.
If I close my eyes,
darkness eclipses the world, until my eyelids lift
bathing it in gold.
And when I toss back my hair
the universe shivers in recognition.

I am today and I am tomorrow.
Crowned queen on the throne of space.
A blink, and fields foam green with wheat.
I am wheat itself. I am green.
The first harvest.
The last.

Translated from the Arabic by Sarah Maguire and Anna Murison Boyd

Garaad-daran

Garaad-daran naftaydaay!
Geeri iyo nololeey!
Guluf lagu negaadaay!
Gabno laga dhergaayeey!
Gabbal dumay habeenoo
Hadh gadiidan yahayeey!
Lammaan aan is-geyinoo
Guri qudh ah u hooydaay!

Googgaada xaajada
Gaaxdeedu waxay tahay,
Maan garan xogtaadee,
Maxaad uga gol leedahay?

Ma wax gaar ah baad too
Goonidiisa jira oo
Garab aan u baahnayn?
Mise gobol dad-weynaha
Ka go'aynnin baad tahay?

Maadigaa ah Gaarriye?
Mise laba gudboonoo
Is-geleynin baad tiin?
Gurrac-loo-abuuryeey,
Bal geddaada ii sheeg.

Garaad-daran naftaydaay!
Gurey iyo cadceedaha
Isku gedo miyaad tiin?
Gacal miyaad wadaagtaan?
Bal Giriig warkiisiyo
Guutadii Fircoon iyo
Waxa boqor la gawracay,

236

Self-Misunderstood

MAXAMED XAASHI DHAMAC 'GAARRIYE' ·
SOMALIA/SOMALILAND

I can't understand you, curious self,
nor grasp how you're both life and death,
grabbed land and peaceful settlement,
grudging milker that makes me full,
sun set at evening whilst casting
noon's shortest shadow: how can you be
two who can't marry
yet share the same house?

How can I set this riddle and
give away its answer if
I fail to understand your secret
or even what you mean by it?

Are you something separate,
a stand-alone that leans
upon no man's shoulder,
or such a part of the people
that you can't be parted from them?

And are you that which is Gaarriye
or two opposing halves
he cannot fit together?
I call you, crooked creation:
bear witness to your character.

I can't get to grips with you, gregarious self
are you the same age as Gurey
and his fellow constellations?
Are you all kin?

And what about the history of the Greeks,
the Pharaoh's army and
the goring of kings,

Ama aad gariir iyo
Guri ba'ay u taagnayd,
Googoos u mariyoo;

Giddi waaxyahaygiyo
U galaydh xubnaha oo;
Midba gees u taagoo
Ka gur sheekadoodoo;
Malaayiin gu' oo tegey
Ku dheh gebaggebeeyoo;
Geeddigoodi dheeraa
Mid kastaa guduudiga,
Halkay galabba joogtiyo
Goorteey kulmeenee
Gaarriye sameeyeen,
Godolkeeda ii mari.

Garaad-daran naftaydaay!
Sida gacanka Waaheen
Hadba gaaf-wareegaay!
Arrin aad gorfeysiyo
Waxaad shalay u guuxdaad,
Maantana ka giigtaa
Gol-daloolo yeeshee;
Miyaad dhalan-geddoontoo
Dib bay kuu gardaadsheen?
Ma runtaa gaboowdoo
Geedkeedu waareyn?
Guul-darradu dhankay tahay?

Guud ahaan waxaad tahay
Dadku kugu go'doonyoo
Isla waa go'aanoo,
Mid baad geesi adagoo
Gabbanayn la tahayoo;
Maan-gaab lumaayiyo
Mid baa ceel ganuuniyo
Kuu haysta gocoroo;
Mid baa kugu goblama oo

238

what about the groans of war,
the dynasties you saw destroyed?
Bear witness to it all.

My limbs and all their molecules,
call them to the stand:
line them up in ranks,
collect their statements;
those million monsoons that marched past,
tell them to complete
the tale of that trek
which each one took, the night-walking
and the assignations,
where they were each afternoon
when they made Gaariye:
make their stories flow like milk.

I can't seem to fix you, quarrelsome self,
you're like that riverbed, Waaheen,
shifting between long drought, brief spate –
that business you concluded yesterday,
signed, sealed and celebrated,
today you snatch it back
and poke it full of holes.
Did you tear up all natal traits,
redraft infancy and all its rites?
Or did truth grow old, and find
its essence not eternal after all?
Where does the failure lie?

Your usual impact is to put
the people in two minds,
to keep them from deciding:
one casts you as the hero
they could never see back down;
while another thinks you short of wits –
your way lost, your well dry –
a barren camel; another one
misses you as he'd miss his own son –

Gurxankiisu damihayn
Haddii saxar ku gaadhoo;
Gaadaa wax boobiyo
Mid baad good la tahayoo;
Mid baad garab laxaadliyo
Ruux guda abaaloo,
Loo galo wanaag iyo
Gaashaan la tahayoo;

Garaadlaay xogtaadii
Cidi gaadhi waydee
Dadkan kugu gabaabsiyey
Kumaa helay guntaadoo
Gacan-qaad la siiyaa?
Miyey gabi habaabeen?
Maadigaa wax gabayoo
Hadba geed is-mariyoo,
Goobba midab la joogoo
Gallibaxa habeenkii?

Garaad-daran naftaydaay!
In kastoon gucleeyoo,
Garmaamada haldhaagiyo
Gammaankaba ka jiitoo
Cirka sare galaa-baxo,
Adigay la gooshoo

Iga gaabinaynoo,
Goobtaan is-taagaba
Adigaa galluubane,
Ma gashaygu baaqdoo
Lagu yidhi ka soo goo?
Mise gaari inan oo
Guur-u-meer ah baad tahay?
Maxaad gama' u diiddee
Iga daba-gureysaa?

Dambiyaal waxaan galo
Ama geysto fool-xumo,

if a speck of grit scratched you
he could not be consoled;
one casts you as cobra,
trustless as a looter; while another
has you as the strong shoulder,
a sure repayer of kindness,
deserving of good deeds,
a shelter and a shield.

Unquantified soul, secret from yourself,
ungraspable for others –
they all fall short in the fathoming.
Did anyone ever track you down
and shake you by the hand
or did they all end up lost?
Or could it be you who fails them?
Hiding within your shapeshifting,
a different colour for each place,
each night a new beast, a different face?

I can't get to grips with this garrulous self
even if my lope outstrips
the galloping of ostriches or horses,
even if I vanish from their horizons,
enter and depart from orbit
in the same instant you are with me,
you never fall short of my side.
Wherever I stand, whenever I stop,
you stand and stop with me
as though I carried round a debt
and someone said, 'Collect it!'
as though you were a good catch,
a woman looking for a husband.
Why is it you never sleep,
following me everywhere?

Whatever crime I commit,
whatever ugliness I enter into;
each shameful deed

Gabigoodba ceebaha
Aan gaar u leeyahay,
In kastoon is-giijoo
Weji kale gashada oo
Dadka been ku gaasiro,
Adigaa giraanoo
Gunta iimahaygoo,
Hoos ii guhaadshee;
Godobtiyo xumaantada
Inaad tahay ninkeed-gaba,
Maxaad iigu garataa?

Garaad-daran naftaydaay!
Gumaysaad ku nooshoo
Dadkaa kugu garaacdoo,
Guddoonkooda mooyee
Kaa gareysan maayaan
Waxad adigu goysee;

Maad galabsan hawlaha
Kugu gaardiyaayee,
Galbiskii adoogaa
Goco oo ilmeeyoo,

Hooyadaa u goohoo
Galabtay ku dihatiyo
Eerso uur-galkaagii

that is my very own –
even though I gird myself to lie,
pull on another mask
to leave people at a loss –
you record each defect
as though set down on tape,
insidiously fill me with guilt,
obligation, injury:
you see through me as a wife does –
but why understand me by my flaws?

Curious, gregarious, garrulous self,
did you fail to grasp the stifling norms?
To quarrel with those who rap our knuckles
for whom only their diktats
need be acknowledged,
and not what you conclude:

You don't deserve the problems
that barrack and assail you.
Remember the marriage ceremony
of your father and weep;
bewail your mother because of
the afternoon you entered her womb
and the world, blame her.

Translated from the Somali by W. N. Herbert and Martin Orwin

La langue de ma mère

Je n'ai pas vu ma mère depuis vingt ans
Elle s'est laissée mourir de faim
On raconte qu'elle enlevait chaque matin
son foulard de tête
et frappait sept fois le sol
en maudissant le ciel et le Tyran
J'étais dans la caverne
là où le forçat lit dans les ombres
et peint sur le parois le bestiaire de l'avenir
Je n'ai pas vu ma mère depuis vingt ans
Elle m'a laissé un service à café chinois
dont les tasses se cassent une à une
sans que je les regrette tant elles sont laides
Mais je n'en aime que plus le café
Aujourd'hui, quand je suis seul
j'emprunte la voix de ma mère
ou plutôt c'est elle qui parle dans ma bouche
avec ses jurons, ses grossièretés et ses imprécations
le chapelet introuvable de ses diminutifs
toute l'espèce menacée de ses mots
Je n'ai pas vu ma mère depuis vingt ans
mais je suis le dernier homme
à parler encore sa langue

My Mother's Language

ABDELLATIF LAÂBI · MOROCCO

It's been twenty years since I last saw my mother
She starved herself to death
They say that each morning
she would pull her headscarf off
and strike the floor seven times
cursing the heavens and the Tyrant
I was in the cave
where convicts read in the dark
and painted the bestiary of the future on the walls
It's been twenty years since I last saw my mother
She left me a china coffee set
and though the cups have broken one by one
they were so ugly I didn't regret their loss
even though coffee's the only drink I like
These days, when I'm alone
I start to sound like my mother
or rather, it's as if she were using my mouth
to voice her profanities, curses and gibberish
the invisible litany of her nicknames
all the endangered species of her sayings
It's been twenty years since I last saw my mother
but I am the last man
who still speaks her language

Translated from the French by André Naffis-Sahely

قردٌ على الشبّاك

(1)

الولدُ الذي كان يلهو في السرير

أمّه تطبخُ مجروحةً

يرمي بالدوائرِ واللغوِ

من النافذة الصغيرةُ

تبتسمُ

(يسطع العالمُ كلّه)

"يُبَرْطِمُ" – ماذا يظنُّ ؟!

على الشبّاك قردٌ

وراء البابْ

لكنه لم يزلْ يهوي إلى ظلمةٍ بعيدةٍ

لا يدلِّي صراخاً

يعلِّي مخالبَهُ – الولدُ

الأخضرُ

المُستَفَزُّ

(2)

لم تعلِّمه البكاءَ–بغتةً– الغناءُ

خضراءُ–كما شاءت

تعلِّمه الأقاصي والشسوعُ

وتناديه: الرحابةُ

خلفه تلٌّ من الوصفِ

أمامه نهرٌ وجرعةُ ليلٍ

قوافلُ تدعوه لينأى

(أين هذا الخيطُ

A Monkey at the Window

AL-SADDIQ AL-RADDI · SUDAN

(1)
The little boy, playing in bed
while his wounded mother cooks,
is throwing words and circles
out of the window.

> She smiles
> (the whole world lights up)
> he chatters excitedly – What can he see?

There's a monkey at the window –
behind the door!
> But he is falling
> into darkness.
> > And though he never raises a cry
> he holds up his claws – this dark
> > stormy
> > > boy.

(2)
She never taught him how to cry, only how to sing.
Happy in herself – just as she wished to be –
she taught him endless space and vastness
and she calls him: open-hearted.

Behind him a mountain of metaphors
in front, a river, a mouthful of night
and a train of caravans calling him away.
(Where is that thread

تلك النارُ

أين الملكاتْ؟!)

(3)

راكضاً في زقاقٍ

يدلق الزيتَ

على السروالِ- هذا الولدْ!

بالَ على السروالِ

من أثرِ الضحك

وهو يركضُ في الأبدْ

هذا الزقاقُ

عصابةُ الجراءِ

تواطؤُ الغيوبْ

(4)

البابُ مصنوعٌ- يوحي بيَدٍ تَعْرَقُ

المفتاحُ أنتَ

صريرُ الكونِ- سِرُّكَ

الوحيدْ

تسندُ عليه قفا مستقبلٍ وترائيات

وتحملُ عنه أكولةَ "الأرْضَةِ"

في قلبِكَ

رائحةَ البَلَلِ

مطارقَ الأعداءِ والأقاربْ

(طالت غيبةُ الضوءِ

يدهنُ الأشياءَ بالصحوِ

طالَ حضورُ الطلاءْ)

248

that fire
the skill?)

(3)
Running – down an alleyway
he splashes cooking oil all down his shorts this boy!

He wets himself
with laughter
running through Eternity –
      through this alleyway
      this pack of dogs
      the conspiracies of fate!

(4)
The solid front door remembers
the hand that made it –
              You are
                  the key –
and the creak of the universe –
it's your sole secret.
You lean your future and your dreams against it.
For its sake you endure the woodworms
gnawing through your heart
the reek of damp
the hammering of enemies and relatives.
(Long is the absence of light
      that paints things awake –
      Long is the presence of paint!)

You come home exhausted – from wherever you've been
the wind at your side – just as you wished –
toyed with by traumas.

تدخلُ مِنْ أيِّ شئتَ– مثقوبَ العناءِ
تصاحبكَ الريحُ– شئتَ
تداعبك الصدماتْ!

كانَ ينْظمُ عقداً من الأصدافِ
يلوّنه بخرافاته
ويصادقُ الضفادعَ الغريبةْ
وهي ترقبه بصمتٍ
وراء الباب/ على الشبّاكِ
(تُهْرَعُ كي تُعلِّي
لايُدلِّي
أيَّ شَيْءٍ)!

(5)

بالغابةِ   ألوحيدةُ تعرفُ الأصواتْ
كانت تناديها عيونُ الغالين
تشدُّها أناشيدُهُم
بحنانِ أناملهم
ورهيفِ توحُّدها
تقعُدُ صامتةً
قُربَ أيَّ شَيْءٍ
تدفِّئُ الشايَ
أو تصنعُ العصيدةْ

في الحديقة
بالبيت الغريبِ– بيتها
تدعو مواعينَ الغسيلِ
إلى صباح الصوت
تدلكُ كلَّ شَيْءٍ في مكانه
تراقبُ المذياع

250

Once he made necklaces from seashells
and colouring them with his own fairytales
once he made friends with strange frogs
– and all the while she's watching him
from behind the door /from out the window
(when she runs to pick him up
        he will not raise
        a cry!)

(5)
In the forest the lonely one knows all the voices
beckoned by the eyes of loved ones
their songs are luring her
with their tender fingers
and her own translucent solitude.
        She sits in silence
        close to every thing
        brewing tea
        stirring the porridge.

In the garden
of a strange home, her home
she welcomes pots and pans
to the sounds of morning.
        Scrubbing everything in its proper place
        one eye on the radio

يدعوها إلى رملٍ بعيد

صحراءَ

لكن لوثُها يمتدُّ نهراً

...كي يغنِّي

والوَلدْ؟!

... ...

في غابةٍ خضراءَ

...أو حمراءَ

في صحراءَ

من كان يناديها– أبدْ؟!

        that calls her to those distant sands
        the desert.
But her colours flow like a river
so she can sing. . . .
                 And that boy?
... ...
In a green forest
or a red forest
or a desert
now who calls him to Eternity?

Translated from the Arabic by Sarah Maguire and Hafiz Kheir

Trazo del tiempo

Entre el viento y lo oscuro,
entre el gozo ascendente
y la quietud profunda,
entre la exaltación de mi vestido blanco
y la oquedad nocturna de la mina,
los ojos suaves de mi padre que esperan; su alegría
incandescente. Subo para alcanzarlo. Es la tierra
de los pequeños astros, y sobre ella,
sobre sus lajas de pirita, el sol desciende. Altas nubes
de cuarzo, de pedernal. En su mirada, en su luz envolvente,
el calor del ámbar.
Me alza en brazos. Se acerca.
Nuestra sombra se inclina ante la orilla. Me baja.
Me da la mano.
Todo el descenso
es un gozo callado,
una tibieza oscura,
una encendida plenitud.
Algo en esa calma nos cubre, algo nos protege
y levanta,
muy suavemente,
mientras bajamos.

Marks of Time

CORAL BRACHO · MEXICO

Between wind and dark,
between a rush of joy
yet deepest calm,
between my lovely white dress flying
and the dark, dark hole of the mine,
are my father's eyes, so gentle, waiting; his dancing
happiness. I go to meet him. This is a land
of little stars, of pyrite crystals,
wherever it's touched by the sunset. Clouds
of quartz, and flint, up high. His bright gaze,
all-embracing,
has the warmth of amber.
He lifts me up into his arms. He comes in close.
Our one shadow drifts over to the edge of the mine. He puts me down.
He gives me his hand.
The whole way down
is just one joy, in silence:
one dark warmth,
one richness, aglow.
Something in that quietness holds us under its wing, it protects
and uplifts us,
very softly,
as we go down.

Translated from the Spanish by Katherine Pierpoint and Tom Boll

پَر

آرام، آرام می آیی
بر نوک پاها
درست وقتی رویا
صدای پایت را می شنود

چشم هایت خمار مَنند
وقتی گربه وار
زیر لحافم می خزی
خواب و بیدار
حریر خوابم را می بوسی

در فاصله ی رساندن دست هایت
به دور گردنم
روی بالش من به خواب می روی

میان خواب و بیداری
به محض خالی شدن از رویا
پُر می شوم از تو

A Feather

SHAKILA AZIZZADA · AFGHANISTAN

for Sepideh

Just as my dream
hears the sound of your steps,
that's when you enter
quietly, quietly on tiptoe.

You crawl under the sheet
like a kitten, your eyes
drinking me in.
Asleep or awake,
you lap the silk of my dreams.

In the moment it takes
to put your arms round my neck,
you're fast asleep on the pillow.

And I, half-asleep, half-awake,
just when I am drained of dreams,
am filled with you and replenished.

Translated from the Dari (Persian) by Mimi Khalvati and Zuzanna Olszewska

Sepideh: the poet's daughter.

Lukisan Wanita 1938

Lukisan dengan lengkap citarasa
giwang, gelang, untaian kuning hijau
selendang, menyembunyikan kehamilan

kehamilan maut yang nanti menjemput
luput diredam
kehamilan hidup yang nanti merenggut
goresan dendam
gejolak dan kemelut keprihatinan
gagal direkam
pada sapuan dan garis wajah yang
menyerah, pada alur sejarah

Lukisan dengan sapuan akhir
yang cemerlang, kelengkapan wajah
diperoleh dalam bingkai kenangan

Juli 1989

A Woman's Portrait 1938

TOETI HERATY · INDONESIA

The painting conveys her exquisite taste:
ear studs, bracelets, green and yellow selendang;
the sash conceals her pregnancy.

The death she is carrying can't be disguised.
The life she carries will grasp and cling on.
Yearning, restlessness and the turmoil of fear
are not recorded in the brush-strokes,
pencil outline of a face
surrendering to the flow of history.

The painting, with its final brilliant gesture,
only fully reveals this face
when it is framed by memory.

July 1989
Translated from the Indonesian by Carole Satyamurti and Ulrich Kratz

دوو گیان

ئەو چی دی ناو قەدی باریک نیە
وەکو دەستە خوشکەکانی.
لەنجەو لاری لەیادچووەو
ناوێڕێ سوار
کورسی کورسیو
بەلەمەکەی سەرچنار بێت
وەک سەردەمی دەزگیرانیی.

ئەو دوو گیانە..
بۆیە جوانترە لە هەموو کچەکانی دەوروبەری
لەو پیاوانەش کە ئێواران
بەلای خەمیدا دەڕۆنو
لەناو ژنانی گەڕەکدا
شێوەی ئەو عاشقترینە،
هەروەها زیندووترینە.

دیمەنی سکی وادەکات
مرۆڤ حەزی لەخواردنی شووتی بێت!
فێریش ببێت
بەدیار چنینی گوڕەوییو
بلوزێکی بچووکەوە
خەون بە گریانو خەندەی
کۆرپەیەکەوە ببینیت.

ئەو چیدی ناوقەدی وەکو
شمشاڵ نییە
تێپەڕی سەردەمی تەنوورەو
سترێنچو
کابۆی جێنز
بینازن ئێستا قەڵەمی لێوو
پاژنەی بەرزو ئاوینە
بەجێما ویستگەی لەبەرکردنی
جلی خەو و جلی مەڵە.

260

Pregnancy

KAJAL AHMAD · KURDISTAN

Unlike her friends,
she can't boast a waist any more.
Her hips don't swing and sway.
She doesn't dare
to ride the wheel
and the ship of Serchnar
as she used to when she was engaged.

She is pregnant
which is why she's prettier than the girls around her,
prettier than the men who at evening
pass by her lament.
Among the neighbourhood women,
she looks the most love-stricken
and the liveliest.

Looking at her
makes you long for watermelon.
And you learn to dream
of a baby's cry or laughter
as you knit a sock
or a little jumper.

Her waist isn't as slim
as a reedpipe any more.
The time for skirts
expands
and for jeans
disappears.

Lipstick's now ignored
along with high heels and mirrors.
Her heyday for wearing
ballgowns and swimsuits is over.

ئەو چی دی
لەگەڵ هەناوی خۆیدا
قسەدەکات
ئاگای لەئێمەو خۆی نیە.

خوایە بەخێری بگێڕیت
نۆ مانگ گەڕان بە کۆلانی
ژیانو مردنا
خوایە بەخێری بگێڕیت
ئەم قەدەرەی لەڕێی ژنە.

Now she talks
to her own womb.
Unaware of us or of herself.

May God make it good,
this nine-month search
on the roads of life and death.
May God make it good,
this fate which women face.

Translated from the Kurdish by Mimi Khalvati and Choman Hardi

Serchnar: City in Iraqi Kurdistan; the wheel and ship are fairground rides.

Dookh

Haddaanad gabayga deelqaafka iyo, dari ka saaraynnin
Dalabtiyo haddaan laga midh tirin, diniqa aan muuqan
Meeshii dahsoonayd haddaan, lagu daqiiqeeynnin
Doogtiyo haddaan lagu lafgurin, dakharradii raagay
Darar lagama maaloo tixuu, dufan ma yeeshaane,
Aan dareersho caawoo kalaan, daribta saafaaye.

Inkastuu darmaan quruxsan iyo, daaddax ugu yeedho
Ama uu ammaan deexdo oo, 'dawlo!' ku yidhaahdo
Hadal dhegaha deeqaaya oo, dabacsan oo fiican
Dun xariir ah iyo shaal hadduu, dahab ku saarsaaro
Daraandaryo araggaaga hooy, damacu waa yaabe,
Oo aanu dookhaaga noqon, waa dariiq xidhane.

Hadduu daaro waaweyn dhisoo, dabaqyo kuu jeexo
Dal dhan oo muraayad ah dhammaan, adiga kuu deyro
Sancadaw dambeeysiyo hadduu, dalabka kuu keeno
Naftu waxay yara doonayso uu, deregga soo saaro,
Oo aanu dookhaaga noqon, waa dariiq xidhane.

Inkastoo adduun door ah iyo, duunyo lagu sheego
Inkastuu dulqaad badan yahoo, deeqsi lagu sheego
Duub iyo malaaq uu yahoo, dooje lagu sheego
Digriiga iyo maastariga iyo, derejo weyn haysto
Digriigyo Quraankiyo hadduu, diinta yahay xaafid,
Oo aanu dookhaaga noqon, waa dariiq xidhane.

Inkastuu dillaacshoo qalbiga, daabac ku xardhaayo
Xididdada dil-dilayee wadnuhu, dirayo dhiiggooda
Dahriga iyo laabtaba ku dhigo, Deeqa magacaaga
Diiwaankii Cilmoo kale galoo, deli ka laallaado
Suugaanta duugga ah murtida, damashi kuu qaado
Daaweeynta heesaha intaa, daram garaacaayo,
Oo aanu dookhaaga noqon, waa dariiq xidhane.

Taste

CAASHA LUL MOHAMUD YUSUF · SOMALIA/SOMALILAND

If this poem isn't free of flaws or clunkiness,
if it contains disharmony or defects,
if it doesn't illuminate what's hidden
and isn't used to staunch old injuries,
its verses won't nourish, are a withered breast.
Let me recite this with spirit. It's night; it's time.

Though he may call you fair names, a 'lovely mare',
and praise you up onto a pedestal, all-powerful,
and slip soothing words in your ear, sweet to hear,
dazzle your eyes and make desire rear up,
if he's not to your taste, he's just a blocked path.

Though he may place you in a skyscraper
and fill your world with glass
or fashion, or your demands,
arriving at your door with every whim,
if he's not to your taste, he's just a blocked path.

Though he's said to be wealthy, with a portfolio of property,
and is known for his patience and generosity
and like a tribal chief, is spoken of with honour,
and has his Master's degree and letters after his name,
if he's not to your taste, he's just a blocked path.

No matter that he wears his heart on his chest
and shows you the blood's beat in his veins
and prints your name on his skin
and writes love poems like Cilmi, from the edge,
and sings enchanted ancient lyrics full of wisdom,
if he's not to your taste, he's just a blocked path.

Haddii uu dalxiis kuugu diro, dunida guudkeeda
Diyaarado hawada sarena aad, kula damaanshaaddo
Durdur iyo hadduu kugu dul furo, ilo dareeraaya
Deeradiyo cawshiyo ugaadh, quruxda daa'uuska
Doog iyo cagaar soo ifbaxay, darinta kuu daadsho
Ama Daallo oo roobku heley, Dalawa kuu maalo
Oo doobi kuu buuxiyoo, kuna daryeelaayo
Dayrtiyo Gugaba kuu da'oo, adiga kuu deexdo
Daruur hoortay uu kuu noqdiyo, malakba doocaanka,
Oo aanu dookhaaga noqon, waa dariiq xidhane.

Inkastuu darwiish adag yahiyo, geesi diriraayo
Dirica iyo wiil hoog yahoo, degello naafeeyo
Dumukha iyo qorigaba ridoo, diiradda u saaro
Halka lagu dagaalamo hadduu, doorar ka ciyaaro
Ama u daqiiqaaya oo uu, duubiyada gooyo,
Oo aanu dookhaaga noqon, waa dariiq xidhane.

Xeedhyo duuban oo duqus leh oo, geedo lagu daadshay
Hilbo duban kuwii diirranaa, qaar dux lagu shiilay
Daboolkiyo lingaxa lagu xidhood, uumi lagu daaro
Ubbadii dahaadhnayd haddii, diiqo lagu siiyo
Haddaan milix yar lagu daadinayn, kaama daadego'e,

Dookhana sidaasoo kalaan, loo dirqiyahayne
Damiirkaagu meeshaanu rabin, dooni kari maysid.

London, 21.08.2011

Though he takes you on a tour around the world
and wants you by him on the plane,
and shows you fountains and pulsing streams
in places teeming with deer, antelope, peacock,
and lays carpets for you on lush low grass
and takes you to stunning Daallo just after rain
and gives you bowls of camel-milk, wanting your comfort,
wanting to look after you through spring and autumn,
conjuring rainclouds and Yemeni honey,
if he's not to your taste, he's just a blocked path.

Though he might be a holy Dervish, a fighter for God,
a fearless young man who can destroy dark forces,
skilful with guns, never missing his target,
commended for bravery in battle,
who crushes his enemies and tears up their bodies,
if he's not to your taste, he's just a blocked path.

You might be treated to a bowl of spiced food,
barbecued meats and meats cooked with fat
steamed to perfection underneath a tight lid,
or a ghee pot with its beautifully crafted case,
but if there's no salt to season, you won't eat with relish.
Taste cannot be won by compulsion.
You cannot go against your own heart.

Translated from the Somali by Clare Pollard and Said Jama Hussein

باران های اول اردیبهشت

بهتر است مشغول خود باشید
یا شاغل به آنچه معافتان کند   از کار دشوار عاشقی
حرفه‌ای که آدم را وا می‌دارد   تونل‌هایی بلند و کور
پشت جمله‌های کوتاه حفر کند
با چشم لک‌لک دنیا را ببیند
زبان مارمولک‌ها را یاد بگیرد
یا مورچه‌ای گیج باشد   که دانه‌های درشت را
از دیوار صاف بالا می‌برد
و از این همه مواجبش تنها
بادهای آخر پاییز باشد و
باران‌های اول اردیبهشت

The First Rains of Spring

AZITA GHAHREMAN · IRAN

It is better to bustle away,
to be busy with some work or other
and keep love at bay.
For when it takes hold
we find significance everywhere we look,
the pelican's point of view seems persuasive,
we long to learn the language of lizards,
even an ant's dizzying ascent looks meaningful.
And what have we gained from it?
Only the last winds of autumn,
the first rains of spring.

Translated from the Farsi (Persian) by Maura Dooley and Elhum Shakerifar

तुम कहोगे, रात

तुम कहोगे, रात
और रात हो जायेगी

तुम कहोगे, दिन
और धुल जायेगा दिन

तुम कहोगे, रंग
और उड़ती चली आयेंगी
तितलियाँ पृथ्वी भर की

तुम सोचोगे, प्रेम
और दिगंत खोल देगा
एक इन्द्र-धनुष गुप्त

तुम होगे, संतप्त
और जल जायेगी
उसकी त्वचा
दूसरे शहर में

                         तुम कहोगे, रात
                         और झरती चली जायेगी स्मृति
                         तुम कहोगे, दिन
                         और रिक्त हो जायेगी पृथ्वी

तुम रहोगे , चुप
और चटक जायेंगी
शिलाएँ चंद्रमा तक

तुम करोगे, अदेखा
और वह जा फँसेगी
अदृश्या
हवा के कंठ में

You Will Say Night

GAGAN GILL · INDIA

You will say night
and night will be

You will say day
and day will be washed

You will say colour
and all the butterflies
of the earth will come flying

You will think love
and the horizon will open
a hidden rainbow

You will be tormented
and in another city
her skin
will burn

> *You will say night*
> *and memory will fall away*
> *You will say day*
> *and the earth will be empty*

You will be silent
and rocks will explode
as far away as the moon

You will not look at her
and she will be caught
invisible
in the throat of the wind

तुम कहोगे, रात
और बनने लगेगा
आप-ही-आप
रेत में एक घर

तुम कहोगे, दिन
और उघड़ जायेगी यह देह
जरा की कुतरी हुई

You will say night
and a house
will rise
in the sand

You will say day
and this body, gnawed by old age
will be naked

Translated from the Hindi by Jane Duran and Lucy Rosenstein

之二七 • 隱

你懷疑愛情是
貪婪的吃角子老虎

你重複同一動作
投幣投幣投幣投幣一千次

愛情重複同一反應
或不反應

一千次
愛情吞沒你全部

慾望的積蓄
那傳言中的完整月亮

從沒出現
一次都沒有

27 • *metaphor*

CHEN YUHONG · TAIWAN

you suspect love is
a voracious one-armed bandit

you keep on
feeding it a coin a coin a coin a coin a thousand times

love keeps up its response:
no response

a thousand times
love swallows all of you

that hoard of desire –
the rumoured whole moon

has never appeared
not even once

Translated from the Chinese by Chenxin Jiang and The Poetry
Translation Centre Workshop

نہ کوئی خواب نہ سہیلی تھی
اِس محبّت میں میں اکیلی تھی

عشق میں تم کہاں کے سچّے تھے
جو اذیّت تھی ہم نے جھیلی تھی

یاد اب کچھ نہیں رہا لیکن
ایک دریا تھا یا حویلی تھی

جس نے اُلجھا کے رکھ دیا دل کو
وہ محبّت تھی یا پہیلی تھی

میں ذرا سی بھی کم وفا کرتی
تم نے تو میری جان لے لی تھی

وقت کے سانپ کھا گئے اُس کو
میرے آنگن میں اِک چنبیلی تھی

اِس شب غم میں کِس کو بتلاؤں
کِتنی روشن مِری ہتھیلی تھی

There Was a Time When I Loved Alone

NOSHI GILLANI · PAKISTAN

There was a time when I loved alone
Without dream or friend

There was a time when your love was untrue
When I endured such torment that

I don't remember anything now but
There was a river . . . or a villa . . .

You confused my heart so much
That love shrank to a riddle

Yet had I been the slightest bit disloyal
You would almost have taken my life

Time is like the snakes
Devouring jasmine in my courtyard

Who can I tell, this sad evening
How bright the line of fate once was on my hand?

Translated from the Urdu by Lavinia Greenlaw and Nukhbah Taj Langah

सन्नाटे में दूर तक

उन्होंने मुझे
ढेले की तरह फेंका था
वे नहीं जानते थे
मैं एक आत्मवस्तु हूँ
वे यह भी नहीं जानते थे
कि मैं एक जीवित वस्तु हूँ
वे मुझे
ढेले की तरह फेंकते रहे
अपने रास्ते से अलग
उस 'परित्यक्त पथ' पर, जो
संयोग से मेरा था।
और इस तरह मैं
अपने रास्ते की
दूरी तय करती रही।
हर बार झर जाता कोई कण
आसक्ति का कोई भाव, सुख की कोई संलग्नता
धरती से जुड़ी कोई आशा
आदमी में फैला कोई स्वप्न
हर बार झर जाता
मेरे अस्तित्व का कोई कण
और अब मेरी बारी थी
पीछे छूट चुका था विश्व —

Deep in the Stillness

AMRITA BHARATI · INDIA

He threw me away
like a clod of earth.
He didn't know
I was a thing with a soul.
He didn't know
I was alive.

He kept on throwing me
like a clod of earth
out of his way –
onto that neglected path
that happened to be mine.
And so I kept travelling
along my own way.
Each time some fragment broke off –
some infatuation, some addiction to happiness,
some earthly hope,
some dream squandered on man.
Each time some fragment of my being
would break off.
And now it was my turn.
The world was already left behind –

रेतीले अंधड़ से भरे मरूस्थल की तरह
तूफ़ानी महासमुद्र और
सूने नगर की तरह –
पीछे छूट चुका था
हर पग नीची सीढ़ियाँ उतरता आदमी
और अब यह मेरी बारी थी।
धरती के आख़िरी टुकड़े पर खड़े हो मैंने
अपने को
पूर्ण वस्तु की तरह समेटा था
और प्रक्षेपित किया था
सन्नाटे में
यह मेरी नीरवता थी –
व्याप्त और विस्तृत।
अब विश्व या तो एक सपना था
या दूर प्रतिभासित होता
एक जल-पुष्प
इस पारावार में
सन्नाटे में दूर तक
मेरी ही आहट थी।

like a desert in a sandstorm,
like an ocean in a hurricane,
like a desolate city.
Man, step by step descending,
was already left behind.
And now it was my turn.
Standing on the last patch of earth
I gathered myself into a whole thing
and hurled myself into the stillness.
This was my silence –
pervasive and expansive.
Now the world was either a dream
or a sea-flower
imagined at the end of the ocean.
Deep in the stillness.
Only the sound of my footsteps.

Translated from the Hindi by Lucy Rosenstein and the Poetry Translation Centre Workshop

نظربند

پیراهن زفافم را
از میخ خاطره های سپید می آویزم
ابریشم نگاهم را
از شانه هایش

دل کنده ام از سینه اش
که هنوز بوی شیر مرا دارد؟

با دل انگشت هایش
بر گردنم
بیدار می شود
غوغای وسوسه ای کهنه در آغوشش

دل می گیرم از او
چشم اندازم پر می شود
از پشتش
که تخت است و برازنده ی
شال شاهی

به یاد نمی سپارم
که دمی دیگر
چادر عروسش را برمی گیرد

شماره نمی کنم
نفس هایش را

The Bridal Veil

SHAKILA AZIZZADA · AFGHANISTAN

I've hung my wedding dress
on a hook of white memories,
my gaze like silk on his shoulders.

I've torn my heart from his chest
which still smells of my milk.

He'd wake,
his fingers pulsing on my neck,
the same old clamour of lust in his arms.

I've torn my heart away
but my eyes are filled with him,
his back, broad and resplendent
in a bridegroom's shawl.

I won't remind myself
that, with the next breath,
he'll take off her veil.

I won't count
his breaths.

Translated from the Dari (Persian) by Mimi Khalvati and
Zuzanna Olszewska

موسموں کی تبدیلی

موسموں کی تبدیلی
کوئی راز ہی کھولے
خوف کے جزیرے میں
راستہ دکھانے کو
اُس کی درد آنکھوں کی
روشنی ہی اب بولے

A Change of Season

NOSHI GILLANI · PAKISTAN

A change of season
Exposes something
Hidden in her fear:
A way across that island
Lit by the pain in her eyes

*Translated from the Urdu by Lavinia Greenlaw and
Nukhbah Taj Langah*

Qui zunihuarálu' naa

Qui zunihuarálu' naa.
Qui zaguza diou' xquendanabane'.
Naro'ba' yu'du' biaani' bisananelu' naa,
nanaadxi' ne nayeche'.

Xadxípe' bisindá'naxhilu' bi stinne',
xadxípe' guleezalu' naa lade ca za
ne xidxaa guidiládilu'.

Racaditi ru' ca naya' guietenala'dxica'
beelaxiaa dxitaxa'nalu'.
Ricaala'dxiru' guidiruaa'
runi guiropa' rii dxiñabizu xi'dxu'.

Paraa chiguniná guendarietenala'dxi' naa ya'.
Paraa, neca zelu', gácananaladxe' lii ya'.
Ti nisadó' benda riaquibiaani' bisananelu' naa,
ti nisadó' benda caguite yeche'.

You Will Not Manage to Hurt Me

VÍCTOR TERÁN · MEXICO

You will not manage to hurt me.
You will not break my existence.
The cathedral of light that you left me is immense,
warm and joyful.

You scented my existence for a long time.
You introduced me to paradise
with your lukewarm and naked body.
My hands still shake at the memory
of your fleshy ass.
My lips still tremble
when I remember the sweet taste of your nipples.

With these memories, how can I feel hurt?
Though you left me, how can I abhor you?
You left me with an ocean of dazzling fish,
an ocean of incessant fish.

Translated from the Zapotec by David Shook

287

کمین گربه

شگوم ندارد
این واژه ها

نگو در بهشت
میان لب های من باز می شود

پای خدا
در چاک سینه های من لغزیده است

می آیم

باز
نفس هایت
درمن می دمند
ریه هایت
از عطر من پر می شوند
زبانت بر پوستم
باران باران
بارانی می شود

وا می روم

و باز
آنگونه که می آیی
با هوای دریدن
در نی نی چشم هایت

بی هیچ شکی

به گربه ی سیاه می مانی
که پیشترک
از کمینگاهش
راه را بر من برید
تا دم درت
گنجشک فلج شده
از تسلیم را
شکار کرده باشد

Cat Lying in Wait

SHAKILA AZIZZADA · AFGHANISTAN

They don't bode well,
these words.

Don't tell me the door to Paradise
opens between my lips.

In the cleft between my breasts,
God himself tripped.

I'll come

and again
your breath will breathe
inside me,
your lungs will fill
with my scent,
your tongue will
rain, rain,
rain again on my skin.

I'll give in.

And this time,
when you come with that glint
in your eye, bent
on tearing me apart, you'll be,

without a shadow of a doubt,

like the black cat that leapt
out of hiding, cut
across my path just now,
hunted down
the sparrow at your door
till she fell
stunned and captive.

Translated from the Dari (Persian) by Mimi Khalvati and Zuzanna Olszewska

امْرَأَةُ النِّعْنَاع

بُجَرْجِرُ الشَّبَقَ مِنْ وَجَعِ الشَّوْكِ
تُوَشْوِشُها.. تَمْلَأُكَ وَقْتاً مُشْمِساً
تَسُوقُ فِيْ حَاشِيَتِها شَذَا اللَّحْظَةِ العَابِرَةْ
تُمَسِّدُ أَلَقَها بِرَائِحَةِ رَبِيعْ
تَرْسِمُ حُدُودَ اللَّهاثِ دَائِماً
لا يُرْضِيها سِوى القُرَّيصُ البَرِّيْ
وَحْدَهُ يَرْصِفُ نُعُومَةَ اللُّغَةِ بِشَوْكِهْ

طَعْمُهُ يُرَطِّبُ حَلاوَةَ المَشْهَدْ
يَخْتَلُ الجَسَدَ المَتْرُوكَ لِلبَياضْ
يَنْتَزِعُ عِفَّةَ النِّعْنَاعَةِ بِخَشْخَشَةِ أَوْرَاقِهِ الجَبَلِيَّةْ
يَتْرُكُ نُدُوبَهُ فِيْها
شَوْكُهُ.. أَلَقُهُ المُتَلاحِقْ
يُوقِفُ مَجرَى التَّنَفُّسِ وَقْتاً كَأَنَّهُ الأَبَدْ
ثُمَّ يُدَغْدِغُ مِرفَقَ النِّعْنَاعَةِ بِوَخزَةٍ حَاسِمَةْ

Woman of Mint

FATENA AL-GHARRA · PALESTINE

She hauls her desire from the anguish of thorns,
whispering, Sunlight abides in you.
She is followed by the aroma of a fleeting moment
which she ignites with the perfume of Spring.
Not once does she gasp for breath.
Only wild nettle sates her desire:
his hair alone will make her easy.
His presence delights the scenery.
He populates vacancy.
He takes the pure mint with the force of his leaves,
scarring her deep inside.
His sting . . . his victory.
Her breath stopped, as if for eternity.
Then he tickles her elbow with his sting.

Translated from the Arabic by Sarah Maguire and Sara Vaghefian

فەلسەفەی میوەفرۆشێک

هاوڕێم تۆ وەک قەیسییەک بوویت
هەر کە ویستم تامتبکەم
هاتم کرۆکو ناوەرۆکم فڕێدایت

دۆستی دێرین
تۆ هەندێجار لالەنگیت!
هەر لە خۆتەوە ڕووتدەبییەوە
جاریش هەیە هەروەکو سێو
بەبێ تویکڵو
بەتویکڵیشەوە دەخورێیت!

دراوسێکەم
تۆ هەر وەکو چەقۆی میوەیت!
کاتێ نییه لەسەر سفرە
مالێ ئێمە نەبینرێیت
بەلام دەبێ لێمببوریت
من حەزم لێت نییه!

نیشتمانی ئازیزم بەلام تۆ لێمۆێیت
هەموو دنیا کە ناوتهات
ناو دەمیان پڕ دەبێت لەئاو
کەچی من موچڕکم پیا دێت!

ئەی ئەوەی ناتناسم
بێگومانم لەوەی شووتیت
تاوەک چەقۆ بە ناختا ڕۆنەچم
ناتوانم بزانم تۆ چیت!

The Fruit-Seller's Philosophy

KAJAL AHMAD · KURDISTAN

My friend! You were like an apricot.
At the first bite,
I spat out the core and crux.

*

My old flame! Sometimes
you're a tangerine,
undressing so spontaneously,

and sometimes you're an apple,
edible
with or without the peel.

*

Neighbour!
You're like a fruit knife.
There's never a time
when you're not
at our dinner table.
But forgive me if I say –
you're a waste of time.

*

Dear homeland, you're like a lemon.
When you are named,
the world's mouth waters
but I get all goosepimply.

*

You, stranger!
I'm sure you're a watermelon.
I won't know what you're really like
till I go through you like a knife.

Translated from the Kurdish by Mimi Khalvati and Choman Hardi

با گلی سرخ

با گلی سرخ
از میان پیراهن‌های سیاه
و پرچم های ژنده‌ی پیاده‌رو بگذر
راهی دیگر نیست
با گل سرخت
از گوشه‌ی چپ کاغذ
پایین بیا
از لابلای خط‌ها و سطرها
عبور کن
و سمت خاطراتم بپیچ
مرا ملاقات کن
در خانه‌ای زرد و فرسوده
که لولاهای زنگ زده دارد
و دریچه‌های پوشیده از پیچک و علف
نجواهای درهم و کشدار،غبار اشیااند
لفاف غمناک سالیان
برگرد ترس ها
با گل سرخت
بیا، بیا
و چنانکه نبینند
سوی در بهشت
اشارت کن.

With a Red Flower

AZITA GHAHREMAN · IRAN

Wearing a poppy
leave behind those black clothes,
the flags of mourning,
the tired, disconsolate streets.
This is the only way forward.
Wearing your red flower
climb from between these handwritten lines,
turn from the empty space of this paper
and step into my memories.

Come! Meet me
in that shabby old house,
where now the pipes are rusty,
the shutters lost in ivy and long grass,
where cobwebs and whispers have
settled over everything,
where, after all these years,
sorrow is the only dustsheet.

Come back to me, hide your fears,
wearing your red flower, come back,
but take care that no one sees
the route that brought you here from Heaven.

Translated from the Farsi (Persian) by Maura Dooley and Elhum Shakerifar

پھُول کے دل پہ ضرب کاری ہے
خوشبوؤں کی ہوا سے یاری ہے

ہم سے قاتل کے خال و خد پوچھو
ہم نے مقتل میں شب گزاری ہے

تم جو چاہو تو ہم پلٹ جائیں
یہ سفر اب بھی اختیاری ہے

سو گئیں شہر کی سبھی گلیاں
اب مِرے جاگنے کی باری ہے

شام کی بے یقین آنکھوں میں
کیفیت ساری انتظاری ہے

وصل کو کیسے معتبر سمجھیں!
ہجر کا خوف دِل پہ طاری ہے

آج تو دل کی بات کہنے دو
آج کی شام تو ہماری ہے

The Flower Is Torn at the Heart

NOSHI GILLANI · PAKISTAN

The flower is torn at the heart
Its fragrance befriends the breeze

Who can tell who destroyed it?
We have spent this evening under sentence

No one has to go on this journey
I can still turn round, if you want

Every street in this city is asleep
It's my turn to stay awake

In the uncertain view of this evening
The whole thing wavers

How can we honour our union
When my heart is gripped by fear of separation

My heart desires above all
That we make this evening ours

Translated by Lavinia Greenlaw and Nukhbah Taj Langah

მაისის თაფლი

რა ადვილია რომ მიყვარდე
ანუ მაგრად მოვმუწო პირი
რომ ჩემს მუცელში მოზუზუნე
მუშა ფუტკრებმა
არ შეგატოვონ ფაქიზი და მკიფე ნესტარი,
მიყვარდე, ნიშნავს, რომ დაგიცვა
ჩემი კოცნისგან.

რა ადვილია, რომ მიყვარდე
კანის ფორებში – ფიჭის უჯრებში
გამოვჩეკო თბილი ჭუპრები:
შეხება
სუნი
მახსოვრობა
ჩვევა
შეჩვევა –
დავაფრთიანო
მოგცე სხვასთან ყოფნის უფლება.

რა ადვილია რომ მიყვარდე,
ყოველ დილით დავუხშო ბაგე
უსქესო ფუტკრებს
- შთაგონების მუშა ქალწულებს
მტვრითა და ცვილით ამოვლესო
ჩემი სკის კარი
მიყვარდე – ნიშნავს იყო შორს და
ჩემგან დაცული.
რა ადვილია, როგორც ოქროს მიწაში დაფლვა,
არადა ისე უმიზეზოდ დამწიფდა თაფლი.

May Honey

DIANA AMPHIMIADI · GEORGIA

How easy it is to love you –
in other words, to seal my lips
so that the worker bees
can't leave their tender sting
in my stomach.
To love you means to protect you
from my kiss.

How easy it is to love you –
in each pore of my skin;
to hatch the warm chrysalis
in each cell of the honeycomb.
Touch, smell, memory, habit, familiarity –
to give wings to them all,
to give you the right to be with another.

How easy it is to love you –
to seal the mouth
of the sexless bees each morning
(those virgin muses)
to block with dust and dew
the opening of my beehive.
For me to love you,
you must remain at a distance,
protected from me –
it's as easy as burying gold in the ground.
But honey is here without any reason.
And so are you.

Translated from the Georgian by Natalia Bukia-Peters and The Poetry Translation Centre Workshop

لهاثْ

كأنَّها تَقتربُ من البابِ
تسمعُ دقات قلبِكَ
أو
كأنك في انتظارِها
تَحْضُرُ طيورُ الضُّحى
وتَصْطَفُّ على النافذةْ

. . . .

ساعةٌ من الصَّبرِ
غابةٌ من الهديلِ والشقشقةْ.

Breathless

AL-SADDIQ AL-RADDI · SUDAN

Your heart thumps —
as if she were already
at your door.

Or — as if expecting her —
all the birds in the midday sky
arrive to clamour at your window.

....

An age of patience.
A forest of fluttering.

Translated from the Arabic by Sarah Maguire and Hafiz Kheir

Cajabey

Cajebeey cajiibeey!
Cawo iyo ayaaneey!
Caqligaad xadaysaa,
Caku! barashadaadii
Iyo caabuqaagee.

Sida faras cag fududoo
Cadda-horor yaqaanoo
Gulufkiyo colaadaha
Ninka lihi cad-goostaa,
Raggu kuu cugtamayaa;
Anna caashaqaagaan
Hadba weel u culayaa,
Cimri-dherer hadhkaagaan
Riyo kula caweeyaa.

Dhulka oo cagaaroo
Cosobkii dul-saarraa
Isagaan car-jabin weli,
Cabbanaan daraaddeed
Ciidda hoose raantiyo
Kula ciiray fooddoon,
Cagta meel la saaroo
La cuskado lahaynoo,
Calcalyada xareeddii
Halka godan cuslays iyo,
Fiid-cawl horraantii
Cirka oo daruuruhu
Midab wada cillaan iyo
Ku dhigeen canjiidaha,
Xilli ay cadceeddii
Dhar cashmiira xidhan tahay
Sagal caasha saaraad
La wadaagtey caanoo,
Haddaan caado kale jirin
Cidi kaama garateen.

302

Amazement

MAXAMED IBRAAHIN WARSAME 'HADRAAWI' ·
SOMALIA/SOMALILAND

O dazzling darling:
happy happenstance and fair fortune
to you, mind mesmeriser –
since we became acquainted
you've been my only fever.
You're like a light-footed charger
canny at midnight combat,
the fight by close engagement
where the rider takes revenge –
men constantly look keen.
I'm an empty pail that's purified
by your love's burning twigs;
every night I go out with
the dream of your long-held image.

When the green of the ground,
its surface fresh
and still unploughed,
when the brow of its growth bows
and it collapses under the weight
of its own bounty,
and there's no space to plant a foot,
not even room to lean;
when just-fallen rain gathers
making the earth's curves heavy;
when in the light red light of evening
the sky's collecting clouds
the exact hue of henna
bearing the sun's brand;
when the sun itself is clothed in
the very colour of cashmere,
when rain-promising rays hang on its neck:
your looks are cousin to all this
and who if not accustomed to it
could tell you two apart?

Geed cal iyo buur dheer
Carro-hodan ku yaalloo
Cokanoo irmaanoo
Dhirta kale ka caynoo
Cimilada agtiisiyo
Rugtu qurux ku caan tahay;
Dusha sare caleentii
Laamaha is-celisoo
Hoobaan casuus lihi
Cartamayso dhinacyada,
Ubaxuna tin iyo cidhib
Kaga dhigay cabbaadhyada,
Shimbiraha ka ciyayaa
Intay heeso curiyeen
Isku camal wareereen,
Dabadeeto carashada
Markii laysku cayn go'ay
Isu ciidan doonteen.

Hal cabbaar ah goortay
Isu calan-walleeyeen
Cadho kala maqnaayeen,
Cadcadiigsi geedkii
Ciddiyaha ku qariyeen,
Codka luuqda heestiyo
Carrabkoodu kala tegey,
Carcaraha is-daba maray
Cudur jirey ku baabba'ay.

Dhallin caano diiddoo
Guryihii ka caagtiyo,
Cadraddiyo barbaartii
Sida goob ciyaareed
Ugu soo carraabeen,
Calaf waa halkiisee,
Hadallada caweyskaas,
'Ku calmaday!' u badan tahay.

You're that tree topping a tall mountain
rooted in fertile soil
sated with water and ready to give fruit;
its climate differing from
that of all other trees,
its setting renowned for its beauty,
its topmost canopy and branches
holding each other up;
its fruit so ripe and red
each roars to each on every flank;
and blossoming from hair to heel
like the lovely lines that ring the throat;
the birds chorusing
till all their songs
are intermingled,
then holding a song war –
singing themselves into a stalemate
and seeking reinforcements.
After a while, when each
waves feather flags to each,
anger driving them apart,
their claws digging crossly
in the bark of the tree,
the making of the melodies
straining their tongues,
they stray from the tunes
till the imbalance is corrected.
The young people too won't eat
and refuse to go home,
unmarried girls hurry there
as though to a place of dancing,
young men too – maybe
they're fated to marry,
chattering in the eager evening –
who would not choose you?

You share your nature with
this bliss-filled universe,
if God will not be angry

Carshigaa nastahan baad
Biyo wada cabteenoo,
Haddaan lay cadaabayn
Rabbi ii cadhoonayn,
Dadku inuu ku caabudo
Madowgiyo caddaankuba
Ku caleemo saaraan,
Sow kuma canaanteen!

or throw me into Hell
I would compel
the people to worship you,
let both black and white
crowd to crown you now!

*Translated from the Somali by W. N. Herbert, Said Jama Hussein
and Maxamed Xasan 'Alto'*

Hilo en una tela de araña

Un arroyo imantado por la brisa y la luz,
un transcurrir cobrizo es el hilo que fluye
en la tela de araña. Charcos de plata cambian
de unas hojas a otras, de unas huellas
a otras sobre la tierra blanda. Te veo cruzar
entre dos líneas. Lo amo,
digo.
Entre dos ramas del azar
fluye el arroyo,
su hilo hechizado por el mar de la luz,
por el licor
de su corriente. Es el agua que embriaga
el atardecer. Es el fuego que fluye
sin cesar hacia el este. Bajo su fiel
solar
te pienso.

Thread in a Spider's Web

CORAL BRACHO · MEXICO

A little stream, drawn by the magnets of air and light,
and flowing like time, like copper forming,
is the thread
in a spider's web. Pools of silver shimmer
from one leaf to another, from one path trodden
to another on the soft ground. I see you go across,
over there, between two lines. 'I love him',
I say.

The little stream forks; flows between
two possibilities.
Its thread is in thrall to this sea of light,
this liquid,
coursing. This water makes the evening sing, heady
and drunk. Its fire flows
on into the east forever. Held in the sun's
fine balance
I think of you.

Translated from the Spanish by Katherine Pierpoint and Tom Boll

فراشنا القديم

أنتظرِكِ في ظلٍّ أبيض

مضاء بكبريت أعواد الشجرة

التحتها افترقنا

حين تأتين

ينبتُ الماءُ في عروقي

كما السحاب من البحر

وأسير بين فخذيكِ مُترنحاً

نحو ضمادة جرحي النازف دائماً

فراشُنا الرملُ ساكنُ الأعماق القديم

غير مُحدد كإشاعة

معاً على هذا الحرير

تملأ الرغبةُ أصواتنا طيوراً

كما تملأ الليالي صداقةٌ جديدة

أنتِ وأنا حوارُ ساعةٍ متأخرة

تحت ثدي الأفق

في حانةٍ بحرية

نرضعُ الإنتظار

نأتي إلى هذا الشاطئ

لنعلّمَ الفجرَ الوقوف على قدم واحدة

ونذهبَ إلى الغابة

لنحتطبَ أشجار الإحتمال

الحجرُ يلد الحجر

وأنا دائماً أنتظرِكِ

خلف لا شيء

يوقف كُرة الأرض

المتدحرجة من جبل الكون.

Our Old Bed

ABDULLAH AL-RIYAMI · OMAN

I wait for you in a bright shadow
lit by matches struck from the tree
under whose branches we said goodbye
When you arrive
fluids purl along my veins
the way clouds arise from the sea
And I stumble between your thighs
towards the cure
for this unstaunchable wound
Our bed is of sand
formed from ancient sediments
soft as a rumour
Together on this silk
desire fills our voices like flocking birds
like a new friendship filling the night
You and I are a late-night conversation
in a tavern by the sea
at the fount of the horizon
Nurtured by longing
we come to this shore
to teach the dawn new tricks
And we go to the forest
to gather wood from new trees
Stone gives birth to stone
and I will wait for you forever
knowing that nothing can stop the earth
rolling down the mountain of life.

Translated from the Arabic by Sarah Maguire, Nariman Youssef,
Anna Murison Boyd and Hafiz Kheir

Como lava candente

El sol viajó desde el Oriente
en sus alas de viento
las semillas brotan
y se hacen palabras
para alumbrar en este día
amado mio

bañar tu alma quiero
con el roció de mis aguas
un abecedario de vocales
donde se entra y no se olvida

viento quiero ser
para calmar las olas enfurecidas del mar
manos para acariciar al volcán
y apagar el fuego de tus palabras
 curare para calmar tus iras de Iwia
lágrimas para entrar en tus ojos de niño
destapándome y erupcionando como lava candente
y rodar como piedra hecha fuego
a tus brazos de sal

Ser el tiempo para permanecer y juntos
recorrer un nuevo camino
ser el ojo de agua
para saciar la sed de tu alma
y beber los secretos de Arutam

Like Red-Hot Lava

MARÍA CLARA SHARUPI JUA · ECUADOR

The sun travelled from the East
on its wings of wind
the seeds sprout
becoming words
to light up this day
my beloved

I want to bathe your soul
in the dew of my waters
an alphabet of vowels
where one enters and is never forgotten

I want to be the wind
to appease the raging waves of the sea
hands that caress the volcano
and douse the fire of your words
Poison to calm the wrath of *Iwia*
the tears that fill your childlike eyes
revealing myself and erupting like red-hot lava
to roll like a stone turned to fire
into your salty arms

I want to be time stood still
to take a new path together
to be the hot spring
that quenches the thirst of your soul
that drinks in the secrets of *Arutam*

*Translated from the Spanish by Nataly Kelly and The Poetry Translation
Centre Workshop*

Iwia: A cannibal spirit that devours humans.
*Arutam: An all-powerful being, in many senses akin to the Christian
concept of the Holy Spirit.*

نجمة

(1)

مَسَّني ضُوْءٌ
شَرَخَتْ زُجَاجَ أَحْلامِي
خَرَجْتُ مِنْ الفَضَاءْ

إِلَيَّ مِنْ بَعيدٍ
تُعَبِّئُ نَجْمَةٌ تَعَبِي
تَعُجُّ إِليكِ حَجًّا عامِراً
مِنْ الهواءْ

وفيَّ مِنْ خيوطٍ، كُوَّةٌ
خَضْرَاءُ، فيكِ
ولي خيلٌ – مِنْ الإِيحَاءِ
جُنْدٌ
مَنْ أَضَاءْ

مَسَّني وخَرَجْتُ
هَشَّمتُ البَيَاضَ كَتبتُ
خلفي أُحْرِقَتْ كُتُبٌ
بَيَاضٌ مِزَقٌ
قَنَاديلُ سَوَادٌ
أَشْرَقَتْ في غَيِّها، سَدَرَتْ
بنفسجةٌ على صَدْرِ السَّمَاءْ

A Star

AL-SADDIQ AL-RADDI · SUDAN

(1)

Awoken by light, I scratch the glass
of dreams, and find myself
stepping free of shadows and silence.

In the distance a star was absorbing
my tiredness, and itself heading like a pilgrim
towards you, leaving blank its place in the heavens.

In the green pits of our being our inner
threads yearn; this radiance, that makes me feel I own
herds of horses, am as inspired as any knight –

what is its source? Shocked
into words, I defied the book-burners, the suffocators
of thought and feeling, all who'd censor and shroud knowledge.

And a violet blossomed fiercely in the bosom of the sky.

يّتُهَا النّجْمَةُ السِّيدَةْ
على سريرِكِ، قُرْبَ لُهَاثِ أَحْلامِكِ

عَنْ كَتَبٍ مِنْ مناديلِ عِطْرِكِ
"بِالضَّبطْ"
السَّاعَةَ الثَّالِثَةَ – الفَجْرَ
بعد نُهُوضِكِ مُرْبَّحَةً بِبقايا نُعَاسٍ مُهَاجِرٍ
وأَرَقٍ لا يُقِيمْ

تَسْكُنُ – تَحْتَ المِلاءَةِ
ذِكْرَى عِنَاقٍ له شَخِيرُكِ الهادِئُ
وهو يُؤَكِّدُ بِوَحْكِ للنوم
بِالقَلَقِ نُجَاهَ حنينَكِ فِيهِ للمرآةْ

تَسْكُنُ نُطْفَةُ نُورٍ
مِنْ جَسَدٍ أَلَّهَ صَبْوَتَهُ
في الغَمْرِ، وسَمَّى ما سَمَّى

تَسْكُنُ تَحْتَ الوِسَادَةِ رَائِحَةٌ خَضْرَاءُ
تَخُصُّكِ فِيَّ
وتَسْكُنُ عَائِلَةُ الأَسْمَاءِ النُّورِيَّةِ
للشَيْءِ الغَامِضِ
تَسْكُنُ سَيِّدَةُ الأَسْمَاءْ
تَسْكُنُ سَيِّدَةُ الأَشْيَاءْ

(2)

Star Woman,
the memory of our embrace still lives
in this bed, adjacent to your dreams
and desires, and near these handkerchiefs
drenched in your scent.
                              You woke in the dawn
                              at three exactly, drowsing,
                              still dazed . . .
Beneath the sounds of your breathing
lurks a worry: where is your mirror?
And this droplet of light
reflecting a passion
that found a name for everything . . .

Under the pillows also, an aroma
alive and ours – and the long list
of names we have bestowed
on this affair. Surely
a goddess lives there too, the one
who knows the names of all things.

Translated from the Arabic by Mark Ford and Hafiz Kheir

Abres y cierras

Abres un filo de navaja
para que gotee la transparencia.

Cierras el sonámbulo cubo de la noche
y un río de sombra se derrama.

Abres y cierras el diafragma líquido
de mi corazón -y amanezco

en el decuplicado y lento
destello de tus manos.

Open and Shut

DAVID HUERTA · MEXICO

You open the blade of a flick knife
so it drips transparency.

You shut the restless cube of night
and a stream of shadow ramifies.

You open and shut the liquid diaphragm
of my heart – and at dawn I arrive

in the stately, tenfold
starlight of your hands.

Translated from the Spanish by Jamie McKendrick

این خواستن و این من

این پروانه
از کجا پیدا شد   چه طور این طور کهربایی
کی
بر دستهٔ فنجان نشست
چه وقت بر رکاب زیرپوش تو
و من
در کجای از لبخندت بی دست و پا شدم
درچه جای از صدات ولو؟

این قاصدک
از کی آمد   و چرا این قدر زنگاری
تا اول
ناف تو را طواف کند   بعد رد لب های مرا وارسی؟

زن
باید اتفاقی افتاده باشد   نباشد بی وقت
که تو
هی به مردگانت نهیب می زنی   هی پدرانت را پس
و خط
بر کلمات پوک
حرف های پوسیده   جملات نخنما و صداهای مطنطن

این پروانه
این قاصدک   این خواستن و این من؟

320

This Craving and this Me

MASOUD AHMADI · IRAN

This butterfly
where did it come from?
How so amber?   When did it alight on the cup handle?
When   on the strap of your petticoat?
And me   where did I stumble
as you smiled?
Where in your voice
did I lose myself?

This flower
when did it arrive   and why   so turquoise
to first circle your navel
and then examine where my lips have been?

Woman,
something must have happened   or not
for you to reject the past
ward off your ancestors
and expunge
the hollow words
tired phrases   tattered lines   and pompous voices

This butterfly
this flower   this craving and this me?

Translated from the Farsi (Persian) by Alireza Abiz and
The Poetry Translation Centre Workshop

'تتلیاں پکڑنے کو ۔۔۔۔'

کِتنا سہل جانا تھا
خوشبوؤں کو چُھو لینا
بارشوں کے موسم میں شام کا ہر اِک منظر
گھر میں قید کر لینا
روشنی ستاروں کی مٹھیوں میں بھر لینا

کِتنا سہل جانا تھا
خوشبوؤں کو چُھو لینا
جگنوؤں کی باتوں سے پھُول جیسے آنگن میں
روشنی سی کر لینا
اس کی یاد کا چہرہ خوابناک آنکھوں کی
جھیل کے گلابوں پر دیر تک سجا رکھنا
کِتنا سہل جانا تھا

اے نظر کی خوش فہمی! اس طرح نہیں ہوتا
'تتلیاں پکڑنے کو دور جانا پڑتا ہے'

322

To Catch Butterflies

NOSHI GILLANI · PAKISTAN

I once thought it easy
To seize fragrance
To capture the evenings of monsoon
While sitting at home
To clutch starlight in my hand

I once thought it easy
To seize fragrance
To light the flower that is my courtyard
With the whisper of fireflies
To hold his memory in my dreaming eyes
Like roses cast upon a lake
I had thought it easy . . .

How I fooled myself! How could it happen?
'To catch butterflies, you have to go far enough.'

Translated from the Urdu by Lavinia Greenlaw and Nukhbah Taj Langah

Guidúbilu' runebia'ya',

Guidúbilu' runebia'ya',
guidúbinaca peou'.
Pa ñácalu' ti guidxi
ratiicasi ninabadiidxa' cabe náa
naa nulué' pa neza riaana ní.
Riuuládxepea' guidúbilu',
riuuladxe' guuya' guiní'lu', guxídxilu',
guzeque yannilu'. Dxiña yaga guiropa' dani
zuguaa ndí' xtilu', ra guyaa' dxiqué
rigucaa' ruaa bidó'. Ñacaladxe' rua'
ñuá' ne niree ndaani' guixhidó' xtilu',
ni guya' dxiiña' guiluxe guendanabani ndaani'.
Biza'naadxi' bido' guzana lii, qui gápalu'
ra guidiiñeyulu'. Binnindxó' nga naa
ti bibane' lii, guca' lii. Yanna ma cadi naa
ridxiiche' gudxigueta lú ca nguiiu ra zedi'dilu',
ma cadi naa racalugua' cueelu' lari.
Ti bidxiña lubí nga lii, ti balaaga' guie'
ziguite yeche' lu guiigu' ti siadó'.

Gabati' lii nou' qui ñunebia'ya', nou'
qui ñuuladxe. Pa ñándasi ñácarua'
biaani' ruxheleruaa ruuya' ca nduni
yuxido' quichi' beelaxa'nalu'. Pa ñándasi
nibeza rua'
         ndaani' guidxi sicarú
                ni nácalu'.

I Know Your Body

VÍCTOR TERÁN · MEXICO

I know your body,
entirely I know you.
If you were a city
I could give perfect directions
to wherever they asked me.
I like all of your body,
I like to see you talk, laugh
move your head. Your two well-rounded hills
are the honey of bees, where my lips celebrate to the gods.
I would have liked to continue storming your forest,
lodgings made deliberately for a nice death.
You were created with love,
your body is worthy of praise. What an honour to have lived,
to have been. I am no longer bothered
when men turn to look at you,
I am no longer impatient when you undress.
You are a stag in the air. A raft of flowers
that snakes across the river by morning.

There is no part of your body that I do not know, there is no
part that I do not like. I want to keep being
the light stunned at the look of your white
roundness of flesh. I want to keep
living
in the beautiful city
that you are.

Translated from the Zapotec by David Shook

Mejentsamek anamrukia

Aya mejentsamek anamrukia wakanchirmijai
wenechirui mejentsakia
ewejrum wincharpatniujai intiashur atirturia
aya uwejmijai sekuta kunkunti nekartuakia
piskatruinia aya makich atirturia
kajkeruinia shakap jurutsakia
misuch ajasan aya amin nakajme

Jearui pujuskia
újumachik aámuram peertusia
sapijmiamur aesturakia
ame sejkiram keamujai

Wekamur aéntruria
ame papanrumi kanaitirijai
entsa supichik ana nui weanturkakia
kanu anunteiri naikmiti

Mejentsamek anamrukia
nijiamanch nawamujai
nuya sawini tseasmakmajai
Arutma nekamteirijai

Arant tupanteip enenteichirua
shintiartasan wakerajai
ewejchiram tujucha anin nui
winchuman
initrum achiakmena nui
jichirmin kaya ainis anin nui, kanaran juaktasan ku wakerajai

Make Me Drunk with Your Kisses

MARÍA CLARA SHARUPI JUA · ECUADOR

Make me drunk with your kisses, my love
kiss my lips
untangle my hair with your silken fingers
explore with your hands the sacred song of the vanilla flower
untie the *makich* anklet
remove the *shakap* belt from my hips
naked, I await you

Live in my home
take me with the tenderness of your words
burn my fears
with the fire of your skin

Trace my path
with the oars of your raft
come to the shores of the beach,
my harbour of sand

Make me drunk with your kisses
with the *chicha*
fermented in saliva
with the wisdom of *Arutam*

Don't go, my love
I want to wake
in your arms like cotton
to dive
into your depths
to fall asleep
in the jewel of your eyes

Translated from the Shuar by Nataly Kelly and The Poetry Translation Centre Workshop

Makich: A ceremonial anklet.
Shakap: Ceremonial belt made of seeds.
Chicha: Specially fermented maize drink made by chewing and spitting.

در یک بامداد رنگین

بوسیدمش
تمام اندامش لرزید
چنان شاخهٔ پرشگوفتهٔ بادام در باد
چون ماه چون ستاره
که می لرزد در آب
بوسیدمش
تمام اندامش لرزید
گونه هایش رنگ دیگر گرفتند
نگاه هایش رنگ دیگرگرفتند
و آفتاب از گریبان مهربانی او طلوع کرد
و هزار و یک شب انتظار
پایان یافت
و من در یک بامداد رنگین
باحقیقت عشق
همخوابه می شدم

جولای ۲۰۰۲
شهر پشاور

On a Colourful Morning

PARTAW NADERI · AFGHANISTAN

I kissed her –
her whole body shivered
Like a branch of almond blossom in the wind
Like the moon, like a star
    trembling on the water
I kissed her –
her whole body shivered
Her cheeks showed one colour
her gaze revealed another
And the sun rose from her tender heart
And the thousand-and-one nights of waiting
ended
And on a colourful morning
I shared a bed
    with the meaning of love

July 2002, Peshawar City
Translated from the Dari (Persian) by Sarah Maguire and Yama Yari

Lá lu'

Ridxí ne huaxhinni, lá lu'.
Siadó', huadxí, lu gueela',
nisi lá lu' riree xieque
ndaani' bichuga íque'
sica tuuxa zeguyoo
runi biniti guendabiaani',
nisi lá lu' riree chuuchi
lu ludxe'
sica benda ndaani' ná'
ti guuze'.

Guindisa' ti gui'chi', lá lu'.
Cuaque' ti xiixa, lá lu'.
Gabati' nalu' nuaa'
cadi daabi guichi lá lu'
íque bicuini naya'
ne ratiicasi zedide'
málasi gó la'na'
guendarietenala'dxi' lú lu'
ñee xquendanabane'.

Ma yanna nga nabaana
ne huidxe mápeca saa guidxi.
Zándaca ridxí zaxhaca la'dxi'
sá' nanda huaxhinni.
Zándaca naa guibane' ti dxi
ne guirá' ca yaya xtí' xquendagute',
zapa ruá' ti nisadó' guendaricaala'dxi'
ndaani' ladxiduá' guzeete' lá lu',
zápa' rua' neca xtuudxi huiini' bi
guzayaniá' ti dxumisú birixhiaa
gusitenala'dxi' lii guendaranaxhii stinne'
sica rusietenala'dxi' laanu ne xquendayaya
dxi ma zeedadxiña xhí nisaguié.

Your Name

VÍCTOR TERÁN · MEXICO

Day and night, your name.
In the morning, the afternoon, at dusk
only your name spins
through my head
like a man strait-jacketed
for having lost his mind;
only your name slips
over my tongue
like a fish between the hands
of a fisherman.

I lift a paper, your name.
I put something away, your name.
There is nowhere I go
that I do not have the thorn of your name
nailed to the tip of my finger
and no matter where I go,
the memory of your face silently bites
the leg of my existence.

It is time for Lent
and May's festival is near.
Perhaps the day is fed up
with chasing the night.
Maybe one day I'll wake up
to the scandal of my death;
despite it all I'll have an ocean of sighs
in my soul, to whisper your name;
I'll undoubtedly have one last breath
capable of filling a basket with winged ants
that will proclaim the love I have,
like the commotion that announces
coming rains.

Translated from the Zapotec by David Shook

لنگه جوراب زرد

آه

این باران لعنتی چه می کند

با این اواخر تیر

گل های ابریشم   اقاقیای نر   خرزهره های هنوز نه خیلی محتضر

و با این بید مجنون

که اخیراً به بلوغ رسید   به سبز سیر

با پنجره ها   بام ها

با حرف هایی که کم تر به یاد می آیند

گوشی را نگذار

تا سرفهٔ ناودان را بشنوی   عطسهٔ گنجشک ها

و آه یکی از مرا که هنوز به فکر توست

آه

این باران لعنتی چه می کند

با این اواخر تیر

برگ های بعضاً معلق   نیمکت های زمین گیر

و جای خالی آن زن

که جا گذاشت   در کنج ذهن من

نگاهی مورب

لبخندی اریب   و لنگه جورابی زرد

The Yellow Stocking

MASOUD AHMADI · IRAN

Ah
what is that blessed rain doing
to these late days of July
the Persian silk tree   the black locust tree
that late-blooming fireweed
and this weeping willow
which only just turned a deep green

To windows   rooftops
to words we remember less

Don't hang up
wait to hear the gutter's cough   the sparrow's sneeze
and the sigh of a me who still thinks of you

Ah
what is that blessed rain doing
to these late days of July
the leaves poised to fall   ancient benches
and the empty chair of a woman
who left   in the corner of my mind
a sidelong glass
a slanted smile   and one yellow stocking

Translated from the Farsi (Persian) by Alireza Abiz and
The Poetry Translation Centre Workshop

Agua de bordes lúbricos

Agua de medusas,
agua láctea, sinuosa,
agua de bordes lúbricos; espesura vidriante -Delicuescencia
entre contornos deleitosos. Agua –agua suntuosa
de involución, de languidez

en densidades plácidas. Agua,
agua sedosa y plúmbea en opacidad, en peso –Mercurial;
agua en vilo, agua lenta. El algaacuática de los brillos –En las ubres del
gozo. El alga, el
hálito de su cima;

-sobre el silencio arqueante, sobre los istmos
del basalto; el alga, el hábito de su roce,
su deslizarse. Agua luz, agua pez; el aura, el ágata,
sus desbordes luminosos; Fuego rastreante el alce

huidizo –Entre la ceiba, entre el cardumen; llama
pulsante;
agua lince, agua sargo (El jaspe súbito). Lumbre
entre medusas.
-Orla abierta, labiada; aura de bordes lúbricos,
su lisura acunante, su eflorescerse al anidar; anfibia,
lábil –Agua, agua sedosa
en imantación; en ristre. Agua en vilo, agua lenta –El
alumbrar lascivo

en lo vadeante oleoso,
sobre los vuelcos de basalto. –Reptar del ópalo entre la
luz,entre la llama interna. –Agua
de medusas.
Agua blanda, lustrosa;

Water of Jellyfish

CORAL BRACHO · MEXICO

Water of jellyfish,
milky, snaking water
of ever-changing shapes; glossy water-flesh; melting
into its lovely surroundings. Water – sumptuous waters
receding, languid

and layered into calm. Water,
water silken, dusky, dense as lead – mercurial;
      floating free, idling. The seaweed in there,
sparkling, in pleasure's very breast. The
        seaweed, crests a-bubbling;

– above the over-arching silence, above the long spits
of basalt rock; the water-weed, its familiar caresses,
its gentle flux. Water of light, of fish; the breeze, the
        agate
spilling its light. The shy elk flicker like flame –

through the cotton-silk trees, through the shoals
of little fish a flame is pulsing,
water slinking, lynx-like; water of bream (jasper's
        sudden reds and browns).
Such glory here,
among the jellyfish medusas.
– Parted lips of coastline, the breeze's gentle
        movements,
lulling softly, settling into crystals, amphibious,
lubricious – water, silken and
magnetic; poised. Water, coasting – lascivious radiance

wading, oily,
over crumbling basalt. Light crawls, opal,
through its own inner flames. – Water
of jellyfish.
Sweet fresh-water shine;

agua sin huella; densa,
mercurial
su blancura acerada, su dilución en alzamientos de
grafito,en despuntar de lisa; hurtante, suave. −Agua viva

su vientre sobre el testuz, volcado sol de bronce
envolviendo-agua blenda, brotante. Agua de medusas, agua táctil
fundiéndose
en lo añil untuoso, en su panal reverberante. Agua
amianto, ulvaEl bagre en lo mullido
-libando; en el humor nutricio entre su néctar delicado; el áureoembalse,
el limbo, lo transluce. Agua leve, aura adentro
el ámbar-el luminar ungido, esbelto; el tigre, su pleamar
bajo la sombra vidriada. Agua linde, agua anguila lamiendo su perfil, su
transmigrar nocturno
-Entre las sedas matriciales; entre la salvia. −Agua

entre merluzas. Agua grávida (-El calmo goce
tibio; su irisable) −Agua
sus bordes

-Su lisura mutante, su embeleñarse
entre lo núbil
cadencioso. Agua,
agua sedosa de involución, de languidez
en densidades plácidas. Agua, agua; Su roce
-Agua nutria, agua pez. Agua

de medusas,
agua láctea, sinuosa; Agua,

water leaving no traces; dense,
mercurial
      white as steel, parting round the granite stacks,
its flashes of minnows; secretive, smooth. – Water alive,

and rolling; a bronze sun vaulting in close;
– liquid minerals, spurting. Water of jellyfish, a water to
      feel
dissolving into itself
into a slick of indigo, quivering honeycombs. Long
      strands of water, sea-lettuce,
the catfish nibbling
in its rich, streaming bed, whose light nectars
form a golden pond, liminal. Weightless water,
air inside amber,
– a chrism of light, full of grace; the high tide a tiger,
below a wash of shadow. Water at the edge, water-eel,
swallowing itself,
its great journey by night –
along these matrices of silk, through the
sea-sage. – Water

rich with cod. Heavy water (that calm pleasure,
warm; the way it shimmers) –
Water's edge –

its smooth changes, its delight in itself,
its own seductive rise and fall. Water,
silken, receding, layered
into languid calm. Water, water; its gentle stroke
– water of the otter, the fish. Water

of jellyfish,
milky, snaking; water,

Translated from the Spanish by Katherine Pierpoint and Tom Boll

عَرْش

مَرْفُوعَةٌ
عَلَى أَصَابِعَ وَلَا أَصَابِعَ لِلمَوْجِ
مَدْلُوقَةٌ
على النَّهْرِ وَلَا قَامَةَ لِلمَوْجِ

في الثَّانِيَةِ الرَّهِيفَةِ
بَيْنَ أَنْ تَصْعَدَ وَتَسِيحْ
تَخْلُقُ العَالَمَ
تَمْحُو رَسْمَهُ
دون أَنْ تَسْتَرِيحْ!!

338

Throne

AL-SADDIQ AL-RADDI · SUDAN

Aloft
as though lifted on fingertips –
and yet waves have no fingers
Her desire
structures the water –
and yet waves have no structure

In the split second
between crest and collapse
the world is created
and the world is annulled
without end

Translated from the Arabic by Sarah Maguire and Atef Alshaer

ESSAYS ON TRANSLATION

Once their collaborations are completed, we ask our poets and translators to reflect on their experiences of co-translation. The following edited extracts are taken from some of their essays, the complete versions of which can be found on the Poetry Translation Centre website: www.poetrytranslation.org

Jo Shapcott on Translating Farzaneh Khojandi

From my point of view, the creation of the translation team for Farzaneh Khojandi's poetry was magic. First there was Farzaneh's work itself: searingly pure, full of integrity and all the richness of the classical Persian tradition. Then there was Narguess Farzad, a scholar of Persian literature and an enormously sensitive reader of poetry in both languages, contemporary and historical.

Stepping into this totally new area of poetry was daunting. I was aware of the complexity and richness of the tradition Farzaneh writes in, but my knowledge of it was limited. Narguess was the ideal guide, teacher and interpreter for this journey. At our first meeting Narguess gave me a selection of her literal translations of Farzaneh's poems, complete with informative notes, line by line. They were already a graceful read and it was clear at once that her versions were going to be a pleasure to work with. Narguess read to me from the poems in Persian that first time, too, and most subsequent meetings. This proved to be crucial and fruitful – when I first heard Farzaneh read, I felt I had caught some of her music, which was down to hearing Narguess in my head as I worked at the poems.

At the second meeting I came armed with my first effort, nervous and wondering if this was a step too far. The diction and subject matter was so far removed from my own work that, at this early stage, I felt clumsy and always several footsteps behind. The sincerity, the passion, the direct calls to tradition, spirituality, morality, brother, lover, 'O my camel-driver!' seemed worlds away from the modern, urban context of my own work. The first poem I attempted was 'Flute Player' and Narguess was pleased with it, our discussions that day helping me towards meeting Farzaneh's world and concerns.

That talk and our subsequent encounters clarified my task which was to be much less about my own voice and attitudes than any previous 'versioning' I had done, and much more about Farzaneh. Some of the phrases and ideas her poems presented to me were patterned in a high, even florid register, achieving an ornate, sometimes archaic note that I would never attempt in my own work. But I found when I tried to disrupt this effect in the process of translation, Farzaneh – the context from which her work emerges, and the complexity of her ideas – was lost and nothing much was gained. I had to 'allow' gestures and tropes which were not my natural writing medium in order to let the poet through. And, as you can tell, the resulting work is very much a joint translation by the two of us, Narguess and me.

Narguess's role was doubly and trebly important because communication with Farzaneh was difficult. Physical logistics first of all. I learned that Tajikistan exists in the shadow of more powerful neighbouring states which control access to power and other resources. Electricity is intermittent, only a few hours each day. (This was brought home to me powerfully during the tour, when Narguess visited Farzaneh and her husband in their room in the Kensington Hilton one evening, to pick them up, and found them – out of habit – waiting in the dark.) During the period Narguess and I worked on the translations, email contact between Farzaneh and Narguess was understandably erratic because of these restrictions, and not helped by the fact that at the most intense period of our work, Tajikistan was experiencing the hardest winter for years. At one point we lost contact completely for weeks and were quite worried about her.

During this time, I relied on the indefatigable Narguess for general support and answers to my growing number of questions. We battled through pretty well: the only difficulty was that comments and answers from Farzaneh finally came through very close to all the publication deadlines and it was quite a feat – mainly from Narguess, again – to shoehorn everything in. A good example is the line in 'Spring is Coming' in which some quite obscure Tajik vocabulary led Narguess to think it involved a specific type of red duck in bubbling streams, rather than blood coursing through veins which is the sense Farzaneh intended. Once the information came through from Farzaneh, we managed to create a more faithful line in the nick of time.

These practical concerns helped bring home to me the magnitude of the step I had to try to make, linguistically, culturally and geographically, to come to terms with the poems. Paradoxically, any obstacles were a help towards poetic understanding: complacency and comfort would never be options.

Thank you PTC, for Narguess and for Farzaneh.

Lavinia Greenlaw on Translating Noshi Gillani

The literal versions for these poems were made by Nukhbah Taj Langah. Before they arrived, I watched a film of Noshi Gillani reading her work and listened carefully to her cadences. I do not understand any Urdu so I was listening to pure sound. I kept returning to this film during the translation process in order to focus my attempts to capture her music in English. Her cadences helped me to understand how she structured her poems, and her performance gave me a sense of the complex character of her poetry's music.

The impression I got from the sound of her poems was that they were intense, and tense, arrangements of exploded feeling. I had in my head Emily Dickinson's dashes – how they hold the parts of her poems in mid-air – or the artist Cornelia Parker's suspended cutlery and blown-up shed. I also felt that Noshi's voice was emphatically lyrical, and that her music may be made up of fragments/phrases but that it was essentially unbroken. While the observations and images out of which her poems are made stand beside one another rather than follow on in narrative sequence, the music of the poem was forcefully cohesive.

I find her to be an extremely precise poet, especially precise about complexity! As I learnt how to unpack her images, I discovered how complex but exact they were. I felt that I was dealing with a sophisticated and technically ambitious poet who wanted to capture both extreme emotions and constraint/restraint.

On first reading the literal versions, I found almost nothing I could confidently make sense of. I had to interrogate each image and observation until they revealed what they had in common or how they spoke to and of one another. This gave me the overall impetus and movement of the poem. These are not narrative poems so they could not be approached in a linear fashion. I started by asking many detailed questions about exact meaning, believing that interrogating the precision of a metaphor would lead me to its intended effect.

At this point, I worked in two different ways. I would either produce something in English which was evidently awkward but which made the first step towards an English version, or I pursued music, turning a phrase into its more natural and lyrical English equivalent. Both helped to pin down the sense.

Nukhbah Taj Langah on Translating Noshi Gillani

Preparing the literal translations of Noshi's poems was a real challenge for me. This is not simply due to the fact that she is writing in Urdu, but her choice of complex imagery and ideas made translating her poems into English extremely difficult. In addition, the brevity of her poems embodied the intensity of her emotions, and this was one of the qualities of her poetry that I definitely wanted to translate into English.

A beautiful example of her writing style is the poem 'There Was a Heart that Burnt Out: Light', which both Lavinia and I found fascinating to translate.[1] This poem is written as if the poet is in dialogue with light, nature and perhaps god, as indicated in the first couplet:

> There was a hear that burnt out: light
> Light O god, O god light

This idea of being in constant communication with nature, light/god, is wonderfully captured in the final version of the poem by Lavinia by emphasising the word 'light' at the end of most of the lines. Another layer of the poem unravels in the final line, where the poet finds herself in a state of paradox; chasing light and yet continuing to exist in darkness. This paradoxical nature of her existence has almost transformed into a curse in her life which she aims to share with the readers.

There are many other poems which reflect Noshi's passion for playing with paradoxical symbolism and creating ambiguities. I find this aspect of her poems is the most difficult to translate into English and I struggled hard to find the appropriate words to convey these conflicting ideas.

Another aspect of Noshi's poems that I found particularly difficult to translate was her rhyme scheme. Most of the poems are written in free verse, but the ones which had rhyming words at the end of the couplets were virtually impossible to replace rhyming words in English. The best example of Noshi's rhyme scheme is 'The Flower is Torn at the Heart'. In the original poem every second line of each couplet closes with rhyming words. The words she uses are: *yari hai* (line 2), *guzari hai* (line 4), *ikhtiari hai* (line 6), *bari hai* (line 8), *intezari hai* (line 10), *tari hai* (line 12) and *hamari hai* (line 14); yet to translate these words into English and also maintain their rhyme was virtually impossible for me. The way I tackled this situation was to maintain the overall musicality of her poem, its theme and imagery.

1. This poem can be read on the PTC website: www.poetrytranslation.org

Imagery and symbolism are the most crucial aspects of Noshi's poetry; indeed, she blends them together, which has the effect of loading each line with several images, making her expression further convoluted. For instance, in these lines from her poem 'This Prisoner Breathes':

I am trapped in a jungle of voices
In which I cannot spread my wings

These lines present the best example of the conflict that I faced as a literal translator. The first question that struck me from this opening couplet was whether to translate 'jungle of voices' as 'world' which could be Noshi's possible idea, or just maintain the original symbols. I experienced this conflicting feeling in most of her poems, but in the end I preferred to translate exactly her original symbolism into English and leave it to the readers to interpret the poem as they wished.

Later in the same poem, she writes:

Yet you set fire to the boat carrying my feelings
Surround this sea of feeling with desert sand

This is one example of Noshi's complexity of expression: the reader wonders how can a boat carry feelings? Or how did sea, desert sand and fire combine to frustrate the poet? The jungle and desert could also be mystic symbols in her poems and it was therefore impossible to ignore them. Similarly, in this poem there are further complex examples where Noshi loads the line with difficult images, such as her idea of stitching the eyelashes and terrorising the feet with faceless chains. For the literal versions, I felt I had to unpack these complex ideas and make them more comprehensible for the English-speaking reader. This issue has been expertly dealt with by Lavinia after our discussions, by reshuffling these lines to capture the sense of the poem.

In the end, after going through various stages of working on these translations, it was a very rewarding experience for me. Despite knowing both Urdu and English languages proficiently, I discovered the musicality and complexity of both these languages, which we perhaps overlook in our everyday spoken and written experiences. This also deepened my love for poetry as the most appealing form of creative expression and my interest in translation as a way of creating a bridge between cultures.

Mimi Khalvati on Translating Kajal Ahmad

My first reaction on receiving Choman Hardi's literal translations of Kajal Ahmad's poems was how good they were, and how little I would seemingly have to do! I think it helped enormously that Choman is such a good poet herself and, in these first versions, had already caught much of the rhythm and tone of Kajal's work. The sweetness and simplicity of the voice, the political and personal passion, the directness and immediacy of the address, were qualities that struck me most, and which I decided were the most important to preserve. I also liked Kajal's sense of humour and the fable-like quality of the poems, evoking so clearly her cultural heritage. In my translations, I also wanted to preserve some sense of the Kurdish language, while helping the poems to sit naturally in English. In considering the strengths and weaknesses of my own voice, I thought that the biggest danger for me might be in losing some of the simplicity that Choman had achieved so gracefully and, to this end, decided to stick as closely as possible to these first versions.

The main challenges I found in translating Kajal (as well as my own inexperience) were as follows:

1. I found sometimes that the syntax, in its preponderance of short declarative sentences, without linking words or subsidiary clauses, produced a somewhat plodding effect in English. In places, I was able to ease this effect by extending or contracting the syntactical structures, although I was aware of the risk of losing the directness and simplicity.

2. I also felt that, partly because of the lack of punctuation creating an over-dependence on the line-break to act as a syntactical marker, the lineation – in its lack of enjambment and high coincidence of line-break and sense-break – produced either wooden or ragged effects and did not convey the musicality of Kajal's voice. In view of this, I decided not to remain overly faithful to the lineation; to use enjambment with discretion, but where I thought it beneficial; and to use punctuation in a prose style consistently throughout. Generally, the 'liberties' I took were more formal than textual.

Despite the many challenges, or because of them, I have really enjoyed this opportunity to work with Choman on Kajal's poetry, to engage with another language (so near to my mother tongue), and to broaden my horizons while trying to imagine what horizons might mean to a Kurdish poet, without a homeland to delineate them. The differences in our poetries is remarkable, but poetry speaks across them and it is so humbling to see the courage that poets such as Kajal display under such impossible circumstances; as Louise Glück says, women poets must have the courage not always to affirm life!

Daniel Hahn on Translating Corsino Fortes

For the Poetry Translation Centre's 2008 World Poets' Tour I was charged with producing 'literal' versions of a selection of poems by Cape Verdean poet Corsino Fortes, which would then be conjured – by British poet Sean O'Brien – from something unfortunate-sounding and lifeless into a working, singing English-language poem.

Born and brought up on the Cape Verdean island of São Vicente, Corsino Fortes studied in Portugal and spent much of his working life abroad, so while his work is concerned with giving voice to the life of his own country, his perspective is often that of an exile, and exile and redemptive return are among his recurring themes. Significantly he uses the oral language – Cape Verdean Creole – as well as standard Portuguese (sometimes one or the other, sometimes the two blended together), itself a powerful statement reinforcing the idea of the islands' distinctive African nature. Fortes began writing in the dying days of colonial rule, and he uses his work to reclaim, almost to recreate, his newly reborn country. But while the islands' post-colonial nature is constantly conspicuous, these are not obviously political poems, or at least not as we usually understand that term; they do not deal with the country's governments, leaders or freedom-fighting heroes, but present the islands almost mythically – a living place imbued with creative, regenerative forces.

A reasonably representative sample of about a dozen poems was chosen from Corsino's three collections (with the assistance of Stefan Tobler, who was already familiar with Corsino's work), and I produced my 'literals', which sought (impossibly, of course) to render the poem clearly and cleanly into English while resisting any impulse to tidy, to polish, to make any aesthetic or interpretative choices at all; not to narrow down to particular choices but to open up all the possibilities a poem could encompass. The lines were often annotated with divergent possibilities, glosses on the Portuguese-language original or useful background information.

Once these literals had been done and handed over to Sean, my job would be to look over his work with the original in mind, and draw attention to misunderstandings, or moments where I felt the English poem had strayed too far from its Portuguese-language moorings. This is not a common experience for a translator – we usually find ourselves straining slightly *against* the original, pulling against it to see if we can get a bit more slack – but in this process I was (not meaning it to sound antagonistic) 'on the same side' as the original, pulling against the new version, the role usually reserved for the naturally protective translated writer, whose representative I had to be.

The voice in Fortes's work is not one that renders easily in English. It's often declamatory and dramatically musical, which can come off as, at best, a little arch and archaic, at worst portentous and completely hollow. Interesting issues arose, too, of how to distinguish in English (if we should at all?) between the two languages Corsino uses in his writing. In addition, the poems use recurring imagery that clearly resonate with a Cape Verdean reader, that more often than not have no such near-mythical associations for an Anglophone one.

What struck me first when I read Sean's versions was how little he had actually changed; what struck me next was how much of a difference those little changes had made. Changing the odd word occasionally, changing the weighting of a line, moving the spring in the line by one syllable one way or another – and suddenly it sounded like a careful, precise line of fine writing. To someone who's never understood how this happens, it was sort of magical – no, that's not the right word, because it wasn't mysterious exactly, it was sort of the opposite; in fact, it was an insight into the mechanics of poetry: like watching a conjuror in slow motion, one frame at a time, to see how magic is actually achieved.

W. N. Herbert on Translating Maxamed Xaashi Dhamac 'Gaarriye'

I. ARAR (*Introduction*)

What a poet looks for in the act of translating from a language he or she doesn't understand differs from what is sought by the creative translator of verse, working with a culture they know intimately, whether on a linguistic, literary or socio-political level. Poets wish to be changed by what they learn as technicians, as workers in the medium of verse. They want the new perspectives, the different handlings of tone and imagery, the shifts of emphasis in the metrical system, to affect and develop them as writers, not just as readers.

The best solution, I found, when working with Martin Orwin on the poetry of the great Somali writer, Maxamed Xaashi Dhamac 'Gaarriye', was to revert to the role of apprentice (not so far in my case). Confronted with Somali – the language that 'makes Arabic look like Esperanto', as Sarah Maguire introduced it to me – I felt less the apprentice and more the schoolboy. And it was as a novice that I engaged with the practically unique structural device at the heart of Somali poetry: the deployment of a single alliterative sound per (often lengthy) poem.

It was practically as a literary tourist that I experienced Somali culture's obsession with poetry. Its groundedness in orality (most verse is still composed in the head rather than on paper) means that poetry lives or dies in performance, rather than in print; a culture where memory, first supplemented by the cassette, has now been augmented by the MP3 – thus practically bypassing the book altogether. And it was certainly as a student that I learned about the country's complex political background: world opinion on the Somali situation, much distracted by lurid headlines, is informed by very few of the facts.

II. DHEXDHEXAAD (*Middle Section*)

How Martin and I worked on these pieces was, essentially, that I would stumble through each poem line-by-line, while he gave me a summation of its meaning, rhythm and role in relation to the whole poem, and the poem's place in Gaarriye's work as a whole. We would meet up each weekend and work our way intensively through the poems like this, setting his painstaking literals against Gaarriye's Somali and retranslating the latter phrase by phrase, with me taking away his and my notes, and trying to work up a fluent draft before our next meeting.

In relation to the form of Somali poetry, I found that attempting a close match of single-sound alliteration was crippling, for the simple reason that this mode is no longer culturally dominant in English poetry: the role of alliteration in Anglo-Saxon and Middle English verse has subsequently been replaced by rhyme. I therefore found myself emphasising key alliterative words at key moments, but falling back on secondary alliterative groupings at other points, in an attempt to honour the device, but also to allow some degree of modulation in its execution.

In relation to imagery, there is in Somali poetry a continuing emphasis on the rural and nomadic, which reflects how most of the population lives. It's difficult, without copious footnotes, to indicate to a predominantly urban readership the complex symbology of livestock, familial interrelations and particularities of weather, which informs this poetry. Such a reader doesn't have access to the fine gradation of perceptions that inform an ordinary Somali word like *saxansaxo*: 'the scent and coolness carried on the wind from a place where it is raining to a place where it is not'.

Because Gaarriye's work is suffused with such distinctions, and because

Martin and I knew we were preparing texts as much for performance as for the page we sought out solutions which had the ring and rhythm of proverbial utterance, but without sacrificing detail. Thus in 'Uurkubbaale (Seer)', we emphasised a proverbial feel where possible, '"A cloud in the east means rest your feet,/the rain will trek to us . . ."'; and, where a lot of information had to be given, we did our best to keep the tone colloquial: '[a poem] is the finest matting, woven for a bride,/the one the song calls "Refuser of poor suitors".'

I found myself describing these long, loping poems (designed as they are to be heard by large audiences) to friends as 'non-lyric'. By this I meant, not that they failed to be lyrical in either their thought or their musicality (actually, they succeeded, often compellingly so), but that they were manifestly not reliant, as much of our poetry is, on a device of romantic intimacy: one person deploying that musicality to 'sing' to another, with the reader either pretending to overhear, or to be the person addressed.

As I saw in Somaliland, looking out on audiences in their hundreds, raucous in their delight at Gaarriye's driven, witty performances, these are not poems which need to pretend to have listeners. The particular way in which they are 'public' has interesting ramifications for both the translating poet, and the attentive Western audience. Somali poetry is not public simply because it is addressed to a plural audience in a public setting. It is public because all its premises of persona, form, tone and subject are, to a marked extent, shared by both poet and audience. What the Somali poet is performing, in terms of subject, can seem more varied than our lyric mode.

When I was working on these pieces, I asked Martin whether the frequent divisions within a text corresponded to stanzas. He said they did not, and I began to think of them instead as simple verse paragraphs. Then, when I heard Gaarriye and other Somali poets read, I discovered that these short gaps were actually spaces for audience appreciation. As some rhetorical or imagistic or alliterative flourish was presented, which the poet knew would appeal to his audience, he paused for applause. This 'interruption' of the poem occurs very infrequently during a reading in the UK, though any poem which, without such pauses, is felt to go on too long, is often criticised as too 'rhetorical'. Gaarriye's example calls us to reconsider such terms.

For a translator from Somali, textual accuracy is a higher than usual priority. This is one case in which a 'version', for a frequently bilingual Somali audience, decidedly will not do. Martin and I therefore agreed that following the meaning took priority over such gestures as attempting to find a consistent rhythmic equivalent.

III. GEBAGGEBO (*End*)

I noticed, when Gaarriye and I first read together, in Liverpool's Bluecoat Centre, that the large Somali audience were not content to sit still, to be rapt as the master rapped. On the contrary, they clapped, exhorted, got up, took photos with their mobiles, posed in those photos with Gaarriye, called people up, asked Gaarriye to speak to those people, or attempted to capture him reciting down the line. Through all this he indefatigably, indeed insouciantly, continued to perform – and therefore so did I. In other words, I learned that the well-made poem is sufficiently robust. If it is very well-made, it induces applause and, here and there, that rapt look occurs for real, not through politeness. It doesn't require our reverence or more polite forms of appreciation, only the space in which to, as Martin says, 'foreground the words'. Everything else is background noise.

Martin Orwin on Translating Maxamed Xaashi Dhamac 'Gaarriye'

My role in this process was to provide literal translations and as much information as possible to Bill Herbert in order for him to make his versions of the translations of a selection of Gaarriye's poems. The first step was to select poems for translation, which I did in association with Maxamed Xasan 'Alto' and Gaarriye. I chose poems which were both accessible to an English-speaking audience and representative of Gaarriye's oeuvre. 'Seer' deals with poetry itself and the figure of the poet, an important topic in its own right but one which has particular resonance given the importance of poetry to social and political discourse among the Somalis. 'Arrogance' and 'Self-Misunderstood' are examples of poems that address more philosophical matters: humanity in the world, and the self, both physically and psychologically.

Translation for me is essentially an intense, deep reading of a poem. When I produce literal translations for others, the process is different from when I'm making translations to work on by myself. However, in both instances, the basis is as full an understanding of the poem as possible. This is an understanding not just of what the words mean, but includes a feeling of how the language flows across the syntax, its alliteration and metre; and how these three interact with the ideas, images and metaphors of the poem. At this stage, given the limited lexicographical tools and the fact that I am not a mother-tongue speaker of the language, I always work with Somalis who know the poetry being translated. In this case I am very grateful to Gaarriye himself, with whom

I worked over a couple of weeks in Hargeysa, and also to Maxamed Xasan 'Alto', whose help in London was invaluable throughout the whole translation process.

Once this full understanding is achieved, there's a sense in which the words get up off the page and dance. When working on my own, I try to filter the words through the medium of English so that English words come to rest on the page dancing to as close a tune as possible to the original. Making literal translations for someone else involves a different approach. Firstly, decisions need to be made with regard to rendering the meaning of each word. This is particularly difficult when images and metaphors are based on cultural specificities with no equivalent in English. An example of this are these two lines in 'Seer':

Caws baar leh weeyaan This refers to a grass mat with unfinished frills. (The women make mats which are used to cover the framework of sticks forming the nomadic hut, the *aqal*. A new mat is always made for the marriage hut, one that's larger than normal. It's this kind of mat that's referred to here.)

Lana baxay sabool-diid This refers to 'the one who refuses the poor man'. (This name is given to the mat being made. It is a valuable thing which is not used as part of a bride's wealth for just anyone, but for a man of some wealth.) The whole image is a metaphor for poetry itself.

In teasing out these lines I was trying to bring enough out for Bill to make his own version. His final version was: 'It is the finest matting, woven for a bride, / the one the song calls "Refuser of poor suitors".' This succeeds in bringing the essentials of the metaphor out, although the line is inevitably longer, and thus the compromise is to lose some of the concise feel of the original.

Decisions as to how to convey each word are made all the time at this stage. There's often a choice and, for a literal translation, the one which most closely coincides with the actual meaning in my mind is the one that I tend to choose, Many words were of course subsequently discussed at length with Bill, with us both coming up with alternatives, which I'd consider in relation to the original so as to make sure that the meaning and tone of the original were not being lost.

What's much more difficult to convey in a literal translation is the feel of the interaction between syntax, metre and alliteration, which are fundamental stylistic characteristics of Somali poetry of all genres, and which lend so much to how a poem is perceived by the listener. This feel is something which comes with a knowledge of the poetic tradition and lots of listening and reading of poetry. In order that he might have some insight into this I gave Bill articles on Somali poetry in which some of the basics of metrical system and alliteration are explained. The way in which different syntactic constructions in conjunction with the metre create a sense of the flow of the language through sections of a poem is something that's not really been written about; however, I tried to convey this as best I could in my literal translations and in the discussions Bill and I had together.

A simple example of this is the position of the verb. The basic position for the verb in Somali is at the end of the clause, unlike English, and this fact is used in poetry to create sections which hold together in subtle ways, either through parallelism or through extended use of subordinate clauses or nominal phrases leading to a main verb. An example is the lines in 'Arrogance', *Onkodkiyo hillaaciyo* | *Ufadaa dhacaysiyo* | *Uurada waraysoo*, which I rendered in the literal translation as follows: 'The thunder and the lightning and | The *ufo* wind which has blown and (*Ufo* is a particular wind which blows when it rains) | The grey cloud, question them.' To this last line I added the note:

> Lit: interview them, or take them into consideration for yourselves. Better English would put the verb at the beginning of these lines: Question the thunder . . . the grey cloud. This doesn't get some of the movement of the Somali here though, especially given the *jiifto* metrical pattern which is used here.

The final version made by Bill and myself of these lines is as follows:

> Ask the thunder, see what lightning says,
> the rain-bearing wind which blows
> the good grey cloud, ask them.

The use of the verb at the beginning of the clause is much more natural in English, particularly as it is an imperative, but this is balanced by its repetition at the end. We used the syntax of English while still nodding to the original and rounding off the line group with a verb.

Bill was very responsive to and respectful of the originals as presented in the literal translations during our intensive meetings over three or four weekends. Given the limited time left to us, we both began to work up versions which then came together and resulted in the final versions. Bill was very keen to understand as much as possible of each of the images used and the vivid impression given by Gaarriye's often striking use of metaphor and imagery comes through in our final versions.

Clare Pollard on Translating Caasha Lul Mohamud Yusuf

Having been excited by the possibilities of translation for some time – I have collaborated on many Hungarian translations and am working on a new version of Ovid's *Heroides* – I was pleased to be invited to work with a Somali poet by the Poetry Translation Centre. From a purely selfish perspective, I felt I would have a huge amount to learn from a poetic culture so radically different from my own, whilst as soon as I read Caasha's work I also realised that – as young female writers – we have much in common.

At first I worked with Maxamed Xasan 'Alto' and Said Jama Hussein, who provided me with simple, literal translations from the Somali and also met with me to talk through the poems line-for-line and explain the cultural context. In Starbucks and libraries, the complex technicalities of Somali poetry were scribbled down for me on napkins, whilst I also learnt about *khat*, tribal punishments and camel fat. I began to get a glimpse of a Somalia beyond the news headlines, one which for many is the most beautiful, cultured country in Africa: the pearl of Mogadishu, lush Daallo, deer and honey. And I was also told about Caasha – what a remarkable poet she is, how boldly she takes on traditional (and often male) forms such as the *gabay*, her fierce technical prowess, the incredible outpouring of emotion in her work.

As I began to understand the poems, it soon became apparent that it is this remarkable contrast between wild feeling and controlled form – the hot and the cool – which I needed to capture. But how? There are many aspects of Somali poetry which can seem clumsy to an English ear: the politically charged rhetoric (readers in the UK often loathe the sense they're being told what to think), the length and seeming bagginess, the extreme alliteration (entire poems often alliterate on just one letter), the shifts in address, the digressions. In fact, these poems are the opposite of clumsy, they just use techniques which are currently deemed 'unfashionable' on Creative Writing circuits (shifts in address are common in Ovid's work, for example, who can hardly be accused of sloppiness).

It was tempting to make Caasha's work more palatable for an English audience – to be both translator and editor, knocking off the awkward edges. But instead I decided to damn fashion. It would be ridiculous to tidy and tame such powerful poems. I just had to look outside the mainstream lyric for models.

Reading Simon Armitage's *Sir Gawain and the Green Knight* helped — in its alliteration and caesuras, Somali poetry is strikingly reminiscent of Anglo-Saxon verse, and the fact readers have embraced Armitage's version meant that perhaps they could handle Somali translations that alliterated heavily too. In Caasha's 'The Sea-Migrations' I managed to keep the poem alliterating on D – the d-d-d sound giving the poem a ferocity that makes it almost feel like a pummelling:

> They are devoured, picked dry by sharks and sea creatures,
> wild dogs eat them like *darib*, the best camel fat,
> and many dead bodies lie decaying on our shores
> defiled by strangers' eyes, skin peeled off their carcasses,
> their lives end in distress, and there will be no decent burial.

I also realised that Caasha's work has much in common with the best contemporary performance poetry and drew on this to make my co-translations work out-loud, signalling that they are part of an 'oral' tradition. Caasha reads quickly, reminding me of stage-poets who use tumbling, almost hip-hop rhythms. Thinking about performance poetry helped with many aspects of Caasha's work, particularly the way in which it seeks to directly engage the audience and make them question their own lives.

In 'Taste', the use of 'you' creates a real intimacy, as the reader becomes a close female friend sharing insights about men:

> Though he may place you in a skyscraper
> and fill your world with glass
> or fashion, or your demands,
> arriving at your door with every whim,
> if he's not to your taste, he's just a blocked path.

And, of course, meeting Caasha in person was an inspiration. We have now done six readings together for the Poetry Translation Centre and I have enjoyed her company hugely. She is poised, no-nonsense and has a wicked sense of humour. Every reading she turned up breathless at the train station – running slightly late – with a fabulous, coordinating head-scarf. Every reading she blew the audience away with her integrity and passion.

Translating Caasha's poetry is an experience that will definitely impact upon my own writing. It makes me want to tear up a lot of mainstream English poetry's 'rules'. The expansiveness and engagement of Somali poetry makes much work coming from the UK seem a bit cramped: it challenges us to be bolder. And Caasha has made me question many of my ingrained assumptions. When I told her how much of my work involves teaching creative writing, she giggled at the idea. 'Writing can't be taught,' Caasha told me, 'it is a gift from God.' Looking at her poems, I can believe it.

Nick Laird on Translating Reza Mohammadi

I've known about the wonderful work the Poetry Translation Centre does for years, and when they asked me to help translate Reza's poems, I was very keen to give it a go. Before I was asked to work with Reza, my experience of translating was very limited indeed. When I lived for a couple of years in Rome I tried to do versions of a few poems by Montale and Valerio Magrelli, but only to try to help my Italian, and the results were fairly ugly, shapeless, makeshift things. Also, since they were for my eyes only, I had no restrictions on what I could or couldn't do, deviating where I felt it necessary or adding a detail or three. I realized with Reza's work that it was going to be a very different enterprise: I knew no Dari, and very little about Persian culture.

The project took a while to get going as the PTC had some difficulty appointing an intermediary for Reza and me to work with, but finally the very helpful Hamid Kabir was found. He would send me his literal translations and I would email back asking general (and no doubt ludicrous) questions about Dari, its poetic forms and styles, and specific questions relating to meanings and ambiguities in Reza's poems. Then I started tinkering with the literal versions and trying to come up with poems. These early efforts were pretty much a disaster and had to be scrapped. I tend to work through many drafts when I write my own poems, and usually end up a long way off from where I start. I was allowing myself the same latitude with the translations, which wouldn't do at all, and I realised I'd have to start again from scratch.

When I was in London for a few days I arranged to visit Hamid and Reza at the travel agency they both work at in Southall. The agency's like an iceberg, with only a tiny proportion of it above the surface, and on the third or fourth level below I found Hamid and Reza in a back office. Over green tea, we went through a few more questions, with Hamid translating my English for Reza, and then Reza's answers for me. I was never convinced I was fully 'getting' the poetry – but it became slightly easier to live with that mystification when I asked Reza to read a poem or two, in Dari, there in the office.

It was, initially, mildly awkward, but that soon faded as Reza got going. He's a great reader of his work, and it turned out it was deeply beneficial to the whole process to hear how he read. Once he began speaking, I realised I could learn a great deal just from the tone in which he read. It was almost irrelevant that I couldn't understand a word he was saying. I got the tone, the style, the import. He read in this unembarrassed, enthralled, rather grand voice, and if that was how the poet read them, that was also how they were written. Reza reads like he's a channel for something greater than himself, and I realised that rather than trying to tame or domesticate his poems into western ideas of order or neatness, I should just try to present them in a language that did its best to allow their strength and power to come through. I aimed to keep the strangeness in them that I experienced on encountering them, and decided to worry less about technique and more about voice.

I can't judge how the finished translations stand as poems in English, and it would need a bi-lingual reader to judge their fitness against the original, but after having toured with Reza for a week around Britain and read my versions out, I still experience an odd frisson when I read the work, which is both mine and emphatically not. He's a rare and fine poet, Reza, and it's been a weird pleasure to work on his poems, like opening your mouth and finding someone else's voice coming out.

POETS' BIOGRAPHIES

Riffat Abbas (Pakistan, Siraiki) is a poet and academic who is famous among the 14 million Siraiki speakers in Pakistan for following the tradition of writing *kafi*: a form unique to Siraiki literature that unites romance with spirituality. In 2005 Abbas won the Khawaja Ghulam Farid Award for Siraiki poetry for his collection *Ishq Allah Saeen Jagiya*.

Kajal Ahmad (Kurdistan, Kurdish) was born in Kirkuk in 1967. Renowned for her brave attention to women's issues, she has published four very popular collections of poetry. She lives in Sulaimaniya in Kurdistan where she is well known not only for her poetry but also as a political analyst and journalist. Her poems have been translated into Arabic, Persian, Turkish, Norwegian and English.

Masoud Ahmadi (Iran, Farsi) was born in Tehran in 1943. Following the Revolution in 1979, he was imprisoned for four years and banned from working for the government for the rest of his life. Author of a dozen poetry collections, interviews and books for children, he currently has four collections of poetry and a book of essays awaiting approval by the Iranian state censor.

Mbarka Mint al-Barra' (Mauritania, Arabic) writes in both Arabic and in her dialect, Hassaniya. She is well-known in Mauritania and, uniquely, throughout the Arabic-speaking world. She has carried out extensive research into Mauritanian oral poetry, specifically into *tibra'*, love poems recited only by women. Her definitive account of modern Mauritanian poetry was published in 1998 and her collected poems appeared in 2012.

Fateneh Al-Gharra (Palestine, Arabic) was born in Gaza. A journalist and radio presenter, she has also worked with women's projects. She has published four highly acclaimed poetry collections: *There is Still a Sea Between Us* (2002), *A Very Troublesome Woman* (2003), *Except for Me* (2009) and *Betrayals of God* (2011). She lives in Belgium.

Al-Saddiq Al-Raddi (Sudan, Arabic) is widely regarded as one of the leading African poets writing in Arabic. Famous since a teenager, he is admired for the lyric intensity of his poetry and for his principled opposition to Sudan's dictatorship. His *Collected Poems* was published in 2010. A distinguished journalist, he was forced into exile in 2012 and now lives in London.

Abdullah al-Riyami (Oman, Arabic) is an Omani theatrical director, poet and cultural commentator. Born in 1965, he spent his early life in Cairo. He returned to Oman in 2000 where he has been imprisoned many times for criticising the Omani regime. His first collection of poems was published in 1992 and he is co-founder of the avant-garde theatre group A'Shams.

Diana Amphimiadi (Georgia, Georgian) is a poet, publicist, linguist and teacher. The author of four collections of poetry – *Shokoladi* (Chocolate), *Konspecturi Mitologia* (Resumé of Mythology), *Alhlokhedvis Traektoria* (Trajectory of the Short-Sighted) and *Piradi Kulinaria* (Personal Cuisine) – she has been awarded prestigious prizes at the Tsero and Saba literature festivals in Georgia.

Angkarn Chanthathip (Thailand, Thai) was born in Khon Kaen in the north-east of Thailand and currently lives in Bangkok. He has published five volumes of poetry, most recently *The Heart's Fifth Chamber*, which won the prestigious SEA Writers' Award in 2013. His meditative poems are often concerned with people who are displaced and marginalised.

Shakila Azizzada (Afghanistan, Dari) began publishing stories and poems while still a student. Following imprisonment by the Soviet-backed regime, she fled Afghanistan, eventually settling in The Netherlands. The author of plays and short stories, she has published two collections of poems in Dari and Dutch. Her delicate poems are openly concerned with female desire, a subject rarely approached in Dari.

Amrita Bharati (India, Hindi) was born in Najibabad, Uttar Pradesh in 1939. She completed an MA and a PhD in Hindi from Banaras Hindu University. She lives in Pondicherry where she is engaged in translating Sri Aurobindo's work and researching Sanskrit philosophy. She has published seven books of poetry and a volume of prose.

Coral Bracho (Mexico, Spanish) was born in Mexico City in 1951. She has won numerous poetry awards, including the Premio Nacional de Poesía de Aguascalientes for *El ser que va a morir* (1982) and the Premio Xavier Vallaurrutia for *Ese espacio, ese jardín* (2003). She is a member of the Sistema Nacional de Creadores de Arte.

Chen Yuhong (Taiwan, Chinese) was born in Kaohsiung and studied English Literature in Taiwan. She spent a decade in Vancouver before returning to Taipei. She has published many award-winning volumes of poetry; her second collection, *Annotations*, won the Annual Poetry Award in 2004. Her poems were included in Chiuko's anthology *Thirty Major Poets of Taiwan in the Past Three Decades* (2008).

Ch'oe Young-mi (South Korea, Korean) has published four trail-blazing 'post-modern' collections of poetry including *At Thirty, the Party is Over* (1994) and *The Life that Has Not Arrived Yet* (2009). Her signature style – urbanity infused with eroticism that is simultaneously political and personal – emerged from the late 1980s when Korea made the transition from military to democratic government.

Mohammed Ebnu (Western Sahara, Spanish) was born in the Western Sahara in 1968 and studied Spanish language and literature in Cuba. His poetry collections include *Voz de fuego* (Voice of Fire) and *Nómada en el exilio* (Nomad in Exile); his poems appear in two Saharawi poetry anthologies, *Añoranza* (Longing) and *Bubisher*. He is a founder member of the Saharawi Friendship Generation.

Corsino Fortes (Cape Verde, Portuguese) was born in 1933 in Mindelo. He trained to be a teacher, then became a lawyer, was a judge in Angola and served as Cape Verde's ambassador to Portugal. A major figure in postcolonial African literature, he has published three seminal volumes of poetry, collected together in 2001 as *A Cabeça Calva de Deus* (The Bald Head of God).

Armando Freitas Filho (Brazil, Portuguese) is one of Brazil's leading poets; he has experimented with different poetic styles throughout his career. Born in Rio de Janeiro in 1940, his numerous collections include *Palavra* (1963), a collected poems *Máquina de Escrever* (2003) and, most recently, *Dever* (2013). He was awarded the prestigious Jabuti Prize in 1986 and 2010.

Fouad Mohammad Fouad (Syria, Arabic) was born in Aleppo in 1961. The author of four collections of poetry, he has participated in readings and events across the Arabic-speaking world and in France. A doctor and public health researcher, he has been forced into exile by recent events in Syria and is now living and working in Beirut.

Frankétienne (Haiti, French) was born in 1936 in Ravine-Sèche. A leading exponent of the revolutionary poetics known as spiralism, he has published dozens of poetry collections, novels and plays both in French and in Haitian Creole. Hailed as 'the Father of Haitian Letters' by *The New York Times*, Frankétienne was shortlisted for the Nobel Prize for Literature in 2009.

Gagan Gill (India, Hindi) was born in 1959 in Delhi. She completed an MA in English from Delhi University and worked as a journalist and a translator before she established herself as one of the leading voices in contemporary Hindi poetry. She has published four collections of poems and two volumes of prose.

Maxamed Xaashi Dhamac 'Gaarriye' (Somalia/Somaliland, Somali) was born in Hargeysa in 1949 and died in Oslo in 2012. One of the most brilliant poets of his generation, his bold, inquisitive, wide-ranging poems matched his engaging, restless personality. A charismatic reader of his poems, he was the first person to articulate the metrical patterns of Somali poetry, a major intellectual achievement.

Azita Ghahreman (Iran, Farsi) was born in Mashhad in 1962 and has lived in exile in Sweden since 2006. One of Iran's leading poets she has published five collections of poetry including *The Suburb of Crows* (2008) which appeared in Swedish and Farsi. She has edited three anthologies of poets from Khorasan, the eastern province of Iran that borders Afghanistan.

Noshi Gillani (Pakistan, Urdu) is one of the most popular poets writing in Urdu today: the first edition of the most recent of her five collections, *Hawa Chupke se Kehti Hai* (The Breeze Whispers, 2011), sold out in Pakistan in two hours. Born in Bahawalpur, Pakistan in 1964, she moved to San Francisco in 1995 and now lives in Australia.

Maxamed Ibraahin Warsame 'Hadraawi' (Somalia/Somaliland, Somali) is universally acknowledged as the greatest living Somali poet. Born in 1943 in Togdheer, the 'Somali Shakespeare' has composed more than 70 lyric songs and 200 epic poems that have enriched the oral poetry tradition central to Somali culture. His fearless commitment to peace and social justice have made him an inspiration to his people.

Toeti Heraty (Indonesia, Indonesian) is an outstanding Indonesian poet with a powerful vision. A philosopher, an art historian and a human rights activist, she is well known for her opposition to the Suharto regime and for her feminism. She writes subtle poems, both intimate and personal, that also highlight repressive social and emotional conventions.

David Huerta (Mexico, Spanish) lives and works in Mexico City where he was born in 1949. The author of nineteen books of poetry, he is a professor of literature and an essayist. A two-volume edition (more than 1,000 pages) of his collected poems *La mancha en el espejo* (The Stain in the Mirror) was published in 2013.

María Clara Sharupi Jua (Ecuador, Shuar) writes poetry in Spanish and Shuar. Born and raised in the Amazon rainforest, her poetry mixes imagery from nature and the traditions of her indigenous culture which pre-dates that of the Incas. María Clara's work has been published in numerous literary journals and books.

Dilawar Karadaghi (Kurdistan, Kurdish) was born in Sulaimaniya in Iraqi Kurdistan in 1963. He studied at the Academy of Fine Arts in Baghdad. He has published nine collections of poetry and translated various novels, biographies and plays from Arabic, Persian and Swedish into Kurdish. His collected poems were published in two volumes entitled *Jaddey Mekhek* (Clove Road).

Karin Karakaşlı (Turkey, Turkish) is a Turkish writer of Armenian descent. She writes poetry, fiction, children's books and journalism in Turkish. She also works as a translation instructor at the university and as a teacher of Armenian language and literature in an Armenian High School in Istanbul where she currently lives.

Euphrase Kezilahabi (Tanzania, Swahili) is a Tanzanian poet and novelist who is Professor of African Literature at the University of Botswana. In 1974 he published the first collection of free verse in Swahili. His fiction has significantly expanded the genre of the novel in Swahili.

Ateif Khieri (Sudan, Arabic) is one of the leading Sudanese poets of his generation. He has published three acclaimed collections of poetry, *Script of Earth* (1995), *Suspicions* (1999) and *Heartening Country Women* (2006) and two plays. His open opposition to the Sudanese dictatorship forced him into exile and he has lived in Australia since 2006.

Farzaneh Khojandi (Tajikistan, Tajik), the national poet of Tajikistan, is one of the most outstanding poets writing in Persian today with a huge following in Iran and Afghanistan as well as in her native Tajikistan. Her many collections of poetry include *Sign of Love, Oracle from My Ancestors, Droplets from the Oxus* and (in Russian) *Golden Leaves*.

Abdellatif Laâbi (Morocco, French) is a prolific poet, novelist, playwright and translator who has won many prizes for his work, including the Prix Goncourt for his *Collected Poems* in 2009. A political activist, he was imprisoned from 1972 to 1981 by the authoritarian regime of Hassan II. He has lived in Paris since 1985.

Conceição Lima (São Tomé and Príncipe, Portuguese) has published three collections of poetry, *O Útero da Casa* (2004), *A Dolorosa Raiz do Micondó* (2006) and *O País de Akendenguê* (2011). Born in 1961, she studied journalism in Portugal. In 1993 she founded the independent journal, *O País Hoje* (The Country Today). She worked in London for the BBC's African Portuguese Language Services until it was closed in 2011.

Parween Faiz Zadah Malaal (Afghanistan, Pashto) is one of the most popular poets writing in Pashto. Born in Kandahar, she trained as a journalist and worked in Kabul for Radio Afghanistan. In 1988 she left Afghanistan and moved to Pakistan where she has published both short stories and three collections of poetry, including *Da Khazaan Tilayee Ploona* (The Golden Footsteps of Autumn, 2002).

Alamin Mazrui (Kenya, Swahili) is a Kenyan poet and scholar who, following imprisonment by the government of Daniel Arap Moi, has lived in the USA; he teaches in the department of African Languages and Literatures at Rutgers University. He is one of the few poets writing free verse in Swahili to have published a poetry collection.

Reza Mohammadi (Afghanistan, Dari) was born in Kandahar in 1979. His three collections of poetry have gained him many awards, such as from the Afghan Ministry of Culture in 2004 and prizes for being Iran's best young poet in 1996 and 1997. A prolific journalist and cultural commentator, he has published two books on the literature of Afghanistan.

Partaw Naderi (Afghanistan, Dari) was born in Badakhshan in 1952. One of the pioneering modernist poets in Afghanistan, he has published ten collections of poetry and eight books of criticism. He was imprisoned in the notorious Pul-e-Charki prison for three years in the 1980s. After a long period in exile he returned to live in Kabul and became the first president of Afghan PEN.

Abdulla Pashew (Kurdish, Kurdistan) is the most popular living Kurdish poet. Since 1967 he has published nine collections of poetry including a two-volume collected poems. He studied pedagogy in the USSR, taught philology in Libya and since 1995 has lived in Finland. He is the translator of Walt Whitman and Alexander Pushkin into Kurdish.

Mohan Rana (India, Hindi) has been highly praised for the depth of thought and elegant simplicity of his poetry. Born in Delhi in 1964, he has published seven poetry collections in Hindi, most recently, *Ret ka Pul* (Bridge of Sand, 2012), and a dual-language collection, *With Eyes Closed* (2008) with translations by Lucy Rosenstein. He lives in Bath.

Tuvya Ruebner (Israel, Hebrew) has won many awards including the prestigious Israel Prize for Poetry in 2008. He has published numerous collections of poetry as well as translations into German and Hebrew. To mark his ninetieth birthday in 2014 dual-language editions of his poems were published in the USA (*In the Illuminated Dark*) and in Germany (*Wunderbarer Whan*).

Pedro Serrano (Mexican, Spanish) has published five collections of poems. His translations include the anthology of contemporary British poetry *La generación del cordero* (The Lamb Generation) and Shakespeare's *King John*. He teaches at UNAM in Mexico City and is editor of UNAM's influential poetry website Periodico de Poesia. *Peatlands*, translated by Anna Crowe, was published by Arc in 2014.

Víctor Terán (Mexico, Zapotec) was born in Juchitán de Zaragoza in 1958 and is the leading poet of the Zapotec Isthmus of Oaxaca, Mexico. His work has been published extensively in magazines and anthologies throughout Mexico and the world. A three-time recipient of the National Fellowship for Writers of Indigenous Languages, his most recent book is *The Spines of Love*.

Caasha Lul Mohamud Yusuf (Somalia/Somaliland, Somali) is one of the most exciting young poets of the Somali diaspora. She came to the UK in 1990 having fled the Somali Civil War and now lives in London. Her poems first appeared on Somali websites in 2008 and since then she has gained a large audience as well as widespread critical approval and admiration.

TRANSLATORS' BIOGRAPHIES

Alireza Abiz has won many awards for his translations of English-language poets into Farsi, including Seamus Heaney, Derek Walcott and Allen Ginsberg. A lecturer on world poetry and on translation in Iranian universities, he is currently completing a PhD at Newcastle University. His third collection of poetry was published in 2013.

Atef Alshaer studied at Birzeit University in Palestine and at SOAS, where he is now a senior Teaching Fellow; he is also a Visiting Lecturer in Arabic Studies at the University of Westminster. His many publications include *Poetry and Politics in the Modern Arab World* (2013).

Dawood Azami is an award-winning broadcast journalist with the BBC World Service in London. From 2010 to 2011 he was the World Service Bureau Chief in Kabul. A Visiting Lecturer at the University of Westminster and a Visiting Scholar at Ohio State University, he speaks five languages, writes poetry and practises calligraphy.

Tom Boll was Assistant Director of the Poetry Translation Centre from 2004 to 2007. He is the author of *Octavio Paz and T. S. Eliot: Modern Poetry and the Translation of Influence* (Legenda, 2012) and lectures in the Department of Spanish, Portuguese and Latin American Studies at King's College, London.

Natalia Bukia-Peters is a freelance translator, interpreter and teacher of Georgian and Russian. She studied at Tbilisi State Institute of Foreign Languages before moving to New Zealand in 1992 and then to Cornwall in 1994. A member of the Charted Institute of Linguists, she has translated many literary works from English into Russian for the British Council.

Maura Dooley has published several collections of poetry, most recently *Life Under Water* (Bloodaxe Books, 2008). Anthologies of verse and essays she has edited include *The Honey Gatherers: Love Poems* and *How Novelists Work*. She teaches at Goldsmiths College, University of London and is a Fellow of the Royal Society of Literature.

Jane Duran has published four collections of poetry with Enitharmon Press: *Breathe Now, Breathe* (1995), *Silences from the Spanish Civil War* (2002), *Coastal* (2005) and *Graceline* (2010). She co-translated Lorca's *Gypsy Ballads* with Gloria García Lorca and these were published in a bilingual edition by Enitharmon in 2011. She received a Cholmondeley Award in 2005.

Narguess Farzad is Senior Fellow in Persian at SOAS. Her publications include works on the 'Persian poetry of sacred defence' and the grammar of Persian. She is on the governing council of several learned and charitable organisations based in the UK and is actively involved in the promotion and translation of Persian poetry.

Mark Ford has published three collections of poetry, *Landlocked* (1992), *Soft Sift* (2001) and *Six Children* (2011). He has also written a biography of the French poet, playwright and novelist, Raymond Roussel, and translated Roussel's *New Impressions of Africa*. He teaches in the English Department at University College London.

Lavinia Greenlaw has published several collections of poetry, most recently *Minsk*, *The Casual Perfect* and *A Double Sorrow: Troilus and Criseyde*. A prize-winning novelist, she has also published non-fiction, including *The Importance of Music to Girls*. She received the 2011 Ted Hughes Award for her sound work *Audio Obscura* and a Wellcome Engagement Fellowship in 2013.

Sabry Hafez is Distinguished Professor of Comparative Literature at Qatar University and Emeritus Professor of Modern Arabic and Comparative Literature at SOAS. He is Editor-in-Chief of the online journal, Al-Kalimah. His many publications have made a significant contribution to the discipline of world literature studies.

Daniel Hahn is a writer, editor and translator, with thirty-something books to his name. His translations from Portuguese, Spanish and French include fiction from Europe, Africa and the Americas, and non-fiction by writers ranging from José Saramago to Pelé. He is currently compiling the new *Oxford Companion to Children's Literature*.

Choman Hardi was born in Iraqi Kurdistan in 1974 and came to the UK as a refugee in 1993. She has published three collections of poetry in Kurdish and one in English, *Life for Us* (Bloodaxe, 2004). *Gendered Experiences of Genocide: Anfal Survivors in Kurdistan-Iraq*, her post-doctoral research, was published by Ashgate in 2011.

W.N. Herbert is a Professor of Poetry and Creative Writing at Newcastle University whose work is mostly published by Bloodaxe Books. His recent focus has been on translating poetry from Bulgarian, Turkish, Farsi, Chinese and Somali by working with the poet or close associate. Recent work includes *Jade Ladder, Omnesia, The Third Shore, Whaleback City* and *Murder Bear*.

Said Jama Hussein is an essayist and short-story writer whose most recent publication is *Safar Aan Jaho Lahayn* (A Flight into the Unknown). A collection of his translations of Chekhov's short stories was published in 2011. A founding member of Somali PEN, he is actively involved with London's Somali Week Festival and the Hargeysa Book Fair.

Chenxin Jiang studied literature and translation at Princeton University. Her work has received a PEN Translation Fund grant and the 2011 Susan Sontag Prize for Translation. Her writing and translations have appeared in *Poetry London, Words Without Borders, Asymptote* and on the BBC. Book-length translations are forthcoming from HarperCollins and Dalkey Archive Press.

Hamid Kabir was born in Kabul. After finishing school, he read Medicine at Moscow Medical Academy. In 1997 he settled in the UK to study International Business with German. He worked for HSBC Bank and two world-class software-solutions companies before joining Ariana Group as the Chief Executive Officer. He speaks Russian, German, English and Persian.

Nataly Kelly is a Spanish-to-English translator based in the United States. A former Fulbright scholar in sociolinguistics, she studied languages and literature at various universities in Ecuador. She currently serves as the vice-president of market development at Smartling, a translation technology company.

Mimi Khalvati has published seven collections with Carcanet, including *The Meanest Flower*, shortlisted for the T. S. Eliot Prize. Her most recent book, *Child: New and Selected Poems*, was a Poetry Book Society Special Commendation. She is the founder of The Poetry School and a Fellow of the Royal Society of Literature.

Hafiz Kheir was born 1968 in Khartoum and moved to the UK in 1992. A translator and film-maker, he graduated from the Film & Television School at the London Institute in 2000. He studied drama and theatre from 1982 to 1986 at the Youth Palace, Omdurman.

Ulrich **Kratz** has spent many decades exploring the literatures of the Malay-speaking world. He has initiated Malaysian and Indonesian poetry readings in London and is the joint editor and translator of an anthology of Indonesian poetry. He is a SOAS Emeritus Professor in Indonesian and Malay.

Nick **Laird** was born in County Tyrone in 1975. He has many awards for his fiction and poetry including the Betty Trask Prize, a Somerset Maugham award, the Rooney Prize for Irish literature, and the Geoffrey Faber Memorial Prize. His last collection, *Go Giants*, was published in 2013. He teaches at Princeton.

Nukhbah Taj **Langah** is an academic, writer, translator and political activist. Her research focuses on Siraiki and ethnic literary expressions from Pakistan. Her publications include *Poetry as Resistance: Islam & Ethnicity in Postcolonial Pakistan* (2011). She is Head of the English Department and Associate Professor at Forman Christian College University, Lahore.

Kyoo **Lee**, author of *Reading Descartes Otherwise: Blind, Mad, Dreamy, and Bad* (2012), co-editor of *Women's Studies Quarterly* on 'Safe' Issue (2011) and *Critical Philosophy of Race* on 'Xenophobia & Racism' Issue (2014), is currently Associate Professor of Philosophy at the City University of New York. She lives on poetry.

Mahsn **Majidy** was born in Southern Kurdistan. He is a translator and freelance journalist with an MA in Translation and Linguistics from London. He worked as a full-time translator and journalist for the BBC for six years. He is currently completing his PhD thesis on sociolinguistics at the University of London.

Canan **Marasligil** is a writer, literary translator, editor and screenwriter who works in French, Turkish, English, Dutch and Spanish. Her current focus is on contemporary Turkish literature and on comics. Based in Amsterdam, in 2013 she was Translator in Residence at the Free Word Centre in London.

Tracey **Martin** lived in Thailand for fifteen years and is an international development worker, facilitator and poet, as well as occasional translator of Thai poetry. Her poems have been published in several magazines and her short stories broadcast on BBC World Service Radio.

Gwen **MacKeith** translates fiction, poetry and theatre from Spain and Spanish America. She is a contributing editor for Ambit magazine, and has taught at University College London and King's College London. Her translation of *Los Siameses/Siamese Twins,* by the Argentine dramatist Griselda Gambaro was published by Oberon Books and performed in London in 2011.

Oded Manor was born in 1942 in Israel and has lived in London since 1969. He is a humanistic group-worker grounded in the systems approach. While practising in London he received his PhD from LSE, qualified as a counsellor and a social worker and was a principal lecturer at Middlesex University.

Jamie McKendrick has published six books of poems, most recently *Out There* which won the Hawthornden Prize. He has translated two novels by Giorgio Bassani, a verse play by Pier Paolo Pasolini and Valerio Magrelli's poems, *The Embrace*, which won the Oxford-Weidenfeld Prize and the John Florio Prize.

Joel Mitchell lived in Mauritania from 2004-2006 while working with an NGO focused on maternal-child health. His exposure to popular poetry in Mauritania and Sudan has inspired his current work translating contemporary Arabic poetry, particularly in dialect. Joel is currently a PhD candidate at the University of London.

Anna Murison Boyd read Arabic at Edinburgh University and at SOAS. She has lived and studied in Cairo and Damascus and has travelled widely throughout the Middle East. A former professional translator, she now works for IHS Global Consulting Services as Middle East and North Africa Country Risk Manager and Senior Editor.

André Naffis-Sahely was born in Venice and raised in Abu Dhabi. A poet, critic and literary translator, his most recent translation is *Money* by Émile Zola (Penguin Classics, 2014); he is currently working on *The Selected Poems of Abdellatif Laâbi* (Carcanet, 2015).

Sean O'Brien is Professor of Creative Writing at Newcastle University. His version of Aristophanes' *Birds* was staged at the National Theatre in 2002. Awards for his poetry include the T. S. Eliot Prize and three Forward Prizes. His publications include *Dante's Inferno: a Verse Translation* (2006), *November* (2011) and *Collected Poems* (2012).

Bernard O'Donoghue was born in County Cork in 1945 and he still spends part of the year there. Since 1965 he has lived in Oxford where he is now an Emeritus Fellow in English at Wadham College. He has published seven volumes of poetry of which the most recent is *Farmers Cross* (Faber, 2011).

Zuzanna Olszewska is a departmental lecturer in social anthropology at the University of Oxford. She specialises in the ethnography, cultural history and poetry of Iran and Afghanistan, and is the author of a forthcoming book, *The Pearl of Dari: Poetry and Personhood among Young Afghans in Iran* (Indiana University Press).

Martin Orwin studied Arabic, Amharic and Somali at SOAS where he is currently Senior Lecturer in Somali and Amharic. He has a PhD in the phonology of Somali and continues to research the language, in particular the metrical system of the poetry and its relationship with musical performance.

Katherine Pierpoint has won various literary awards including Sunday Times Young Writer of the Year and a Somerset Maugham award from the Society of Authors. Her poetry book, *Truffle Beds* (Faber), was shortlisted for the T. S. Eliot Prize.

Clare Pollard has published four collections of poetry; the most recent, *Changeling*, was a PBS Recommendation. Her play, *The Weather*, premiered at the Royal Court Theatre and her documentary, *My Male Muse*, was a Radio 4 Pick of the Year. Clare's latest book is a translation of Ovid's *Heroines* (Bloodaxe, 2013.)

Katriina Ranne has a PhD in Swahili poetry from SOAS. She translated and edited the first collection of African poetry in Finnish, an anthology of 200 poems from 30 African countries translated from seven languages. Her first novel, *Minä, sisareni*, was published in 2010 and her first collection of poems, *Ohikulkijan tuoksu*, in 2014.

Lucy Rosenstein grew up in Sofia, Bulgaria. She received her MA and PhD in Hindi from SOAS where she taught for several years. She has published widely on Hindi poetry with a particular focus on gender issues and translation. At present she is training to become a counsellor for children.

Carole Satyamurti has published six poetry collections, of which the most recent is *Countdown* (Bloodaxe, 2011). She won the National Poetry Competition in 1987 and received a Cholmondeley Award in 2001. She is currently working on a verse abridgement of the *Mahabharata*, to be published by Norton in 2015.

Elhum Shakerifar studied Persian literature at Oxford. She is the co-director of the award-winning film collective, Postcode Films, and programme manager for the Birds Eye View Film Festival that celebrates women directors. She is a lecturer at the Free University of Berlin and a research fellow in the Department of Anthropology at Goldsmiths University.

Jo Shapcott was awarded the Queen's Gold Medal for Poetry in 2011. Her poetry collections include *Electroplating the Baby* (1988), *Phrase Book* (1992), *My Life Asleep* (1998), *Her Book* (2000) and, most recently, *Of Mutability* (2010), which won the Costa Book Award. *Tender Taxes*, her versions of Rilke, was published in 2001. She teaches Creative Writing at Royal Holloway College.

David Shook is a translator and poet whose first poetry collection, *Our Obsidian Tongues*, was published by Eyewear Publishing in 2013. His recent translations include work by Mario Bellatin and Tedi López Mills. He lives in Los Angeles, where he edits *molossus* and Phoneme Media.

Stefan Tobler is the founder and publisher of And Other Stories, a young publishing house whose acclaimed books include *Swimming Home* and *Black Vodka* by Deborah Levy and *Down the Rabbit Hole* and *Quesadillas* by Juan Pablo Villalobos. His translations include Rodrigo de Souza Leão's *All Dogs are Blue*, *Água Viva* by Clarice Lispector and *Silence River* by Antônio Moura.

Sara Vaghefian was born in the UK of Irish-Iranian descent and grew up speaking English and Arabic. After studying French and Arabic at University College and SOAS, she is currently a graduate student in French and Comparative Literature at UCL.

Francisco Vilhena is an editorial assistant at *Granta* magazine. He coordinated Portuguese-language reading groups for independent publisher, And Other Stories. In 2011 he completed a master's degree in Cultural Memory at the IGRS (University of London) that focused on the relationship between poetry and photography.

Maxamed Xasan 'Alto' is a writer and freelance journalist who has published and edited many books in Somali. In 1980 he left Somalia to join the armed opposition based in Ethiopia. He obtained an MA in Journalism from Moscow State University in 1990. From 2004–10 he was a teaching fellow in Somali at SOAS. He now lives in Helsinki.

Samuel Wilder has lived and worked as a literary translator in Cairo and Beirut since 2006. He is currently a PhD candidate at Cambridge University, where he is studying the transformations of lyric form and the conceptual mapping of love in Arabic poetry of the Umayyad period.

Yama Yari was born in Herat and came to the UK in 1999 where he studied Civil Engineering. With Sarah Maguire, he co-translated Atiq Rahimi's novel, *A Thousand Rooms of Dream and Fear* (2006). After working on Crossrail, Yama returned to Afghanistan and is currently Senior Advisor to the Afghanistan Railway Authority.

Nariman Youssef has translated *The American Granddaughter*, a novel concerned with the war on Iraq, by Inaam Kachachi (Bloomsbury, 2010); the controversial 2012 Egyptian constitution draft (for the English-speaking *Egypt Independent*); and poetry for a number of anthologies. Having grown up in Cairo, Nariman has lived and worked in both Egypt and the UK since 2001.

INDEX OF TITLES AND FIRST LINES

INDEX OF POETS

ACKNOWLEDGEMENTS

The PTC emerged from the poetry translation workshops I began leading in 2002 when I was the Royal Literary Fund's Writing Fellow at SOAS and they have continued to be one of our core activities. A quarter of all the poems included in *My Voice* were translated in our workshops and almost all the poets translated here – some of whom we've gone on to translate at length and invite to the UK – were first introduced to us by translators bringing their poems to a workshop. In other words, the PTC could not possibly have come into existence or continued to flourish without the depth of knowledge of our translators. My greatest debt is to them: this is their anthology. Thanks, too, to all our loyal workshop participants whose patient discussions of the most minute of linguistic details have led to the results you read here.

As you might imagine, assembling an anthology that includes 111 poems by 45 poets from 26 countries writing in 23 different languages has been something of a logistical challenge. I am enormously grateful to the translators and poets who went out of their way to help me with biographical details and permission requests, often from poets in far-flung regions with erratic access to electricity, telephony and the internet: I only wish I could name you individually, but I hope each of you knows how much I value your generosity and thoughtfulness.

I would like to give particular thanks to those who assisted me in creating files of poems in non-Latin scripts: Al-Saddiq Al-Raddi (Arabic), Chenxin Jiang and Nicky Harvey (Chinese), Natalia Bukia-Peters (Georgian), Julie Landau (Hebrew), Lucy Rosenstein (Hindi), Kyoo Lee and Deborah Smith (Korean), Mahsn Majidy and Dilawar Karadaghi (Kurdish), Dawood Azami (Pashto), Alireza Abiz (Persian), Crispin Hughes (Siraiki) and Tracey Martin (Thai).

Thanks to Neil Astley at Bloodaxe Books for his immediate and sustained enthusiasm for *My Voice*; to Susan Wightman of Libanus Press for her formidable typesetting skills; to North Kuras of Exploded View for his dazzlingly beautiful cover (and to everyone who kindly submitted their eleven-word translation of the book's title that forms its watermark); and to Rebecca Carter who gave me the benefit of her outstanding editorial skills and sustained me with warmth and kindness throughout.

Many of these poems first appeared in the seventeen chapbooks we have published since 2008, ten of them in collaboration with Enitharmon Press: warm thanks to Stephen Stuart-Smith and Isabel Brittain for enduring the onslaught with equanimity and good humour.

I am grateful to the editors of the following publications in which some poems were first published: *The Guardian, London Review of Books, Modern Poetry in Translation, POEM, Poems on the Underground, Poetry London, Poetry Review, Prairie Schooner* and *The Times Literary Supplement*.

Although I confess to dreaming up the PTC and micromanaging every detail of its programme – from selecting which poets to translate to choosing the particular shade of pink on this book's cover (Pantone 232C, since you asked) – the PTC would never have become the success that it is without the vital support of many people. My first debt is to Gary McKeone who, when I approached him as Head of Literature at ACE with the germ of the PTC idea, immediately grasped what I aimed to achieve and offered invaluable encouragement from the start. I am also very grateful to Amanda Hopkinson, Kate Griffin, Nick McDowell, Antonia Byatt, Charles Beckett and David Cross at ACE all of whom have been very generous with their advice and expertise. The PTC has also received vital financial support from the Esmée Fairburn Foundation and the Fondation Jan Michalski which is much appreciated.

Gary McKeone has chaired our Board of Trustees with insight and enthusiasm; I would like to offer sincere thanks to him and all our board members, past and present, for their commitment to our work: Lord Victor Adebowale, Rebecca Carter, Emily Heath, Anja Koenig, Laetitia Ransley, Fiona Sampson and Bill Swainson.

I am so lucky to have had Tom Boll as the PTC's Assistant Director from 2004 to 2007. His vision, commitment, depth of knowledge and visceral sense of humour made a crucial contribution to forming the PTC into the organisation it is today. Deborah Bourne turned us from a guerrilla organisation into a fully-fledged charity and company limited by guarantee. Jennifer Chevalier inaugurated our fantastic series of podcasts and poem-podcasts, a task recently taken on by the talented Kirsty Pope. The indefatigable Julia Bird has overcome many international logistical obstacles to organise our hugely successful tours, while Travis Elborough has acted as the perfect poets' chaperone during them. Crispin Hughes has employed his considerable photographic skills to produce a witty and stunning record of our poets and events. North Kuras of Exploded View is responsible for creating the PTC's beautiful website, chapbooks and postcards; few things have been more pleasurable than discussing the most minute of details with him. And the PTC's current team of Sherry Neyhus, Sarah Hesketh and Reem Abu-Hayyeh have worked extremely hard to expand and consolidate our achievements.

My greatest debt is to all the extraordinary poets and translators who have given so much, so generously over the past ten years. I feel deeply moved to be able to count many world-class poets as my friends and to have been given the profound honour, thanks to the brilliance of their translators, of introducing their magnificent poetry to English-speaking audiences. I can't wait for the next decade. Heartfelt thanks to you all.